Lecture Notes in Computer Science   9942

Commenced Publication in 1973
Founding and Former Series Editors:
Gerhard Goos, Juris Hartmanis, and Jan van Leeuwen

More information about this series at http://www.springer.com/series/7407

Dorel Lucanu (Ed.)

Rewriting Logic and Its Applications

11th International Workshop, WRLA 2016
Held as a Satellite Event of ETAPS
Eindhoven, The Netherlands, April 2–3, 2016
Revised Selected Papers

Springer

Editor
Dorel Lucanu
Alexandru Ioan Cuza University
Iaşi
Romania

ISSN 0302-9743   ISSN 1611-3349 (electronic)
Lecture Notes in Computer Science
ISBN 978-3-319-44801-5   ISBN 978-3-319-44802-2 (eBook)
DOI 10.1007/978-3-319-44802-2

Library of Congress Control Number: 2016947924

LNCS Sublibrary: SL1 – Theoretical Computer Science and General Issues

Printed on acid-free paper

This Springer imprint is published by Springer Nature
The registered company is Springer International Publishing AG Switzerland

Preface

This LNCS volume contains the selected papers together with invited papers and tutorials presented at the 11th International Workshop on Rewriting Logic and Its Applications (WRLA 2016), held during April 2–3, 2016, in Eindhoven, The Netherlands.

Rewriting is a natural model of computation and an expressive semantic framework for concurrency, parallelism, communication, and interaction. It can be used for specifying a wide range of systems and languages in various application domains. It also has good properties as a metalogical framework for representing logics. Several successful languages based on rewriting (ASF+SDF, CafeOBJ, ELAN, Maude) have been designed and implemented. The aim of WRLA is to bring together researchers with a common interest in rewriting and its applications, and to give them the opportunity to present their recent work, discuss future research directions, and exchange ideas. WRLA 2016 was a special edition by marking its 20th anniversary since the first edition was held in Asilomar, California, in 1996.

The topics of the workshop include, but are not limited to:

A. Foundations

- Foundations and models of rewriting and rewriting logic, including termination, confluence, coherence and complexity
- Unification, generalisation, narrowing, and partial evaluation
- Constrained rewriting and symbolic algebra
- Graph rewriting
- Tree automata
- Rewriting strategies
- Rewriting-based calculi and explicit substitutions

B. Rewriting as a Logical and Semantic Framework

- Uses of rewriting and rewriting logic as a logical framework, including deduction modulo
- Uses of rewriting as a semantic framework for programming language semantics
- Rewriting semantics of concurrency models, distributed systems, and network protocols
- Rewriting semantics of real-time, hybrid, and probabilistic systems
- Uses of rewriting for compilation and language transformation

C. Rewriting Languages

- Rewriting-based declarative languages
- Type systems for rewriting

- Implementation techniques
- Tools supporting rewriting languages

D. Verification Techniques

- Verification of confluence, termination, coherence, sufficient completeness, and related properties
- Temporal, modal, and reachability logics for verifying dynamic properties of rewrite theories
- Explicit-state and symbolic model-checking techniques for verification of rewrite theories
- Rewriting-based theorem proving, including (co)inductive theorem proving
- Rewriting-based constraint solving and satisfiability
- Rewriting-semantics-based verification and analysis of programs

E. Applications

- Applications to logic, mathematics, and physics
- Rewriting models of biology, chemistry, and membrane systems
- Security specification and verification
- Applications to distributed, network, mobile, and cloud computing
- Specification and verification of real-time, probabilistic, and cyber-physical systems
- Specifications and verification of critical systems
- Applications to model-based software engineering
- Applications to engineering and planning

Following the tradition of the last editions, WRLA 2016 was a satellite event of ETAPS 2016. The workshop programme included the accepted regular papers, two invited talks, and three tutorials. The regular papers were reviewed by at least three reviewers and intensively discussed in the electronic meeting of the Program Committee (PC) members. We sincerely thank all the authors of papers submitted to WRLA 2016; we were really pleased by the quality of the submissions.

These proceedings include the revised versions of the contributions accepted as regular papers, one invited paper, one invited tutorial, and the abstracts of the other invited talks and tutorials. We warmly thank the invited speakers – Hélène Kirchner and Nikolaj Bjorner – and the authors of tutorials – Carolyn Talcott, Salvador Lucas, and Grigore Roşu – for kindly accepting to contribute to WRLA 2016.

We would like to thank the members of the PC and all the referees for their excellent work in the review and selection process. All of this was possible also thanks to the valuable and detailed reports provided by the reviewers. We benefited from the invaluable assistance of the EasyChair system through all the phases of submission, evaluation, and production of the proceedings.

Last but not least, we would also like to thank the ETAPS 2016 Tutorials and Workshops organizers, led by Erik de Vink, for their efficient coordination of and assistance with all the activities leading to WRLA 2016.

July 2016   Dorel Lucanu

Organization

Program Committee

Kyungmin Bae	Carnegie Mellon University, USA
Roberto Bruni	Università di Pisa, Italy
Ştefan Ciobâcă	Alexandru Ioan Cuza University of Iaşi, Romania
Manuel Clavel	Universidad Complutense de Madrid, Spain
Francisco Durán	Universidad de Málaga, Spain
Jörg Endrullis	Vrije Universiteit Amsterdam, The Netherlands
Santiago Escobar	Technical University of Valencia, Spain
Maribel Fernández	KCL, UK
Kokichi Futatsugi	JAIST, Japan
Thomas Genet	IRISA - Rennes, France
Jürgen Giesl	RWTH Aachen, Germany
Deepak Kapur	University of New Mexico, USA
Hélène Kirchner	Inria, France
Alexander Knapp	Universität Augsburg, Germany
Alberto Lluch Lafuente	Technical University of Denmark
Dorel Lucanu	Alexandru Ioan Cuza University of Iaşi, Romania (Chair)
Salvador Lucas	Universidad Politécnica de Valencia, Spain
Narciso Martí-Oliet	Universidad Complutense de Madrid, Spain
José Meseguer	University of Illinois at Urbana-Champaign, USA
Ugo Montanari	Università di Pisa, Italy
Pierre-Etienne Moreau	Inria-LORIA Nancy, France
Vivek Nigam	Universidade Federal da Paraíba
Kazuhiro Ogata	JAIST, Japan
Peter Olveczky	University of Oslo, Norway
Miguel Palomino	Universidad Complutense de Madrid, Spain
Christophe Ringeissen	LORIA-INRIA, France
Grigore Roşu	University of Illinois at Urbana-Champaign, USA
Vlad Rusu	Inria, France
Ralf Sasse	ETH Zürich, Switzerland
Traian-Florin Şerbănuţă	University of Bucharest, Romania
Mark-Oliver Stehr	SRI International, USA
Carolyn Talcott	SRI International, USA
Mark van den Brand	Eindhoven University of Technology, The Netherlands
Martin Wirsing	Ludwig-Maximilians-Universität München, Germany

Additional Reviewers

Aguirre, Luis
Arusoaie, Andrei
Bottoni, Paolo
Marshall, Andrew

Martín, Óscar
Milazzo, Paolo
Moreno-Delgado, Antonio

Abstracts of Invited Talks

All Strings Attached: String and Sequence Constraints in Z3

Nikolaj Bjorner

Microsoft Research
nbjorner@microsoft.com

Abstract. In this talk I describe recent efforts for theory support for strings, sequences and regular expressions in Z3. One of the main conveniences of Satisfiability Modulo Theories (SMT) solvers is their support for theories that are commonly used in program verification and analysis. The theories of arithmetic and bit-vectors have shown to be ubiquitous in almost all applications of SMT, while other theories, such as algebraic data-types, seem to be essential to cover only more sophisticated applications. The theory of strings, sequences and regular expressions have been an occasional but persistent ask from users of SMT tools. Efforts on supporting strings and sequences, have however only been catching on relatively recently, first with tools that solve string constraints under assumptions of bounded lengths (Kaluza, Hampi and the string solver in Pex), followed by a proposal for sequences in the exchange format for SMT solvers and implementations for strings in CVC4, Princess, S3, and Z3Str. A separate line of work has considered Symbolic Automata, where transitions are labeled by formulas over a background theory, and automata operations are performed directly by solving satisfiability constraints. Our approach in Z3 combines some of the approaches taken in string solvers and integrate methods from symbolic automata. I will describe some of our experiences so far, propose new opportunities with using SMT solvers with sequences, and summarise some of the technical challenges ahead.

Program Verification Using Reachability Logic

Grigore Roşu[1], Andrei Ştefănescu[1], and Ştefan Ciobâcă[2]

[1]University of Illinois at Urbana-Champaign, USA
{grosu,stefane1@illinois.edu}
[2]University "Alexandru Ioan Cuza" of Iaşi, Romania
stefan.ciobaca@info.uaic.ro

Abstract. Matching logic is a logic for reasoning about program configuration properties in a language-parametric manner. On top of matching logic we define reachability logic and equivalence logic. Reachability logic enables reasoning about the correctness of both deterministic programs (one-path reachability logic) and non-deterministic programs (all-path reachability logic). Equivalence logic enables reasoning about program equivalence. We introduce K, a semantics framework which has been used to define the operational semantics of real-world languages such as C, Java, and JavaScript. We show how the logics above are integrated in K. In particular, we show how the semantics of C, Java, and JavaScript yield automatic program verifiers for the respective languages. The verifiers can check the full functional correctness of challenging heap manipulation programs implementing the same data-structures in these languages (e.g. AVL trees). We also show how to reason about program equivalence using semantics defined in K.

Pathway Logic: Executable Models of Cellular Processes

Carolyn Talcott

SRI International, USA
clt@csl.sri.com

Abstract. Pathway Logic (PL) is a framework based on rewriting logic for developing and analysing executable models of cellular processes. The long term objective is better understanding of how cells work. Progress towards this goal involves curation of experimental knowledge, assembly of models to study a question of interest, visualisation, and analysis.

In this tutorial we will focus on signal transduction: how cells sense their external and internal environment and make decisions. We will begin with some background and describe the informal models and reasoning often used by biologists.

We will describe the PL representation of cellular signalling systems as Maude modules, and explain how knowledge is curated, including steps toward partial automation.

We will then introduce the Pathway Logic Assistant (PLA) a tool for interacting with PL knowledge bases. Using PLA one can search a knowledge base or assemble and visualise a model. Once a model is assembled one can explore its structure or ask questions such as 'how can a given state be reached?' (the answer is an execution pathway) or 'what if I remove this or add that?'.

We will look under the hood of PLA to see how reflection is used to enable Maude to be part of an interactive system. Reflection is also used to manage multiple representations of the knowledge base and derived models for export/import to integrate with other tools and knowledge bases, for example graph drawing tools or special purpose model checkers.

Contents

Labelled Graph Rewriting Meets Social Networks...................... 1
   Maribel Fernández, Hélène Kirchner, Bruno Pinaud, and Jason Vallet

Use of Logical Models for Proving Operational Termination
in General Logics 26
   Salvador Lucas

A Maude Framework for Cache Coherent Multicore Architectures 47
   *Shiji Bijo, Einar Broch Johnsen, Ka I Pun,
and Silvia Lizeth Tapia Tarifa*

Synchronized Tree Languages for Reachability in Non-right-linear Term
Rewrite Systems 64
   Yohan Boichut, Vivien Pelletier, and Pierre Réty

Formal Specification and Verification of a Selective Defense
for TDoS Attacks 82
   *Yuri Gil Dantas, Marcilio O.O. Lemos, Iguatemi E. Fonseca,
and Vivek Nigam*

Egalitarian State-Transition Systems 98
   Óscar Martín, Alberto Verdejo, and Narciso Martí-Oliet

Towards Generic Monitors for Object-Oriented Real-Time
Maude Specifications.. 118
   Antonio Moreno-Delgado, Francisco Durán, and José Meseguer

Proving Reachability-Logic Formulas Incrementally 134
   Vlad Rusu and Andrei Arusoaie

Maximally Parallel Contextual String Rewriting 152
   Traian Florin Şerbănuţă and Liviu P. Dinu

Metalevel Algorithms for Variant Satisfiability 167
   Stephen Skeirik and José Meseguer

Author Index 185

Labelled Graph Rewriting Meets Social Networks

Maribel Fernández[1], Hélène Kirchner[2(✉)], Bruno Pinaud[3], and Jason Vallet[3]

[1] King's College London, London, UK
maribel.fernandez@kcl.ac.uk
[2] Inria, Rocquencourt, France
helene.kirchner@inria.fr
[3] CNRS UMR5800 LaBRI, University of Bordeaux, Bordeaux, France
{bpinaud,jvallet}@labri.fr

Abstract. The intense development of computing techniques and the increasing volumes of produced data raise many modelling and analysis challenges. There is a need to represent and analyse information that is: complex –due to the presence of massive and highly heterogeneous data–, dynamic –due to interactions, time, external and internal evolutions–, connected and distributed in networks. We argue in this work that relevant concepts to address these challenges are provided by three ingredients: labelled graphs to represent networks of data or objects; rewrite rules to deal with concurrent local transformations; strategies to express control versus autonomy and to focus on points of interests. To illustrate the use of these concepts, we choose to focus our interest on social networks analysis, and more precisely in this paper on random network generation. Labelled graph strategic rewriting provides a formalism in which different models can be generated and compared. Conversely, the study of social networks, with their size and complexity, stimulates the search for structure and efficiency in graph rewriting. It also motivated the design of new or more general kinds of graphs, rules and strategies (for instance, to define positions in graphs), which are illustrated here. This opens the way to further theoretical and practical questions for the rewriting community.

1 Introduction

With the intense development of computing techniques, the last decades have seen an increasing complexity of models needed to study phenomena of the physical world and, at the same time, increasing volumes of data produced by observations and computations. New paradigms of data science and data exploration have emerged and opened the way to analytic approaches, such as data-driven algorithms, analysis and mining (also called data analytics). Social and human sciences are also impacted by this evolution and provide interesting research problems for computer scientists. To illustrate these concepts, we choose to focus our interest on social networks, which have been intensively studied in the last years [12,31,36]. The analysis of social networks, used to represent users and their

© Springer International Publishing Switzerland 2016
D. Lucanu (Ed.): WRLA 2016, LNCS 9942, pp. 1–25, 2016.
DOI: 10.1007/978-3-319-44802-2_1

relations with one another, raises several questions concerning their possible construction and evolutions. Among these questions, the study of network propagation phenomena has initiated a sustained interest in the research community, offering applications in various domains, ranging from sociology [23] to epidemiology [9,17] or even viral marketing and product placement [15]. To solve these problems we need to model and analyse systems that are complex, since they involve data that are massive and highly heterogeneous, dynamic, due to interactions, time, external or internal evolutions, connected and distributed in networks.

We argue in this paper that relevant concepts to address these challenges are: **Labelled Graphs** to represent networks of data or objects, **Rules** to deal with concurrent local transformations, and **Strategies** to express control versus autonomy and to focus on points of interests. Indeed, modelling social networks raises many questions we have to address. First, large networks are involved for which an efficient search of patterns is needed, along with capability of focusing on points of interest and defining appropriate views. Since data are often corrupted or imprecise, one should also deal with uncertainty, which implies that we need to address probabilistic or stochastic issues in the models. The dynamic evolution of data is generally modelled by simple transformations, applied in parallel and triggered by events or time. However, such models should also take into account controlled versus autonomous behaviour. Modelling may reveal conflicts that have to be detected (for instance through overlapping rules) and solved (using precedence, choices, i.e., strategic issues). Memory and backtracking must be provided, through notions of computation history or traces. Last but not least, visualisation is important at all levels: for data analysis, program engineering, program debugging, tests and verification (for instance to provide proof intuition).

In [37], we focused on propagation phenomena and showed how some popular models can be expressed using labelled graph and rewriting. In the current paper, we use this previous work to illustrate our computing model and introduce a generative model for social networks. Indeed, many data sets, extracted from various social networks, are publicly available.[1] However, in order to demonstrate the generality of a new approach, or to design and experiment with stochastic algorithms on a sufficiently large sample of network topologies, it is more convenient to use randomly generated networks. Several generative models of random networks are available to work with (e.g., [5,8,18,39]). Some, like the Erdös–Rényi (ER) model [18], do not guarantee any specific property regarding their final topology, whereas others can be characterised as small-world or scale-free networks. This paper shows how to generate such models using labelled graphs, rules and strategies.

Port graph rewriting systems have been used to model systems in a wide variety of domains, such as biochemistry, interaction nets, games or social networks (e.g., [1,20,21,37]). In the following, we reuse from [19] the formal definitions of port graphs with attributes, rewrite rule and rewriting step, the concept of strategic graph program, as well as the definition of the strategy language and its operational semantics, and enrich them in order to achieve a more complete

---

[1] For instance from http://snap.stanford.edu.

and generic definition. Most notably, the refined definitions permit the use of oriented edges and conditional existence matching, reminiscent of similar solutions found in ELAN [10] and GP [35]. We use the PORGY environment which supports interactive modelling using port graph rewriting; more details concerning the rewriting platform can be found in [33].

Summarising, our contributions are twofold: we present a general modelling framework, based on strategic port graph rewriting, that facilitates the analysis of complex systems, and we illustrate its power by focusing on social networks (more precisely, their generation). For this application, the visual high-level modelling features of port graph rewriting are particularly relevant. Concepts of port graphs, rules and strategies are illustrated on this specific domain. Conversely, the study of social networks, with their size and complexity, stimulates the search for structure and efficiency in graph rewriting. We identify open problems and questions that arise when studying social networks.

The paper is organised as follows. Section 2 introduces the modelling concepts we propose to use: port graphs, morphism, rewriting, derivation tree, strategy and strategic graph programs are defined in their full generality, while illustrated on the special case of social networks. In Sect. 3, we focus on social network behaviour simulation, more precisely on social network generation. In Sect. 4, we conclude by synthesising the lessons learned from this study and giving perspectives for future work.

2   Labelled Graph Rewriting

Several definitions of graph rewriting are available, using different kinds of graphs and rewrite rules (see, for instance, [6,7,16,24,28,34]). In this paper we consider *port graphs* with *attributes* associated with nodes, ports and edges, generalising the notion of port graph introduced in [2,3]. The following definitions, based on [19], have been generalised to use indistinctly either directed or undirected edges. We present first the intuitive ideas, followed by the formal definition of port graph rewriting.

2.1   Port Graphs

Intuitively, a port graph is a graph where nodes have explicit connection points called *ports*, to which edges are attached. Nodes, ports and edges are labelled by records listing their attributes.

A *signature* ∇ used to label the graph is composed of:

- $\nabla_{\mathscr{A}}$, a set of attributes;
- $\mathcal{X}_{\mathscr{A}}$, a set of attribute variables;
- $\nabla_{\mathscr{V}}$, a set of values;
- $\mathcal{X}_{\mathscr{V}}$, a set of value variables.

where $\nabla_{\mathscr{A}}$, $\mathcal{X}_{\mathscr{A}}$, $\nabla_{\mathscr{V}}$ and $\mathcal{X}_{\mathscr{V}}$ are pairwise disjoint. $\nabla_{\mathscr{A}}$ contains distinguished elements *Name*, *(In/Out)Arity*, *Connect*, *Attach*, *Interface*. Values in $\nabla_{\mathscr{V}}$ are assumed to be of basic data types such as *strings, int, bool,*... or to be well-typed computable expressions built using ∇ and basic types.

Definition 1 (Record). *A record r over the signature ∇ is a set of pairs $\{(a_1, v_1), \ldots, (a_n, v_n)\}$, where*

$a_i \in \nabla_{\mathscr{A}} \cup \mathcal{X}_{\mathscr{A}}$ *for $1 \leq i \leq n$, called attributes; each a_i occurs only once in r, and there is one distinguished attribute Name.*

$v_i \in \nabla_{\mathscr{V}}$ *for $1 \leq i \leq n$, called values.*

The function Atts applies to records and returns all their attributes:

$$Atts(r) = \{a_1, \ldots, a_n\}$$

if $r = \{(a_1, v_1), \ldots, (a_n, v_n)\}$. As usual, $r.a_i$ denotes the value v_i of the attribute a_i in r.

The attribute Name identifies the record in the following sense: For all r_1, r_2, $Atts(r_1) = Atts(r_2)$ if $r_1.Name = r_2.Name$.

Definition 2 ((Directed) Port Graph). *Given sets $\mathcal{N}, \mathcal{P}, \mathcal{E}$ of nodes, ports and edges, a* port graph *over a signature ∇ is a tuple $G = (N, P, E, \mathcal{L})$ where*

- $N \subseteq \mathcal{N}$ *is a finite set of nodes; $n, n', n_1, \ldots$ range over nodes.*
- $P \subseteq \mathcal{P}$ *is a finite set of ports; $p, p', p_1, \ldots$ range over ports.*
- $E \subseteq \mathcal{E}$ *is a finite set of edges between ports; $e, e', e_1, \ldots$ range over edges. Edges can be directed and two ports may be connected by more than one edge.*
- $\mathcal{L}$ *is a labelling function that returns, for each element in $N \cup P \cup E$, a record such that:*
  - *For each edge $e \in E$, $\mathcal{L}(e)$ contains an attribute Connect whose value is the ordered pair (p_1, p_2) of ports connected by e.*
  - *For each port $p \in P$, $\mathcal{L}(p)$ contains an attribute Attach whose value is the node n which the port belongs to, and an attribute Arity whose value is the number of edges connected to this port. When edges are directed, ports have instead two attributes, InArity and OutArity, whose respective values are the number of edges directed to and from this port.*
  - *For each node $n \in N$, $\mathcal{L}(n)$ contains an attribute Interface whose value is the set of names of ports in the node: $\{\mathcal{L}(p_i).Name \mid \mathcal{L}(p_i).Attach = n\}$. We assume that $\mathcal{L}$ satisfies the following constraint:*

$$\mathcal{L}(n_1).Name = \mathcal{L}(n_2).Name \Rightarrow \mathcal{L}(n_1).Interface = \mathcal{L}(n_2).Interface.$$

By Definition 2, nodes with the same name (i.e., the same value for the attribute *Name*) have the same set of port names (i.e., the same interface), with the same attributes but possibly with different values. Variables may be used to denote any value.

Two nodes $n, n' \in N$ connected by an undirected edge are said to be adjacent and each other neighbours. However, for a directed edge $(n, n') \in E$ going from n to n', only n' is said *adjacent* to n (not conversely) and is called a neighbour of n. The set of nodes adjacent to a subgraph F in G consists of all the nodes in G *outside* F and adjacent to any node in F. $N(n)$ denotes the set of neighbours of the node n.

The advantage of using port graphs rather than plain graphs is that they allow us to express in a more structured and explicit way the properties of the connections, since ports represent the connecting points between edges and nodes. However, the counterpart is that the implementation, rules and matching operations are more complex. So, whenever possible, it is simpler and more efficient to keep the number of ports for each node to a minimum.

Example 1 (Social Network). A social network [11] is commonly described as a graph $G = (N, E)$ built from a set of nodes (the users) N and a set of edges $E \subseteq N \times N$ linking users. Although in most real-world social relations, two persons relate to each other with a mutual recognition, some social networks present an asymmetric model of acknowledgement, the most popular of them being Twitter, classifying one of the users as a *follower* while the other is a *followee*. Such relations can be very simply represented by orienting edges, thus transforming our initial graph in a directed graph.

In this paper, we model a social network as a port graph, where nodes represent users and edges are connections between them. Edges are directed to reflect the relation between users (e.g., follower/followee) and store the attributes of their relation (e.g., influence level, threshold value...). An alternative solution would be to use undirected edges and nodes with two ports called "In" and "Out" for instance, as in [37], to simulate edge direction. In this paper, the nodes representing users have only one port gathering directed connections. While this is sufficient for simple cases, when facing real social networks, multiple ports are useful, either to connect users according to the nature of their relation (e.g., friends, family, co-workers...) or to model situations where a user is connected to friends via different social networks. The full power of port graphs is indeed necessary in multi-layer networks [27] where edges are assigned to different layers and where nodes are shared. In that case, different ports are related to different layers, which can improve modularity of design, readability and matching efficiency through various heuristics. This is however a topic left for future work.

Example 2 (Propagation). Propagation in a network can be seen as follows: when users perform a specific action (announcing an event, spreading a gossip, sharing a video clip, *etc.*), they become *active*. They inform their neighbours of their state change, giving them the possibility to become active themselves if they perform the same action. Such process reiterates as the newly active neighbours share the information with their own neighbours. The activation can thus propagate from peer to peer across the whole network.

To replicate this phenomena observed in real-world networks, some models opt for entirely probabilistic activations (e.g., [14,42]) where the presence of only one active neighbour is enough to allow the propagation to occur. Other models use threshold values (e.g., [22,26,40]) building up during the propagation. Such values represent the influence of one user on his neighbours or his tolerance towards performing a given action (the more solicited a user is, the more inclined he becomes to either activate or utterly resist).

To express propagation conditions (e.g., a probabilistic model for node activation, or activation after reaching a predefined threshold), it is natural to make use of records with expressions, i.e., include specific attributes whose values are numerical expressions. More specifically:

- Each node n has an attribute *Active* that indicates whether it contributes to the propagation or not. It is coupled with the *Colour* attribute, which takes accordingly green or red values. The node n has also a *Sigma* attribute that measures the maximum influence withstood by n from its active neighbours at the time being.
- An edge e that connects two ports p' and p of the respective nodes n' and n has an attribute *Influence* which indicates the influence of n' (i.e., $\mathcal{L}(p').Attach$) on n (i.e., $\mathcal{L}(p).Attach$). The edge e has also a Boolean attribute *Marked*, initially false, which becomes true when n is inactive, n' is active and n' has tried to influence n.

2.2   Rewriting

We see a *port graph rewrite rule* $L \Rightarrow R$ as a port graph consisting of two subgraphs L and R together with a special node (called *arrow* node) that encodes the correspondence between the ports of L and the ports of R. Each of the ports attached to the arrow node has an attribute $Type \in \nabla_{\mathscr{A}}$, which can have three different values: *bridge*, *wire* and *blackhole*. The value indicates how a rewriting step using this rule should affect the edges that connect the redex to the rest of the graph. We give details below.

Definition 3 (Port Graph Rewrite Rule).   *A port graph rewrite rule is a port graph consisting of:*

- *two port graphs L and R over the signature ∇, respectively called* left-hand side *and* right-hand side, *such that all the variables in R occur in L, and R may contain records with expressions;*
- *an* arrow *node with a set of edges that each connect a port of the arrow node to ports in L or R.*

The arrow node has for Name $\Rightarrow$. Each port in the arrow node has an attribute Type, *which can be of value:* bridge, blackhole *or* wire, *satisfying the following conditions:*

1. *A port of type* bridge *must have edges connecting it to L and to R (one edge to L and one or more to R).*
2. *A port of type* blackhole *must have edges connecting it only to L (at least one edge).*
3. *A port of type* wire *must have exactly two edges connecting to L and no edge connecting to R.*

The arrow node has an optional attribute Where *whose value is a Boolean expression involving the predicate* Edge, *applied to node and port names, and Boolean operators.*

When modelling rumour propagation, the rules never suppress nor add new nodes. Moreover, when there is only one port per node, there is no ambiguity on the rewiring between left and right-hand sides. In that case indeed, the structure and visualisation of the arrow node is much simpler. However, this only holds when the network's structure does not change.

The introduction of the *Where* attribute is inspired from the GP programming system [35] (and from ELAN [10] with a more general definition), in which a rule may have a condition introduced by the keyword where. For instance, a condition where not Edge(n,n') requires that no edge exists between the nodes n and n'. This condition is checked at matching time.

Let us first recall the notion of port graph morphism [19]. Let G and H be two port graphs over the same signature ∇. A *port graph morphism* $f : G \to H$ maps nodes, ports and (directed) edges of G to those of H such that the attachment of ports and the (directed) edges connections are preserved, all attributes and values are preserved except for variables in G, which must be instantiated in H. Intuitively, the morphism identifies a subgraph of H that is equal to G except at positions where G has variables (at those positions, H could have any instance).

Definition 4 (Match). *Let $L \Rightarrow R$ be a port graph rewrite rule and G a port graph. We say a match $g(L)$ of the left-hand side (also called a redex) is found if:*

– *There is a port graph morphism g from L to G; hence $g(L)$ is a subgraph of G.*
– *If the arrow node has an attribute* Where *with value C, C must be true of $g(L)$.*
– *For each port in L that is not connected to the arrow node, its corresponding port in $g(L)$ must not be an extremity in the set of edges of $G - g(L)$.*

This last point ensures that ports in L that are not connected to the arrow node are mapped to ports in $g(L)$ that have no edges connecting them with ports outside the redex, to avoid dangling edges in rewriting steps.

Several injective morphisms g from L to G may exist (leading to different rewriting steps); they are computed as solutions of a *matching* problem from L to (a subgraph of) G.

Definition 5 (Rewriting Step). *According to [19], a rewriting step on G using a rule $L \Rightarrow R$ (where C) and a morphism $g : L \to G$ (satisfying C), written $G \to^{g}_{L \Rightarrow R} G'$, transforms G into a new graph G' obtained from G by performing the following operations in three phases:*

– *In the build phase, after a redex $g(L)$ is found in G, a copy $R_c = g(R)$ (i.e., an instantiated copy of the port graph R) is added to G.*
– *The rewiring phase then redirects edges from G to R_c as follows:*
  For each port p in the arrow node:
  • *If p is a bridge port and $p_L \in L$ is connected to p:*
    for each port $p^i_R \in R$ connected to p,
    find all the ports p^k_G in G that are connected to $g(p_L)$ and are not in $g(L)$, and redirect each edge connecting p^k_G and $g(p_L)$ to connect p^k_G and $p^i_{R_c}$.

- *If p is a wire port connected to two ports p_1 and p_2 in L, then take all the ports outside g(L) that are connected to $g(p_1)$ in G and connect each of them to each port outside g(L) connected by an edge to $g(p_2)$.*
- *If p is a blackhole: for each port $p_L \in L$ connected to p, destroy all the edges connected to $g(p_L)$ in G.*
- *The deletion phase simply deletes g(L). This creates the final graph G'.*

Example 3 (Propagation). Figure 1 shows two rules used for propagation. Active nodes are depicted in green and visited nodes in purple. Red nodes are in an inactive state (however, they may have been visited already). Rule *R1* in Fig. 1(a) indicates that when an activated node n is connected to an inactive node $\overline{n}$, it tries to influence it. If it succeeds, a second rule, Rule *R2* in Fig. 1(b), makes this node active.

In a social network $G = (N, E)$, let n and $\overline{n}$ be two nodes $(n, \overline{n} \in N)$ connected via an edge $e = (n, \overline{n}) \in E$. The node's attribute $\mathcal{L}(\overline{n}).Sigma$, giving the influence withstood by $\overline{n}$ and initially set to 0, is updated such as:

$$\mathcal{L}(\overline{n}).Sigma = \max\left(\frac{\mathcal{L}(e).Influence}{r}, \mathcal{L}(\overline{n}).Sigma\right)$$

where r is a random number between 0 and 1 and $\mathcal{L}(e).Influence$ is the influence of n on $\overline{n}$. The formula is stored as a node attribute in the right-hand side of Rule *R1* in Fig. 1(a) and each corresponding rewriting performs the update. More details are given in [37].

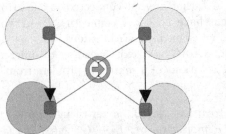
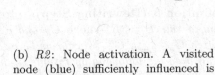

(a) *R1*: Influence trial. An active neighbour (green) influences an inactive node (red) by visiting it (transformation into a blue node).

(b) *R2*: Node activation. A visited node (blue) sufficiently influenced is activated (transformation into a green node).

Fig. 1. Rules used to express a propagation model. For both rules, we use two specific node's *attributes–active* and *visited–* to manage the matching performed, the different colours being visual cues helping users identifying the node state at a glance. Green nodes, or active nodes, must have their attributes *active* equal to 1 and *visited* equal to 0; red nodes, or inactive nodes, must have their attributes *active* equal to 0 and *visited* equal to 0; finally, blue nodes, or visited nodes, must have their attributes *active* equal to 0 and *visited* equal to 1. (Color figure online)

Given a finite set $\mathcal{R}$ of rules, a port graph G *rewrites* to G', denoted by $G \rightarrow_{\mathcal{R}} G'$, if there is a rule r in $\mathcal{R}$ and a morphism g such that $G \rightarrow_r^g G'$. This induces a reflexive and transitive relation on port graphs, called *the rewriting relation*, denoted by $\rightarrow_{\mathcal{R}}^*$. A port graph on which no rule is applicable is *irreducible*.

A *derivation*, or computation, is a sequence $G \rightarrow_{\mathcal{R}}^* G'$ of rewriting steps. Each rewriting step involves the application of a rule at a specific position in the graph. A *derivation tree* from G represents all possible computations (with possibly infinite ones) and *strategies* are used to specify the rewriting steps of interest, by selecting branches in the derivation tree.

2.3 Strategic Graph Programs

In this section, we recall the concept of *strategic graph program*, consisting of a *located graph* (a port graph with two distinguished subgraphs that specify the locations where rewriting is enabled/disabled), a set of rewriting rules, and a strategy expression. We then recall the strategy language presented in [19] to define strategy expressions. In addition to the well-known constructs to select rewrite rules, the strategy language provides position primitives to select or ban specific positions in the graph for rewriting. The latter is useful to program graph traversals in a concise and natural way, and is a distinctive feature of the language. In the context of social networks, the position primitives are also convenient to restrict the application of rules to specific parts of the graph.

Located Graphs and Rewrite Rules. First, we recall that, in graph theory, a subgraph of a graph $G = (N_G, E_G)$ is a graph $H = (N_H, E_H)$ contained in G, that is, $N_H \subseteq N_G$ and $E_H \subseteq E_G$. The definition extends to directed port graphs in the natural way: let $G = (N_G, P_G, E_G, \mathcal{L}_G)$ and $H = (N_H, P_H, E_H, \mathcal{L}_H)$ be port graphs over the signature ∇. H is a subgraph of G if $N_H \subseteq N_G$, $P_H \subseteq P_G$, $E_H \subseteq E_G$, $\mathcal{L}_H = \mathcal{L}_G|_{N_H \cup P_H \cup E_H}$, that is, $\mathcal{L}_H$ is the restriction to H of the labelling function of G.

Definition 6 (Located Graph). *According to [19], a* located graph G_P^Q *consists of a port graph G and two distinguished subgraphs P and Q of G, called respectively the* position subgraph, *or simply* position, *and the* banned subgraph.

In a located graph G_P^Q, P represents the subgraph of G where rewriting steps may take place (i.e., P is the focus of the rewriting) and Q represents the subgraph of G where rewriting steps are forbidden. We give a precise definition below; the intuition is that subgraphs of G that overlap with P may be rewritten, if they are outside Q.

When applying a port graph rewrite rule, not only the underlying graph G but also the position and banned subgraphs may change. A *located rewrite rule*, defined below, specifies two disjoint subgraphs M and M' of the right-hand side R that are respectively used to update the position and banned subgraphs. If M (resp. M') is not specified, R (resp. the empty graph $\emptyset$) is used as default. Below, we use the operators $\cup, \cap, \setminus$ to denote union, intersection and complement of port graphs. These operators are defined in the natural way on port graphs considered as sets of nodes, ports and edges.

Definition 7 (Located Rewrite Rule). *A located rewrite rule is given by a port graph rewrite rule* $L \Rightarrow R$, *and, optionally, a subgraph* W *of* L *and two disjoint subgraphs* M *and* M' *of* R. *It is denoted* $L_W \Rightarrow R_M^{M'}$. *We write* $G_P^Q \rightarrow_{L_W \Rightarrow R_M^{M'}}^g G'_{P'}^{Q'}$ *and say that the located graph* G_P^Q *rewrites to* $G'_{P'}^{Q'}$ *using* $L_W \Rightarrow R_M^{M'}$ *at position* P *avoiding* Q, *if* $G \rightarrow_{L \Rightarrow R} G'$ *with a morphism* g *such that* $g(L) \cap P = g(W)$ *or simply* $g(L) \cap P \neq \emptyset$ *if* W *is not provided, and* $g(L) \cap Q = \emptyset$. *The new position subgraph* P' *and banned subgraph* Q' *are defined as* $P' = (P \setminus g(L)) \cup g(M)$, $Q' = Q \cup g(M')$; *if* M *(resp.* M') *are not provided then we assume* $M = R$ *(resp.* $M' = \emptyset$).

In general, for a given located rule $L_W \Rightarrow R_M^{M'}$ and located graph G_P^Q, more than one morphism g, such that $g(L) \cap P = g(W)$ and $g(L) \cap Q$ is empty, may exist (i.e., several rewriting steps at P avoiding Q may be possible). Thus, the application of the rule at P avoiding Q produces a *set of located graphs*.

Example 4. In influence propagation, banned subgraphs are used to avoid several activations of the same neighbours. Another usage is to select a specific community in the social network where the propagation should take place.

2.4   Strategies

To control the application of the rules, a strategy language is presented in [19]. We recall it in Table 1, including some additional constructs that are needed to deal with directed edges.

Strategy expressions are generated by the grammar rules from the non-terminal S. A strategy expression combines applications of located rewrite rules, generated by the non-terminal A, and *position updates*, generated by the non-terminal U, using *focusing expressions*, generated by F. Subgraphs of a given graph can be defined by specifying simple properties, expressed with attributes of nodes, edges and ports. The strategy constructs, generated by S, are used to compose strategies and are strongly inspired from term rewriting languages such as ELAN [10], Stratego [38] and Tom [4].

We briefly explain below the constructs used in this paper. A full description of the language can be found in [19].

The primary construct is a located rule, which can only be applied to a located graph G_P^Q if at least a part of the redex is in P, and does not involve Q. When probabilities $\pi_1, \ldots, \pi_k \in [0, 1]$ are associated to rules $T_1, \ldots, T_k$ such that $\pi_1 + \cdots + \pi_k = 1$, the strategy $\mathtt{ppick}(T_1, \pi_1, \ldots, T_k, \pi_k)$ picks one of the rules for application, according to the given probabilities.

$\mathtt{all}(T)$ denotes all possible applications of the transformation T on the located graph at the current position, creating a new located graph for each application. In the derivation tree, this creates as many children as there are possible applications.

Table 1. Syntax of the strategy language.

Let L, R be port graphs; M, M' subgraphs of R; W a subgraph of L; $k \in \mathbb{N}$; $\pi_{i=1\ldots k} \in [0,1]$; $\sum_{i=1}^{k} \pi_i = 1$; let *attribute* be an attribute label in $\nabla_{\mathscr{A}}$; $v \in \nabla_{\mathscr{V}}$ a valid expression without variables;		

<table>
<tr><td rowspan="2">Rules</td><td>(Transformations)</td><td>$T ::= L_W \Rightarrow R_M^{M'} \mid (T \parallel T)$
$\mid \texttt{ppick}(T_1, \pi_1, \ldots, T_k, \pi_k)$</td></tr>
<tr><td>(Applications)</td><td>$A ::= \texttt{all}(T) \mid \texttt{one}(T)$</td></tr>
<tr><td rowspan="4">Positions</td><td>(Focusing)</td><td>$F ::= \texttt{crtGraph} \mid \texttt{crtPos} \mid \texttt{crtBan}$
$\mid F \cup F \mid F \cap F \mid F \setminus F \mid (F) \mid \emptyset$
$\mid \texttt{ppick}(F_1, \pi_1, \ldots, F_k, \pi_k)$
$\mid \texttt{property}(F, \rho) \mid \texttt{ngb}(F, \rho)$
$\mid \texttt{ngbOut}(F, \rho) \mid \texttt{ngbIn}(F, \rho)$</td></tr>
<tr><td>(Determine)</td><td>$D ::= \texttt{all}(F) \mid \texttt{one}(F)$</td></tr>
<tr><td>(Update)</td><td>$U ::= \texttt{setPos}(D) \mid \texttt{setBan}(D)$
$\mid \texttt{update}(function\{parameters\_list\})$</td></tr>
<tr><td rowspan="4">Properties</td><td>(Properties)</td><td>$\rho ::= Elem, Expr$</td></tr>
<tr><td></td><td>$Elem ::= \texttt{node} \mid \texttt{edge} \mid \texttt{port}$</td></tr>
<tr><td></td><td>$Expr ::= attribute \ Relop \ v \mid \texttt{true}$</td></tr>
<tr><td></td><td>$Relop ::= == \ \mid \ != \ \mid \ > \ \mid \ <$
$\mid \ >= \ \mid \ <= \ \mid \ =\sim$</td></tr>
<tr><td rowspan="2">Compositions</td><td>(Comparison)</td><td>$C ::= F = F \mid F \mathrel{!=} F \mid F \subset F \mid \texttt{isEmpty}(F)$
$\mid \texttt{match}(T)$</td></tr>
<tr><td>(Strategies)</td><td>$S ::= \texttt{id} \mid \texttt{fail} \mid A \mid U \mid C \mid S; S$
$\mid \texttt{if}(S)\texttt{then}(S)\texttt{else}(S) \mid (S)\texttt{orelse}(S)$
$\mid \texttt{repeat}(S)[(k)] \mid \texttt{while}(S)[(k)]\texttt{do}(S)$
$\mid \texttt{ppick}(S_1, \pi_1, \ldots, S_k, \pi_k)$
$\mid \texttt{try}(S) \mid \texttt{not}(S)$</td></tr>
</table>

$\texttt{one}(T)$ computes only one of the possible applications of the transformation and ignores the others; more precisely, it makes an equiprobable choice between all possible applications.

Similar constructs exist for positions focusing: $\texttt{one}(F)$ returns one node in F and $\texttt{all}(F)$ returns the full F. In the remaining of this paper, when not specified, F stands for $\texttt{all}(F)$.

Focusing expressions are used to define positions for rewriting in a graph, or to define positions where rewriting is not allowed. They denote functions used in strategy expressions to change the positions P and Q in the current located graph. In this paper, we use:

- crtGraph, crtPos and crtBan, applied to a located graph G_P^Q, return respectively the whole graph G, P and Q.
- property(F, ρ) is used to select elements of a given graph that satisfy a certain property, specified by ρ. It can be seen as a filtering construct: if the expression F generates a subgraph G' then property(F, ρ) returns only the nodes and/or edges from G that satisfy the decidable property $\rho = Elem, Expr$. Depending on the value of $Elem$, the property is evaluated on nodes, ports, or edges.
- ngb(F, ρ) returns a subset of the neighbours (i.e., adjacent nodes) of F according to ρ. Note that the direction of the edge is taken into account; to emphasise it, we introduce ngbOut(F, ρ) and its counterpart ngbIn(F, ρ). If edge is used, i.e., if we write ngb$(F, \text{edge}, Expr)$, it returns all the neighbours of F connected to F via edges which satisfy the expression $Expr$.
- setPos(D) (resp. setBan(D)) sets the position subgraph P (resp. Q) to be the graph resulting from the expression D. It always succeeds (i.e., returns id).

The following constructs are also used:

- $S;S'$ represents sequential application of S followed by S'.
- repeat$(S)[\text{max } n]$ simply iterates the application of S until it fails, but, if max n is specified, then the number of repetitions cannot exceed n.
- (S)orelse(S') applies S if possible, otherwise applies S'. It fails if both S and S' fail.
- When probabilities $\pi_1, \ldots, \pi_k \in [0, 1]$ are associated to strategies $S_1, \ldots, S_k$ such that $\pi_1 + \cdots + \pi_k = 1$, the strategy ppick$(S_1, \pi_1, \ldots, S_k, \pi_k)$ picks one of the strategies for application, according to the given probabilities. This construct generalises the probabilistic constructs on rules and positions.

Example 5 (Propagation). (Example 3 cont'd)   To illustrate the strategy language, let us come back to the propagation model in social networks and to the two rules described in Fig. 1. When Rule *R1* in Fig. 1(a) is applied on a pair of nodes active(n)/non active$(\overline{n})$ (green/red): *(a)* we generate a random number $r \in]0, 1]$; *(b)* we store in the attribute $\mathcal{L}(\overline{n}).Sigma$ the new value of $Sigma$ for $\overline{n}$ computed with the previously given formula; and *(c)* using the $Marked$ attribute, we mark the edge e linking n to $\overline{n}$ to prevent the selection of this particular pair configuration in the next pattern matching searches. This ensures that the active node n will not be able to try to influence the same node $\overline{n}$ over and over.

Once every pair of active/inactive neighbours has been tried, if $\overline{n}$ is sufficiently influenced (i.e., $\mathcal{L}(\overline{n}).Sigma \geq 1$), Rule *R2* in Fig. 1(b) is applied and $\overline{n}$ becomes active. This behaviour is expressed with the following strategy:

Strategy 1: Influence propagation in social network.

```
1 repeat(R1);
2 setPos(property(crtGraph, node, Sigma ≥ "1"));
3 repeat(R2)
```

This example illustrates how record expressions may be used to compute attribute values and how they are updated through application of rules.

Probabilistic features of the PORGY strategy language, through the use of the ppick() construct, are illustrated in Sect. 3 for social network generation.

A more complete formal definition of strategic graph programs and their semantics can be found in [19]. Correctness and completeness of strategic port graph rewriting are stated and imply in particular that the derivation tree in which each rewrite step is performed according to the strategy –let us call it the *strategic derivation tree*– is actually a subtree of the derivation tree of the rewrite system without strategy. The strategic derivation tree is a valuable concept because it records the history of the transformations and provides access to generated models. It is, by itself, a source of challenging questions, such as detecting isomorphic models and folding the tree, finding equivalent paths and defining the "best ones", abstracting a sequence of steps by a composition strategy, or managing the complexity of the tree and its visualisation.

From now on, the paper focuses on social networks generation using the introduced labelled graph rewriting concepts and the PORGY environment.

3   Social Network Generation

We focus in the following on generating graphs with a small-world property as defined in [41]. Such graphs are characterised by a small diameter –the average distance between any pair of nodes is short– and strong local clustering –any pair of connected nodes tend to both be connected to the same neighbour nodes thus creating densely linked groups of nodes, also called *communities*. Popularised by Milgram in [30], small-world graphs are a perfect case study for information propagation in social networks due to their small diameter allowing a quick and efficient spreading of information among the users. Furthermore, the graph $G = (N, E)$ produced by the generation process satisfies the following requirements: the number of nodes $|N|$ and directed edges $|E|$ are given *a priori*; G is formed of a sole connected component thus $|E|$ should at least be equal to $|N| - 1$; any ordered pair of nodes (n, n') can only be linked once, thus maximising the possible number of edges in G to $|E|_{max} = |N| \times (|N| - 1)$; finally, the definitive number of communities is left to be randomly decided during the generative operations.

A few previous works have explored the idea of using rules to generate networks. In [25], the authors define and study probabilistic inductive classes of graphs generated by rules which model spread of knowledge, dynamics of acquaintanceship and emergence of communities. The model presented below follows a rather similar approach; however, we have adjusted its generative rules to cope with directed edges and ensure the creation of a graph with a single connected component. This is achieved by performing the generation through local additive transformations, each only creating new elements connected to the sole component, thus increasingly making the graph larger, more intricate and more interesting to study.

Starting from one node, the generation is divided into three phases imitating the process followed by real-world social networks. Whenever new users first join the social network, their number of connections is very limited, mostly to the other users who have introduced them to the social network. Then comes the second phase where the new users reach the people they already know personally, thus creating new connections within the network, which may seem random for any spectator only aware of the present social network. Finally, the new users start to get to know the people with whom they are sharing friends in the network, potentially leading to the creation of new connections.

The method presented below can easily be extended to create graphs with more than one component. One has to use a number of starting nodes equal to the number of desired connected components and ensure that no edge is created between nodes from different components. The generative rules and strategies can then be applied on each component iteratively or in parallel (parallel application of rules is possible but beyond the scope of this paper).

The first step (Sect. 3.1) generates a simple directed acyclic graph representing an initial simple network evolving as new users join it. It is then complemented with additional edges in the second step (Sect. 3.2), as users "import" their pre-existing connections into the social network. Finally, the third and final step (Sect. 3.3) focuses on creating communities as users connect with the friends of their friends within the network.

3.1 Generation of a Directed Acyclic Graph

The first step toward the construction of the directed graph $G = (N, E)$ uses the two rules shown in Figs. 2(a) and (b). Both rewriting operations start with a single node and transform it to generate a second node linked to the first one (thus creating a new node and a new edge with each application). The difference between those two rules lies in the edge orientation as Rule 2(a) creates an outgoing edge on the initiating node, while Rule 2(b) creates an incoming edge.

We can notice the left hand-sides of both rules require the existence of a node prior to their application, thus imposing the starting graph upon which the rules will be applied to have at least one node. As we also seek to ensure that only one connected component exists prior to any transformation, we use a single node as the starting graph.

Strategy 2: *Node generation*: Creating a directed acyclic graph of size N

```
1  //equiprobabilistic application of the two rules used for generating nodes
2  repeat(
3      ppick(one(GenerationNode1), 0.5,
4             one(GenerationNode2), 0.5)
5  )(|N| − 1) // Generation of N nodes
```

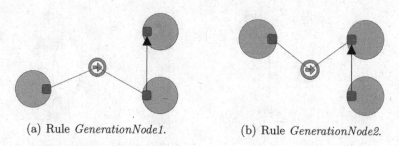

(a) Rule *GenerationNode1*.　　　　　　(b) Rule *GenerationNode2*.

Fig. 2. Rules used for generating and re-attaching nodes to the social network. For both rules, a new node is created in the right-hand side and connected to the pre-existing node. The main difference between the two rules resides in the generated edge orientation: going from the pre-existing node (belonging to the social network) to the newly added node in Rule (a) or oriented in the opposite direction in Rule (b).

The whole node generation is achieved during this first phase and managed using Strategy 2. It repeatedly applies the generative rules $|N| - 1$ times so that the graph reaches the appropriate number of nodes. As mentioned earlier, each rule application also generates a new edge, which means that once executed, Strategy 2 produces a graph with exactly $|N|$ nodes and $|N| - 1$ edges. The orientation of each edge varies depending of the rule applied (either 2(a) or 2(b)), moreover, their application using the `ppick()` construct allows us to ensure an equiprobable choice between the two rules. We focus next on generating additional edges.

3.2 Creating Complementary Connections

We still need to generate $(|E|-|N|+1)$ additional edges in the graph G. However, because we want to ensure the creation of communities during the last phase, we do not wish to create all the remaining edges just now. Depending on how we balance the number of edges created during this phase and the next one, the final graphs will present different characteristics (see Figs. 5 and 6). During this phase, we aim to create either seemingly random connections between the network users or to reciprocate already existing single-sided connections.

We use two rules to link existing nodes thus creating a new additional edge with each application. The first rule (Fig. 3(a)) simply considers two nodes and adds an edge between them to emulate the creation of a (one-sided) connection between two users. The second rule (Fig. 3(b)) reciprocates an existing connection between a pair of users: for two nodes $n, n' \in N$ connected with an edge (n', n), a new edge (n, n') is created; it is used to represent the mutual appreciation of users in the social network. Note that, because each node is randomly chosen among the possible matches, we do not need to create alternative versions of these rules with reversed oriented edges.

In both rules, the existence of edges between the nodes on which the rule applies should be taken into account. Though the rules visual representations do not explicitly indicate it, any edge (n, n') created by either rule cannot already

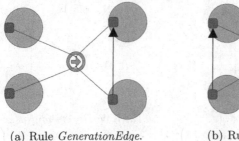 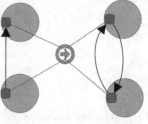

(a) Rule *GenerationEdge*.   (b) Rule *GenerationMirror*.

Fig. 3. First set of rules used to generate additional connections within the social network. Rule (a) is used to create a new connection between two previously created and unrelated nodes, while Rule (b) is applied on a pair of connected nodes and generates a new edge reciprocating the pre-existing connection.

exist in the network, thus forbidding the rules to apply in such case. This requirement can be taken into account by adding a condition "where not Edge(n,n')" introduced in Definition 3. It can also be handled through positions for limiting the elements to be considered during matching. We use the latter solution here. Strategy 3 presents how we proceed. First, we filter the elements to consider during the matching. We randomly select one node among the nodes whose outgoing arity (*OutArity*) is lower than the maximal possible value (i.e., $|N| - 1$), and we banish all of its outgoing neighbours as they cannot be considered as potential matching elements. Then, Rule 3(a) or Rule 3(b) are equiprobably applied to add a new edge from the selected node. Previously banishing neighbours allows only considering pair of nodes not already connected. This ensures that the graph is kept simple (i.e., only one edge per direction between two nodes).

Strategy 3: *Edge generation*: addition of $|E'|$ edges if possible.

```
1 repeat(
2 //select one node with an appropriate number of neighbours
3   setPos(one(property(crtGraph, node, OutArity < |N| − 1)));
4 //for this node, forbid rule applications on its outgoing neighbours
5   setBan(all(ngbOut(crtPos, node, true)));
6 //equiprobable application of the edge generation rules
7   ppick((one(GenerationEdge))orelse(one(GenerationMirror)), 0.5,
8         (one(GenerationMirror))orelse(one(GenerationEdge)), 0.5);
9 )(|E'|)
```

We aim to create $|E'|$ more edges, where $|E'| < (|E| - |N| + 1)$ to keep the number of edges below $|E|$. The use of the ( )orelse() construct allows testing all possible rule application combinations, thus, if one of the rules can be applied, it is found. If neither rule can be applied, the maximum number of edges in the graph has been reached, i.e., the graph is complete. The values given for the number of edges $|E'|$ is too high to create a simple graph. If the strategy went well, we are left with $(|E| - |E'| - |N| + 1)$ remaining edges to create in the next step for enforcing communities within G.

3.3   Construction of Communities

To create a realistic social network, we want to add communities. Thus, some of the links between users have to follow certain patterns. Based on ideas advanced in several previous works (e.g., [13,25,29,32]), we focus our interest on triad configurations (i.e., groups formed by three users linked together) to generate and extend communities via the three rewrite rules introduced in Fig. 4.

The first triad rule (Fig. 4(a)) considers how a first user (A) influences a second user (B) who influences in turn a third user (C). This situation can produce some sort of transitivity as "the idol of my idol is my idol", meaning that A is much likely to influence C. We use here the term "idol" instead of the more classical "friend" because we only consider single-sided relations as a base for the transformation. The second rule (Fig. 4(b)) shows two users (B and C) being influenced by a third user (A). When in this position, the users B and C

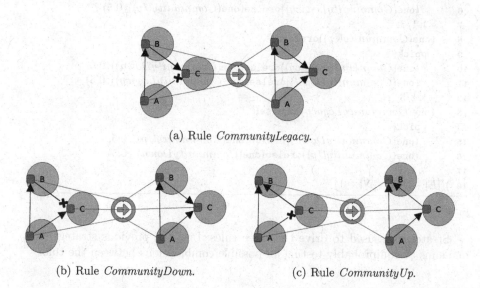

(a) Rule *CommunityLegacy*.

(b) Rule *CommunityDown*.   (c) Rule *CommunityUp*.

Fig. 4. Generation of additional connections based on triads. Rule (a) is used to identify influence chains: when C is influenced by B, itself influenced by A, the rule creates a new connection from A to C. Rule (b) focuses on triads where two users B and C are influenced by a third person A: this common characteristic can lead B and C to develop a relation. Rule (c) is somewhat the opposite of Rule (b): two users A and C influence a third user B, creating a connection between them (from A to C). Two distinctive edge types are used: standard arrow edges for representing existing connections and cross-shaped headed edges for indicating edges which should not exist during the matching phase.

might start exchanging (similar connections, common interests...), thus creating a relation between the two of them (either from B to C or the opposite). The last rule (Fig. 4(c)) depicts one user (B) being influenced by two other users (A and C). This case can happen when A and C are well-versed about a common subject of interest which is of importance to B. An exchange can thus appear between the two influential users (from A to C for instance).

The three rules use a `where not Edge(n,n')` condition to forbid the existence of an edge between two matching nodes. The condition is visually encoded using a cross-shaped headed edge to indicate which edge should be verified as non-existent during the matching operations.

Strategy 4: *Community generation:* remaining edges creation to strengthen communities

---

```
1  repeat(
2    ppick(
3      (one(CommunityDown))orelse(
4        ppick(
5          (one(CommunityUp))orelse(one(CommunityLegacy)), 0.5,
6          (one(CommunityLegacy))orelse(one(CommunityUp)), 0.5)
7        ), 1/3,
8      (one(CommunityUp))orelse(
9        ppick(
10         (one(CommunityLegacy))orelse(one(CommunityDown)), 0.5,
11         (one(CommunityDown))orelse(one(CommunityLegacy)), 0.5)
12       ), 1/3,
13     (one(CommunityLegacy))orelse(
14       ppick(
15         (one(CommunityDown))orelse(one(CommunityUp)), 0.5,
16         (one(CommunityUp))orelse(one(CommunityDown)), 0.5)
17       ), 1/3)
18 )(|E| − |E'| − |N| + 1)
```

Strategy 4 is used to drive the three rules. Like the previous strategy, this one aims at equiprobably testing all possible combinations between the rules.

3.4 Resulting Network Generation

Once the last strategy execution is completed, the social network generation is achieved. For the sake of simplicity, the strategies presented above aim at making equiprobable choices between rules. The probabilities may of course be modified to take into account any specific condition present in the modelled system, moreover, whatever the chosen probabilities are, the following result holds.

Proposition 1. *Given three positive integer parameters* $|N|, |E|, |E'|$, *such that* $|N|-1 \leq |E| \leq |N| \times (|N|-1)$ *and* $|E'| \leq |E|-|N|+1$, *let the strategy* $S_{|N|,|E|,|E'|}$

be the sequential composition of the strategies Node generation, Edge generation *and* Community generation *described above, and* G_0 *be a port graph composed of one node with one port. The strategic graph program* $[S, G_0]$ *terminates with a port graph* G *with* $|N|$ *nodes and* $|E|$ *edges, which is simple, directed and weakly-connected.*

Proof. Let us prove by induction that the generated port graphs are directed, simple (at most one edge in each direction between any two nodes) and weakly connected (connected when direction of edges is ignored). This is trivially true for G_0 and each rewrite step preserves these three properties, thanks to the positioning strategy that controls the outdegree in *Edge generation* (Strategy 3) and the forbidden edges in the rules for *Community generation* (Fig. 4). As the strategic program never fails, since a repeat strategy cannot fail, this means that a finite number of rules has been applied and the three properties hold by rewriting induction. Then by construction, the strategy *Node generation* creates a new node and a new edge at each step of the repeat loop, exactly $|N| - 1$, and is the only strategy that creates new nodes. From here, G has exactly $|N|$ nodes and $|N| - 1$ edges. The strategies *Edge generation* and *Community generation* create a new edge at each step of the repeat loop, so respectively $|E'|$ and $|E| - |E'| - |N| + 1$. As a result, when the strategy S terminates, the number of edges created is equal to $|N| - 1 + |E'| + |E| - |E'| - |N| + 1 = |E|$. □

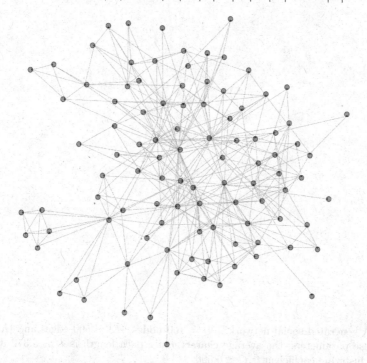

Fig. 5. A generated social network. $|N| = 100$ nodes, $|E| = 500$ edges and $|E'| = 50$. With these parameters, the average characteristic path length is $L \simeq 2.563$ and the average clustering coefficient is $C \simeq 0.426$.

3.5 Implementation, Experimentation and Visualisation

We use the PORGY system [33] to experiment with our generative model. The latest version of the rewriting platform[2] is available either as source code or binaries for MacOS and Windows machines.

Figures 5 and 6 are two examples of social networks generated using a sequential composition of the previous strategies. Although both graphs have the same number of nodes and edges ($|N| = 100$ and $|E| = 500$), they have been generated with different $|E'|$, respectively $|E'| = 50$ for Fig. 5 and $|E'| = 0$ for Fig. 6. This changes the number of purely random edges created in the resulting graph and explains why the first graph seems to visually present less structure than the other one. Conversely, a graph with only randomly assigned edges could be generated with $|E'| = |E| - |N| + 1$.

To ensure that our constructions present characteristics of real-world social networks, we have performed several generations using different parameters and measured the *characteristic path length* – the average number of edges in the

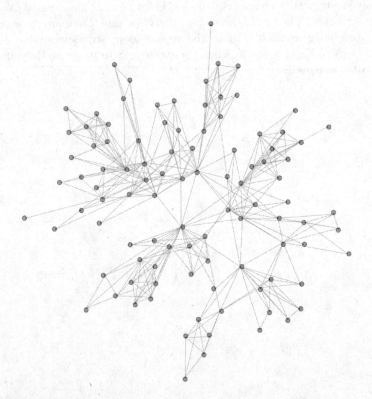

Fig. 6. A generated social network. $|N| = 100$ nodes, $|E| = 500$ edges and $|E'| = 0$. With these parameters, the average characteristic path length is $L \simeq 3.372$ and the average clustering coefficient is $C \simeq 0.596$.

[2] PORGY website: http://tulip.labri.fr/TulipDrupal/?q=porgy.

shortest path between any two nodes in the graph – and the *clustering coefficient* – how many neighbours of a node n are also connected with each other – as defined in [41]. In a typical random graph, e.g., a graph generated using the Erdös–Rényi model [18] or using our method with the parameters $|N| = 100$ nodes, $|E| = 500$ edges and $|E'| = |E| - |N| + 1 = 401$, the average characteristic path length is very short ($L \simeq 2.274$), allowing information to go quickly from one node to another, but the clustering coefficient is low ($C \simeq 0.101$), implying the lack of well-developed communities. However, with the parameters used in Fig. 5 (respectively, Fig. 6), we retain a short characteristic path length $L \simeq 2.563$ (resp. $L \simeq 3.372$) while increasing the clustering coefficient $C \simeq 0.426$ (resp. $C \simeq 0.596$), thus matching the characteristics of small-world graphs: a small diameter and strong local clustering.

The graphs generated using our method can be subsequently used as any randomly generated network. For instance, we have used such graphs in [37] to study the evolution of different information propagation models. PORGY was used in this work to run several propagation scenarios and analyse the resulting outputs with its visualisation tools.

4   Conclusion

Our first experiments and results on generation and propagation in social networks, obtained in [37] and in this work, illustrate how labelled port graph strategic rewriting provides a common formalism in which different mathematical models can be expressed and compared. The ultimate goal is to provide a simulation environment helpful for making decisions, such as choosing good parameters, detecting and preventing unwanted situations, or looking for a better diffusion strategy.

As a first approach to this ambitious challenge, we focused on social networks that already offer a big variety of situations and problems. Several lessons and research directions can be drawn from this study, both for the rewriting community and for the social network community.

First, dealing with this application domain led us to validate the concepts of labelled port graphs on a given signature, of rules that are themselves also labelled port graphs with variables from the given signature, and of strategy constructs added to define positions in graphs in a flexible way. When modelling the evolution of the studied network, the derivation tree (also a port graph) provides support for history tracking, state comparison, state recovery and backtracking. For the social network community, the rewrite rule approach is not quite surprising because some works such as [25] already use rules to generate social networks, although without claiming it. The fact that different models can be expressed in a common formalism provides a good argument for those who are interested to compare various algorithms and models. In such situations, simulations can indeed help for taking decision, for instance to prevent bad situations, or to look for optimal diffusion strategy.

Indeed several issues remain to address. For rewriting, although graph rewriting has been largely studied, addressing social network applications causes a drastic change of scale for the structures. Dealing with millions of nodes and edges requires great attention to size and complexity. There is also room for improvement in data storage and retrieval –in connection with graph data bases–, subgraph matching algorithms –either exact or approximate– for finding one or all solutions, parallel graph rewriting avoiding dangling edges, and probabilistic or stochastic issues for matching and rewriting, for instance, in the context of imprecise data or privacy constraints.

Also related to size, but even more to complexity of information data, there is a need for data structuring and management, that may be carried on by abstraction pattern, focusing on points of interests, hierarchies and views (for instance, through multi-layer graphs). All these notions need a precise and logical definition that may be influenced by well-known programming language concepts.

As programs, data need certification and validation tools and process, not only at one step but all along their evolution. The knowledge developed in the logic and rewriting community should be valuable in this context.

This study has also revealed the importance of visualisation and raises some challenges in this area. Visualisation is important, more widely, for data analysis, program engineering, program debugging, testing or verifying. However, the representation of dynamic or evolving data, such as social networks or richer graph structures, is yet an actual research topic for the visualisation community.

In future work, we plan to address multi-layer networks, based on societal problems. An example is tracking criminal activities. The objective then is to build a new methodology for tracking, based on construction, manipulation and analysis of heterogeneous digital information coming from different sources: legal records of tribunal sentences, social networks coming from exchanges, meetings, phone calls, information on financial flows and even family relations. Beyond the modelisation challenge, in connection with jurists and social scientists, we expect that our formalism of labelled port graphs, rules and strategy will provide an adequate framework for simulations and hypotheses testing.

Acknowledgements. We thank Guy Melançon (University of Bordeaux) and all the other members of the PORGY project. We also thank the anonymous reviewer for carefully reading this paper and making valuable suggestions for improvement.

References

1. Andrei, O., Fernández, M., Kirchner, H., Melançon, G., Namet, O., Pinaud, B.: PORGY: strategy-driven interactive transformation of graphs. In: Echahed, R. (ed.) 6th International Workshop on Computing with Terms and Graphs, vol. 48, pp. 54–68 (2011)
2. Andrei, O., Kirchner, H.: A rewriting calculus for multigraphs with ports. In: Proceedings of RULE 2007. Electronic Notes in Theoretical Computer Science, vol. 219, pp. 67–82 (2008)

3. Andrei, O., Kirchner, H.: A higher-order graph calculus for autonomic computing. In: Lipshteyn, M., Levit, V.E., McConnell, R.M. (eds.) Graph Theory, Computational Intelligence and Thought. LNCS, vol. 5420, pp. 15–26. Springer, Heidelberg (2009)

4. Balland, E., Brauner, P., Kopetz, R., Moreau, P.-E., Reilles, A.: Tom: piggybacking rewriting on Java. In: Baader, F. (ed.) RTA 2007. LNCS, vol. 4533, pp. 36–47. Springer, Heidelberg (2007)

5. Barabási, A.-L., Albert, R.: Emergence of scaling in random networks. Science **286**(5439), 509–512 (1999)

6. Barendregt, H.P., van Eekelen, M.C.J.D., Glauert, J.R.W., Kennaway, J.R., Plasmeijer, M.J., Sleep, M.R.: Term graph rewriting. In: de Bakker, J.W., Nijman, A.J., Treleaven, P.C. (eds.) Proceedings of PARLE, Parallel Architectures and Languages Europe. LNCS, vol. 259-II, pp. 141–158. Springer, Heidelberg (1987)

7. Barthelmann, K.: How to construct a hyperedge replacement system for a context-free set of hypergraphs. Technical report, Universität Mainz, Institut für Informatik (1996)

8. Batagelj, V., Brandes, U.: Efficient generation of large random networks. Phys. Rev. E **71**, 036113 (2005)

9. Bertuzzo, E., Casagrandi, R., Gatto, M., Rodriguez-Iturbe, I., Rinaldo, A.: On spatially explicit models of cholera epidemics. J. R. Soc. Interface **7**(43), 321–333 (2010)

10. Borovanský, P., Kirchner, C., Kirchner, H., Moreau, P.-E., Ringeissen, C.: An overview of ELAN. ENTCS **15**, 55–70 (1998)

11. Brandes, U., Wagner, D.: Analysis and visualization of social networks. In: Jünger, M., Mutzel, P. (eds.) Graph Drawing Software. Mathematics and Visualization, pp. 321–340. Springer, Heidelberg (2004)

12. Carrington, P.J., Scott, J., Wasserman, S.: Models and Methods in Social Network Analysis. Structural Analysis in the Social Sciences. Cambridge University Press, Cambridge (2005)

13. Cartwright, D., Harary, F.: Structural balance: a generalization of Heider's theory. Psychol. Rev. **63**, 277–293 (1956)

14. Chen, W., Collins, A., Cummings, R., Ke, T., Liu, Z., Rincón, D., Sun, X., Wang, Y., Wei, W., Yuan, Y.: Influence maximization in social networks when negative opinions may emerge and propagate. In: Proceedings of the 11th SIAM International Conference on Data Mining, SDM 2011, pp. 379–390 (2011)

15. Chen, W., Wang, C., Wang, Y.: Scalable influence maximization for prevalent viral marketing in large-scale social networks. In: Proceedings of the 16th ACM SIGKDD International Conference on Knowledge Discovery and Data Mining, KDD 2010, pp. 1029–1038. ACM (2010)

16. Corradini, A., Montanari, U., Rossi, F., Ehrig, H., Heckel, R., Löwe, M.: Algebraic approaches to graph transformation - part I: basic concepts and double pushout approach. In: Handbook of Graph Grammars and Computing by Graph Transformations. Foundations, vol. 1, pp. 163–246. World Scientific (1997)

17. Dodds, P.S., Watts, D.J.: A generalized model of social and biological contagion. J. Theor. Biol. **232**(4), 587–604 (2005)

18. Erdős, P., Rényi, A.: On the evolution of random graphs. Publ. Math. Inst. Hungar. Acad. Sci. **5**, 17–61 (1960)

19. Fernández, M., Kirchner, H., Pinaud, B.: Strategic port graph rewriting: an interactive modelling and analysis framework. Research report, Inria, January 2016

20. Fernández, M., Kirchner, H., Namet, O.: A strategy language for graph rewriting. In: Vidal, G. (ed.) LOPSTR 2011. LNCS, vol. 7225, pp. 173–188. Springer, Heidelberg (2012)

21. Fernández, M., Kirchner, H., Pinaud, B.: Strategic port graph rewriting: an interactive modelling and analysis framework. In: Bosnacki, D., Edelkamp, S., Lluch-Lafuente, A., Wijs, A. (eds.) Proceedings of the 3rd Workshop on GRAPH Inspection and Traversal Engineering, GRAPHITE 2014. EPTCS, vol. 159, pp. 15–29 (2014)

22. Goyal, A., Bonchi, F., Lakshmanan, L.V.S.: Learning influence probabilities in social networks. In: Proceedings of the 3rd ACM International Conference on Web Search and Data Mining, WSDM 2010, pp. 241–250. ACM (2010)

23. Granovetter, M.: Threshold models of collective behavior. Am. J. Sociol. **83**(6), 1420 (1978)

24. Habel, A., Müller, J., Plump, D.: Double-pushout graph transformation revisited. Math. Struct. Comput. Sci. **11**(5), 637–688 (2001)

25. Kejžar, N., Nikoloski, Z., Batagelj, V.: Probabilistic inductive classes of graphs. J. Math. Sociol. **32**(2), 85–109 (2008)

26. Kempe, D., Kleinberg, J.M., Tardos, É.: Influential nodes in a diffusion model for social networks. In: Caires, L., Italiano, G.F., Monteiro, L., Palamidessi, C., Yung, M. (eds.) ICALP 2005. LNCS, vol. 3580, pp. 1127–1138. Springer, Heidelberg (2005)

27. Kivelä, M., Arenas, A., Barthelemy, M., Gleeson, J.P., Moreno, Y., Porter, M.A.: Multilayer networks. J. Complex Netw. **2**(3), 203–271 (2014). doi:10.1093/comnet/cnu016. http://comnet.oxfordjournals.org/content/2/3/203.abstract

28. Lafont, Y.: Interaction nets. In: Proceedings of the 17th ACM Symposium on Principles of Programming Languages (POPL 1990), pp. 95–108. ACM Press (1990)

29. Leskovec, J., Huttenlocher, D., Kleinberg, J.: Signed networks in social media. In: Proceedings of the SIGCHI Conference on Human Factors in Computing Systems, CHI 2010, pp. 1361–1370. ACM (2010)

30. Milgram, S.: The small world problem. Psychol. Today **2**, 60–67 (1967)

31. Newman, M., Barabási, A.-L., Watts, D.J.: The Structure and Dynamics of Networks. Princeton Studies in Complexity. Princeton University Press, New Jersey (2006)

32. Nick, B., Lee, C., Cunningham, P., Brandes, U.: Simmelian backbones: amplifying hidden homophily in facebook networks. In: 2013 IEEE/ACM International Conference on Advances in Social Networks Analysis and Mining (ASONAM), pp. 525–532, August 2013

33. Pinaud, B., Melançon, G., Dubois, J.: PORGY: a visual graph rewriting environment for complex systems. Comput. Graph. Forum **31**(3), 1265–1274 (2012)

34. Plump, D.: Term graph rewriting. In: Ehrig, H., Engels, G., Kreowski, H.-J., Rozenberg, G. (eds.) Handbook of Graph Grammars, Computing by Graph Transformations. Applications, Languages, and Tools, vol. 2, pp. 3–61. World Scientific, Singapore (1998)

35. Plump, D.: The graph programming language GP. In: Bozapalidis, S., Rahonis, G. (eds.) CAI 2009. LNCS, vol. 5725, pp. 99–122. Springer, Heidelberg (2009)

36. Scott, J., Carrington, P.J.: The SAGE Handbook of Social Network Analysis. SAGE, New York (2011)

37. Vallet, J., Kirchner, H., Pinaud, B., Melançon, G.: A visual analytics approach to compare propagation models in social networks. In: Rensink, A., Zambon, E. (eds.) Proceedings of the Graphs as Models, GaM 2015. EPTCS, vol. 181, pp. 65–79 (2015)

38. Visser, E.: Stratego: a language for program transformation based on rewriting strategies system description of Stratego 0.5. In: Middeldorp, A. (ed.) RTA 2001. LNCS, vol. 2051, pp. 357–361. Springer, Heidelberg (2001)
39. Wang, L., Du, F., Dai, H.P., Sun, Y.X.: Random pseudofractal scale-free networks with small-world effect. Eur. Phys. J. B - Condens. Matter Complex Syst. **53**(3), 361–366 (2006)
40. Watts, D.J.: A simple model of global cascades on random networks. Proc. Nat. Acad. Sci. **99**(9), 5766–5771 (2002)
41. Watts, D.J., Strogatz, S.H.: Collective dynamics of 'small-world' networks. Nature **393**, 440–442 (1998)
42. Wonyeol, L., Jinha, K., Hwanjo, Y.: CT-IC: Continuously activated and time-restricted independent cascade model for viral marketing. In: 2012 IEEE 12th International Conference on Data Mining (ICDM), pp. 960–965 (2012)

Use of Logical Models for Proving Operational Termination in General Logics

Salvador Lucas$^{(\boxtimes)}$

DSIC, Universitat Politècnica de València, Valencia, Spain
slucas@dsic.upv.es
http://users.dsic.upv.es/~slucas/

Abstract. A *declarative programming language* is based on some logic $\mathcal{L}$ and its operational semantics is given by a proof calculus which is often presented in a *natural deduction style* by means of inference rules. *Declarative programs* are theories $\mathcal{S}$ of $\mathcal{L}$ and *executing* a program is proving goals φ in the inference system $\mathcal{I}(\mathcal{S})$ associated to $\mathcal{S}$ as a particularization of the inference system of the logic. The usual soundness assumption for $\mathcal{L}$ implies that every *model* $\mathcal{A}$ of $\mathcal{S}$ also satisfies φ. In this setting, the *operational termination* of a declarative program is quite naturally defined as *the absence of infinite proof trees* in the inference system $\mathcal{I}(\mathcal{S})$. Proving operational termination of declarative programs often involves two main ingredients: (i) the generation of logical models $\mathcal{A}$ to *abstract* the program execution (i.e., the provability of specific goals in $\mathcal{I}(\mathcal{S})$), and (ii) the use of *well-founded relations* to guarantee the absence of *infinite branches* in proof trees and hence of infinite proof trees, possibly taking into account the information about provability encoded by $\mathcal{A}$. In this paper we show how to deal with (i) and (ii) in a uniform way. The main point is the synthesis of logical models where *well-foundedness* is a side requirement for some specific predicate symbols.

Keywords: Abstraction · Logical models · Operational termination

1 Introduction

A recent survey defines the *program termination problem* as follows [4]: "using only a *finite* amount of time, *determine* whether a given *program* will always finish *running* or could *execute* forever." Being an intuitively clear definition, some questions should be answered before *using* it: (Q1) What is a *program*? (Q2) What is *running/executing* a program? (Q3) How to *determine* the property (in *practice!*)? In *declarative programming*, early proposals about the use of logic as a *programming framework* provide answers to the first two questions: (A1) programs are *theories* $\mathcal{S}$ of a given logic $\mathcal{L}$; and (A2) executing a program $\mathcal{S}$ is proving a goal φ as a deduction in the inference system $\mathcal{I}(\mathcal{L})$ of $\mathcal{L}$, written $\mathcal{S} \vdash \varphi$ [15, Sect. 6].

Partially supported by the EU (FEDER), Spanish MINECO TIN 2013-45732-C4-1-P and TIN2015-69175-C4-1-R, and GV PROMETEOII/2015/013.

© Springer International Publishing Switzerland 2016
D. Lucanu (Ed.): WRLA 2016, LNCS 9942, pp. 26–46, 2016.
DOI: 10.1007/978-3-319-44802-2_2

Example 1. The following Maude program is a *Membership Equational Logic* specification [16] somehow *sugared*, as explained in [13]. Sort Node represents the nodes in a graph and sorts Edge and Path are intended to classify paths consisting of a single edge or many of them, respectively [3, pages 561–562]:

```
fmod PATH is
  sorts Node Edge Path .
  subsorts Edge < Path .
  ops source target : Edge -> Node .
  ops source target : Path -> Node .
  op _;_ : [Path] [Path] -> [Path] .
  var E : Edge .
  vars P Q R S : Path .
  cmb E ; P : Path if target(E) = source(P) .
  ceq (P ; Q) ; R = P ; (Q ; R)
     if target(P) = source(Q) /\ target(Q) = source(R) .
  ceq source(P) = source(E) if E ; S := P .
  ceq target(P) = target(S) if E ; S := P .
endfm
```

The *execution* of PATH is described as *deduction* of goals $t \rightarrow_{[s]} u$ (one-step *rewriting* for terms t, u with sorts in the *kind* $[s]$), $t \rightarrow^*_{[s]} u$ (many-step rewriting), or $t : s$ (*membership*: claims that term t is of sort s) using the inference system of the *Context-Sensitive Membership Rewriting Logic* [5] in Fig. 1 (see also [13]). Here, a new kind [Truth] with a constant tt and a function symbol eq : [Node] [Node] -> [Truth] are added to deal with *equalities* like target(E)=source(P) as *reachability conditions* eq(target(E),source(P)) $\rightarrow^*$ tt. And a new membership predicate $t :: s$ arises where terms t are not rewritten before checking its sort s. Also note that the *overloaded* functions source and target (which are used to describe edges in a graph by establishing their *source* and *target* nodes, respectively) receive a *single* rank [Path] -> [Node] and the different overloads are modeled as rules $(M1^E_{\text{src}})$, $(M1^E_{\text{tgt}})$, $(M1^P_{\text{src}})$, and $(M1^P_{\text{tgt}})$.

The notion of *operational termination* [11] (often abbreviated OT in the subsequent related notions and definitions) provides an appropriate *definition* of termination of declarative programs: a program S is operationally terminating if *there is no infinite proof tree* for any goal in S. We have recently developed a *practical* framework for proving operational termination of declarative programs [14]. In our method, we first obtain the *proof jumps* $A \Uparrow B_1, \ldots, B_n$ associated to inference rules $\frac{B_1 \cdots B_n \cdots B_{n+p}}{A}$ in $\mathcal{I}(S)$ (where $A, B_1, \ldots, B_n, \ldots, B_{n+p}$ are logic formulas, $n > 0$, and $p \geq 0$). Proof jumps capture (infinite) paths in a proof tree T as sequences (*chains*) of proof jumps. A set of proof jumps τ is called an OT *problem*. We call it *finite* if there is no infinite chain of proof jumps taken from τ. The *initial* OT problem τ_I consists of all proof jumps obtained from the inference rules in $\mathcal{I}(S)$ as explained above. Thus, (A3) *determining* that S is operationally terminating is equivalent to proving τ_I *finite*. This answers Q3.

$$(SR_N) \quad \frac{t \to_{[Node]} u \quad u : Node}{t : Node} \qquad (SR_E) \quad \frac{t \to_{[Path]} u \quad u : Edge}{t : Edge}$$

$$(SR_P) \quad \frac{t \to_{[Path]} u \quad u : Path}{t : Path} \qquad (M1_P) \quad \frac{X :: Edge}{X :: Path}$$

$$(M1_{\mathsf{src}}^{E}) \quad \frac{X :: Edge}{source(X) :: Node} \qquad (M1_{\mathsf{tgt}}^{E}) \quad \frac{X :: Edge}{target(X) :: Node}$$

$$(M1_{\mathsf{src}}^{P}) \quad \frac{X :: Path}{source(X) :: Node} \qquad (M1_{\mathsf{tgt}}^{P}) \quad \frac{X :: Path}{target(X) :: Node}$$

$$(M2_N) \quad \frac{t :: Node}{t : Node} \qquad (M2_E) \quad \frac{t :: Edge}{t : Edge}$$

$$(M2_P) \quad \frac{t :: Path}{t : Path}$$

$$(R_N^*) \quad \frac{}{t \to_{[Node]}^* t} \qquad (R_P^*) \quad \frac{}{t \to_{[Path]}^* t}$$

$$(R_T^*) \quad \frac{}{t \to_{[Truth]}^* t} \qquad (T_N) \quad \frac{t \to_{[Node]} u \quad u \to_{[Node]}^* v}{t \to_{[Node]}^* v}$$

$$(T_P) \quad \frac{t \to_{[Path]} u \quad u \to_{[Path]}^* v}{t \to_{[Path]}^* v} \qquad (T_T) \quad \frac{t \to_{[Truth]} u \quad u \to_{[Truth]}^* v}{t \to_{[Truth]}^* v}$$

$$(C_{\mathsf{src}}) \quad \frac{t \to_{[Path]} u}{source(t) \to_{[Node]} source(u)} \qquad (C_{\mathsf{tgt}}) \quad \frac{t \to_{[Path]} u}{target(t) \to_{[Node]} target(u)}$$

$$(C_{\mathsf{sq}_1}) \quad \frac{t \to_{[Path]} u}{t\,;\,v \to_{[Path]} u\,;\,v} \qquad (C_{\mathsf{sq}_2}) \quad \frac{t \to_{[Path]} u}{v\,;\,t \to_{[Path]} v\,;\,u}$$

$$(C_{\mathsf{eq}_1}^{N}) \quad \frac{t \to_{[Node]} u}{eq(t,\,v) \to_{[Truth]} eq(u,\,v)} \qquad (C_{\mathsf{eq}_2}^{N}) \quad \frac{t \to_{[Node]} u}{eq(v,\,t) \to_{[Truth]} eq(v,\,u)}$$

$$(M1_{\_;\_}) \quad \frac{E :: Edge \quad P :: Path \quad eq(target(E), source(P)) \to_{[Truth]}^* tt}{E;\,P :: Path}$$

$$(Re_1) \quad \frac{P :: Path \quad Q :: Path \quad R :: Path \quad eq(target(P), source(Q)) \to_{[Truth]}^* tt \quad eq(target(Q), source(R)) \to_{[Truth]}^* tt}{(P;\,Q);\,R \to_{[Path]} P;\,(Q;\,R)}$$

$$(Re_2) \quad \frac{E :: Edge \quad P :: Path \quad S :: Path \quad P \to_{[Path]}^* E;\,S}{source(P) \to_{[Node]} source(E)}$$

$$(Re_3) \quad \frac{E :: Edge \quad P :: Path \quad S :: Path \quad P \to_{[Path]}^* E;\,S}{target(P) \to_{[Node]} target(S)}$$

$$(Re_4) \quad \frac{N :: Node}{eq(N,\,N) \to_{[Truth]} tt}$$

Fig. 1. Inference rules $\mathcal{I}(\texttt{PATH})$ for $\texttt{PATH}$

The OT Framework provides an incremental proof methodology to *simplify* OT problems τ in a divide-and-conquer style to eventually prove termination of the program (Sect. 2). In order to *remove* proof jumps $\psi : A \Uparrow B_1, \ldots, B_n$ from τ we often use *well-founded relations*: if there is a well-founded relation $\sqsupset$ on *formulas* of the language of $\mathcal{S}$ such that, for all substitutions σ,

$$\text{if } \mathcal{S} \vdash \sigma(B_i) \text{ for all } i, 1 \le i < n, \text{ then } \sigma(A) \sqsupset \sigma(B_n), \tag{1}$$

then we can *remove* ψ from τ to obtain a new OT problem τ' *whose finiteness implies that of* τ [14]. For the sake of *automation*, recasting (1) as follows:

$$\forall \boldsymbol{x}(B_1 \wedge \cdots \wedge B_{n-1} \Rightarrow A \sqsupset B_n) \tag{2}$$

would, be interesting to apply theorem proving or semantic methods to prove (1). In [14] we anticipated that *logical models* are useful for this purpose.

In order to provide a general treatment of the aforementioned problems which is well-suited for automation, we need to focus on a sufficiently simple but still powerful logic which can serve to our purposes. In [6] *Order-Sorted First-Order Logic* (OS-FOL) is proposed as a sufficiently general and expressive framework to represent declarative programs, semantics of programming languages, and program properties (see Sect. 3). In [10] we show how to systematically generate models for OS-FOL theories by using the *convex polytopic domains* introduced in [12]. In Sect. 4 we extend the work in [10] to generate appropriate interpretations of *predicate symbols* that can be then used to synthesize a model for a given OS-FOL theory $\mathcal{S}$.

Unfortunately, even with $\mathcal{S}$ an OS-FOL theory, (2) *is not* a formula of the theory $\mathcal{S}$: the *new* predicate symbol $\sqsupset$ is *not* in the language of $\mathcal{S}$. And (2) is not *well-formed* because predicate $\sqsupset$ is applied to *formulas* A and B_n rather than *terms* as required in any first-order language. Section 5 shows how to solve this problem by using *theory* transformations. It also shows how to obtain *well-founded* relations when the general approach to generate interpretations of predicate symbols described in Sect. 4 is used. Section 6 illustrates the use of the new developments to prove operational termination of PATH in the OT Framework. Automation of the analysis is achieved by using AGES [8], a web-based tool that implements the techniques in [10] and also in this paper. Section 7 concludes.

2   The OT Framework for General Logics

A *logic* $\mathcal{L}$ is a quadruple $\mathcal{L} = (Th(\mathcal{L}), Form, Sub, \mathcal{I})$, where: $Th(\mathcal{L})$ is the class of *theories* of $\mathcal{L}$, *Form* maps each theory $\mathcal{S} \in Th(\mathcal{L})$ into a set $Form(\mathcal{S})$ of *formulas* of $\mathcal{S}$, *Sub* is a mapping sending each $\mathcal{S} \in Th(\mathcal{L})$ to its set $Sub(\mathcal{S})$ of *substitutions*, with a containment $Sub(\mathcal{S}) \subseteq [Form(\mathcal{S}) \rightarrow Form(\mathcal{S})]$.

Remark 1. In [14, Sect. 2] we further develop the generic notion of substitution we are dealing with. In this paper we focus on first-order theories where the notion of substitution is the usual one: a mapping from variables into terms which is extended to a mapping from terms (formulas) into terms (formulas) in the usual way.

Finally, $\mathcal{I}$ maps each $\mathcal{S} \in Th(\mathcal{L})$ into a subset $\mathcal{I}(\mathcal{S}) \subseteq Form(\mathcal{S}) \times Form(\mathcal{S})^*$, where each $(A, B_1 \ldots B_n) \in \mathcal{I}(\mathcal{S})$ is called an *inference rule* for $\mathcal{S}$ and denoted $\frac{B_1 \ldots B_n}{A}$. In the following we often use $\boldsymbol{B_n}$ to refer a sequence $B_1, \ldots, B_n$ of n formulas. A proof tree T is either

1. an *open goal*, simply denoted as G, where $G \in Form(\mathcal{S})$. Then, we denote $root(T) = G$. Or
2. a *derivation tree* with root G, denoted as $\frac{T_1 \;\; \cdots \;\; T_n}{G}(\rho)$ where $G \in Form(\mathcal{S})$, $T_1, \ldots, T_n$ are proof trees (for $n \geq 0$), and $\rho : \frac{B_1 \ldots B_n}{A}$ is an inference rule in $\mathcal{I}(\mathcal{S})$, such that $G = \sigma(A)$, and $root(T_1) = \sigma(B_1), \ldots, root(T_n) = \sigma(B_n)$ for some substitution $\sigma \in Sub(\mathcal{S})$. We write $root(T) = G$.

A finite proof tree without open goals is called a *closed* proof tree for $\mathcal{S}$. If there is a closed proof tree T for $\varphi \in Form(\mathcal{S})$ using $\mathcal{I}(\mathcal{S})$ (i.e., such that $root(T) = \varphi$), we often denote this by writing $\mathcal{S} \vdash \varphi$.

A proof tree T for $\mathcal{S}$ is a *proper prefix* of a proof tree T' (denoted $T \sqsubset T'$) if there are one or more open goals $G_1, \ldots, G_n$ in T such that T' is obtained from T by replacing each G_i by a derivation tree T_i with root G_i. A proof tree T for $\mathcal{S}$ is *well-formed* if it is either an open goal, or a closed proof tree, or a tree $\frac{T_1 \ \cdots \ T_n}{G}(\rho)$ where there is i, $1 \leq i \leq n$ such that $T_1, \ldots, T_{i-1}$ are *closed*, T_i is *well-formed but not closed*, and $T_{i+1}, \ldots, T_n$ are *open* goals. An *infinite proof tree* T for $\mathcal{S}$ is an infinite sequence $\{T_i\}_{i\in\mathbb{N}}$ of finite trees such that for all i, $T_i \sqsubset T_{i+1}$. We write $root(T) = root(T_0)$.

Definition 1 [11]. *A theory $\mathcal{S}$ in a logic $\mathcal{L}$ is called* operationally terminating *iff no infinite well-formed proof tree for $\mathcal{S}$ exists.*

A *proof jump* ψ for $\mathcal{S}$ is a pair $(A \Uparrow \boldsymbol{B}_n)$, where $n \geq 1$ and $A, B_1, \ldots, B_n \in Form(\mathcal{S})$; A and B_n are called the *head* and *hook* of ψ, respectively. The *proof jumps* of $\mathcal{I}(\mathcal{S})$ are $\mathcal{J}_\mathcal{S} = \{(A \Uparrow \boldsymbol{B}_i) \mid \frac{\boldsymbol{B}_n}{A} \in \mathcal{I}(\mathcal{S}), 1 \leq i \leq n\}$.

Remark 2. Given an inference rule $\frac{B_1, \ldots, B_n}{A}$ with label ρ and $1 \leq i \leq n$, $[\rho]^i$ denotes the i-th proof jump $A \Uparrow B_1, \ldots, B_i$ which is obtained from ρ.

An $(\mathcal{S}, \mathcal{J})$-*chain* is a sequence $(\psi_i)_{i\geq 1}$ of proof jumps $\psi_i : (A^i \Uparrow \boldsymbol{B}^i_{n_i}) \in \mathcal{J}$ together with a substitution σ such that for all $i \geq 1$, $\sigma(B^i_{n_i}) = \sigma(A^{i+1})$ and for all j, $1 \leq j < n_i$, $\mathcal{S} \vdash \sigma(B^i_j)$. An *OT problem* τ in $\mathcal{L}$ is a pair $(\mathcal{S}, \mathcal{J})$ with $\mathcal{S} \in Th(\mathcal{L})$ and $\mathcal{J} \subseteq Jumps(\mathcal{S})$; τ is *finite* if there is no infinite $(\mathcal{S}, \mathcal{J})$-chain; τ is called *infinite* if it is *not* finite. The set of all OT problems in $\mathcal{L}$ is $OTP(\mathcal{L})$. The *initial OT problem* τ_I of a theory $\mathcal{S}$ is $(\mathcal{S}, \mathcal{J}_\mathcal{S})$.

Theorem 1 [14]. *A theory $\mathcal{S}$ is* operationally terminating *iff $(\mathcal{S}, \mathcal{J}_\mathcal{S})$ is finite.*

An *OT processor* $\mathsf{P} : OTP(\mathcal{L}) \to \mathcal{P}(OTP(\mathcal{L})) \cup \{\text{no}\}$ maps an OT problem into either a *set of OT problems* or the answer "no". A processor P is *sound* if for all OT problems τ, if $\mathsf{P}(\tau) \neq \text{no}$ and all OT problems in $\mathsf{P}(\tau)$ are finite, then τ is finite. A processor P is *complete* if for all OT problems τ, if $\mathsf{P}(\tau) = \text{no}$ or $\mathsf{P}(\tau)$ contains an infinite OT problem, then τ is infinite. By repeatedly applying processors, we can construct a tree (called *OT-tree*) for an OT-problem $(\mathcal{S}, \mathcal{J})$ whose nodes are labeled with OT problems or "yes" or "no", and whose root is labeled with $(\mathcal{S}, \mathcal{J})$. For every inner node labeled with τ, there is a processor P satisfying one of the following: (i) $\mathsf{P}(\tau) = \text{no}$ and the node has just one child that is labeled with "no". (ii) $\mathsf{P}(\tau) = \varnothing$ and the node has just one child that is labeled with "yes". (iii) $\mathsf{P}(\tau) \neq \text{no}$, $\mathsf{P}(\tau) \neq \varnothing$, and the children of the node are labeled with the OT problems in $\mathsf{P}(\tau)$.

Theorem 2 (OT-Framework). *Let $(\mathcal{S}, \mathcal{J}) \in OTP(\mathcal{L})$. If all leaves of an OT-tree for $(\mathcal{S}, \mathcal{J})$ are labeled with "yes" and all used processors are sound, then $(\mathcal{S}, \mathcal{J})$ is finite. If there is a leaf labeled with "no" and all processors used on the path from the root to this leaf are complete, then $(\mathcal{S}, \mathcal{J})$ is infinite.*

3   Order-Sorted First-Order Logic

Given a set of *sorts* S, a many-sorted signature is an $S^* \times S$-indexed family of sets $\Sigma = \{\Sigma_{w,s}\}_{(w,s) \in S^* \times S}$ containing *function symbols* with a given string of argument sorts and a result sort [7]. If $f \in \Sigma_{s_1 \cdots s_n, s}$, then we display f as $f : s_1 \cdots s_n \to s$. This is called a *rank* declaration for symbol f. Constant symbols c (taking no argument) have rank declaration $c : \lambda \to s$ for some sort s (where λ denotes the *empty* sequence). An order-sorted signature $(S, \leq, \Sigma)$ consists of a poset of sorts $(S, \leq)$ together with a many-sorted signature (S, Σ). The *connected components* of $(S, \leq)$ are the equivalence classes $[s]$ corresponding to the least equivalence relation $\equiv_\leq$ containing $\leq$. We extend the order $\leq$ on S to strings of equal length in S^* by $s_1 \cdots s_n \leq s'_1 \cdots s'_n$ iff $s_i \leq s'_i$ for all i, $1 \leq i \leq n$. Symbols f can be *subsort-overloaded*, i.e., they can have several rank declarations related in the $\leq$ ordering [7]. Constant symbols, however, have only one rank declaration. Besides, the following *monotonicity condition* must be satisfied: $f \in \Sigma_{w_1,s_1} \cap \Sigma_{w_2,s_2}$ and $w_1 \leq w_2$ imply $s_1 \leq s_2$. We assume that Σ is *sensible*, meaning that if $f : s_1 \cdots s_n \to s$ and $f : s'_1 \cdots s'_n \to s'$ are such that $[s_i] = [s'_i]$, $1 \leq i \leq n$, then $[s] = [s']$. An order-sorted signature Σ is *regular* iff given $w_0 \leq w_1$ in S^* and $f \in \Sigma_{w_1,s_1}$, there is a least $(w,s) \in S^* \times S$ such that $f \in \Sigma_{w,s}$ and $w_0 \leq w$. If, in addition, each connected component $[s]$ of the sort poset has a top element $\top_{[s]} \in [s]$, then the regular signature is called *coherent*.

Given an S-sorted set $\mathcal{X} = \{\mathcal{X}_s \mid s \in S\}$ of *mutually disjoint* sets of variables (which are also disjoint from the signature Σ), the set $\mathcal{T}_\Sigma(\mathcal{X})_s$ of terms of sort s is the least set such that (i) $\mathcal{X}_s \subseteq \mathcal{T}_\Sigma(\mathcal{X})_s$, (ii) if $s' \leq s$, then $\mathcal{T}_\Sigma(\mathcal{X})_{s'} \subseteq \mathcal{T}_\Sigma(\mathcal{X})_s$; and (iii) for each $f : s_1 \cdots s_n \to s$ and $t_i \in \mathcal{T}_\Sigma(\mathcal{X})_{s_i}$, $1 \leq i \leq n$, $f(t_1, \ldots, t_n) \in \mathcal{T}_\Sigma(\mathcal{X})_s$. If $\mathcal{X} = \varnothing$, we write $\mathcal{T}_\Sigma$ rather than $\mathcal{T}_\Sigma(\varnothing)$ for the set of *ground* terms. Terms with variables can also be seen as a special case of ground terms of the *extended* signature $\Sigma(\mathcal{X})$ where variables are considered as *constant* symbols of the appropriate sort, i.e., $\Sigma(\mathcal{X})_{\lambda,s} = \Sigma_{\lambda,s} \cup \mathcal{X}_s$. The assumption that Σ is sensible ensures that if $[s] \neq [s']$, then $\mathcal{T}_\Sigma(\mathcal{X})_{[s]} \cap \mathcal{T}_\Sigma(\mathcal{X})_{[s']} = \varnothing$. The set $\mathcal{T}_\Sigma(\mathcal{X})$ of order-sorted terms is $\mathcal{T}_\Sigma(\mathcal{X}) = \cup_{s \in S} \mathcal{T}_\Sigma(\mathcal{X})_s$.

Following [6], an order-sorted signature *with predicates* Ω is a quadruple $\Omega = (S, \leq, \Sigma, \Pi)$ such that $(S, \leq, \Sigma)$ is an coherent order-sorted signature, and $\Pi = \{\Pi_w \mid w \in S^+\}$ is a family of *predicate symbols* $P, Q, \ldots$ We write $P : w$ for $P \in \Pi_w$. Overloading is also allowed on predicates with the following conditions:

1. There is an equality predicate symbol $= \in \Pi_{ss}$ iff s is the top of a connected component of the sort poset S.
2. *Regularity*: For each w_0 such that there is $P \in \Pi_{w_1}$ with $w_0 \leq w_1$, there is a least w such that $P \in \Pi_w$ and $w_0 \leq w$.

We often write Σ, Π instead of $(S, \leq, \Sigma, \Pi)$ if S and $\leq$ are clear from the context. The formulas φ of an order-sorted signature with predicates Σ, Π are built up from atoms $P(t_1, \ldots, t_n)$ with $P \in \Pi_w$ and $t_1, \ldots, t_n \in \mathcal{T}_\Sigma(\mathcal{X})_w$, logic connectives (e.g., $\wedge$, $\neg$) and quantifiers ($\forall$) as follows: (i) if $P \in \Pi_w$, $w = s_1 \cdots s_n$, and $t_i \in \mathcal{T}_\Sigma(\mathcal{X})_{s_i}$ for all i, $1 \leq i \leq n$, then $P(t_1, \ldots, t_n) \in Form_{\Sigma,\Pi}$ (we often call it an *atom*); (ii) if $\varphi \in Form_{\Sigma,\Pi}$, then $\neg\varphi \in Form_{\Sigma,\Pi}$; (iii) if $\varphi, \varphi' \in Form_{\Sigma,\Pi}$, then $\varphi \wedge \varphi' \in Form_{\Sigma,\Pi}$; (iv) if $s \in S$, $x \in \mathcal{X}_s$, and $\varphi \in Form_{\Sigma,\Pi}$, then $(\forall x : s)\varphi \in Form_{\Sigma,\Pi}$. As usual, we can consider formulas involving other logic connectives and quantifiers (e.g., $\vee$, $\Rightarrow$, $\Leftrightarrow$, $\exists$,...) by using their standard definitions in terms of $\wedge$, $\neg$, $\forall$. A closed formula, i.e., whose variables are all universally or existentially quantified, is called a *sentence*.

Order-Sorted Algebras and Structures. Given a many-sorted signature (S, Σ), an (S, Σ)-algebra $\mathcal{A}$ (or just a Σ-algebra, if S is clear from the context) is a family $\{\mathcal{A}_s \mid s \in S\}$ of sets called the *carriers* or *domains* of $\mathcal{A}$ together with a function $f_{w,s}^{\mathcal{A}} \in \mathcal{A}_w \to \mathcal{A}_s$ for each $f \in \Sigma_{w,s}$ where $\mathcal{A}_w = \mathcal{A}_{s_1} \times \cdots \times \mathcal{A}_{s_n}$ if $w = s_1 \cdots s_n$, and $\mathcal{A}_w$ is a one point set when $w = \lambda$. Given an order-sorted signature $(S, \leq, \Sigma)$, an $(S, \leq, \Sigma)$-algebra (or Σ-algebra if $(S, \leq)$ is clear from the context) is an (S, Σ)-algebra such that (i) If $s, s' \in S$ are such that $s \leq s'$, then $\mathcal{A}_s \subseteq \mathcal{A}_{s'}$, and (ii) If $f \in \Sigma_{w_1,s_1} \cap \Sigma_{w_2,s_2}$ and $w_1 \leq w_2$, then $f_{w_1,s_1}^{\mathcal{A}} \in \mathcal{A}_{w_1} \to \mathcal{A}_{s_1}$ equals $f_{w_2,s_2}^{\mathcal{A}} \in \mathcal{A}_{w_2} \to \mathcal{A}_{s_2}$ on $\mathcal{A}_{w_1}$. With regard to many sorted signatures and algebras, an (S, Σ)-homomorphism between (S, Σ)-algebras $\mathcal{A}$ and $\mathcal{A}'$ is an S-sorted function $h = \{h_s : \mathcal{A}_s \to \mathcal{A}'_s \mid s \in S\}$ such that for each $f \in \Sigma_{w,s}$ with $w = s_1, \ldots, s_k$, $h_s(f_{w,s}^{\mathcal{A}}(a_1, \ldots, a_k)) = f_{w,s}^{\mathcal{A}'}(h_{s_1}(a_1), \ldots, h_{s_k}(a_k))$. If $w = \lambda$, we have $h_s(f^{\mathcal{A}}) = f^{\mathcal{A}'}$. Now, for the order-sorted case, an $(S, \leq, \Sigma)$-homomorphism $h : \mathcal{A} \to \mathcal{A}'$ between $(S, \leq, \Sigma)$-algebras $\mathcal{A}$ and $\mathcal{A}'$ is an (S, Σ)-homomorphism that satisfies the following additional condition: if $s \leq s'$ and $a \in \mathcal{A}_s$, then $h_s(a) = h_{s'}(a)$.

Given an order-sorted signature with predicates $(S, \leq, \Sigma, \Pi)$, an $(S, \leq, \Sigma, \Pi)$-*structure* (or just a Σ, Π-structure) is an order-sorted $(S, \leq, \Sigma)$-algebra $\mathcal{A}$ together with an assignment to each $P \in \Pi_w$ of a subset $P_w^{\mathcal{A}} \subseteq \mathcal{A}_w$ such that [6]: (i) for P the identity predicate $\_ = \_ : ss$, the assignment is the identity relation, i.e., $(=)_{\mathcal{A}} = \{(a, a) \mid a \in \mathcal{A}_s\}$; and (ii) whenever $P : w_1$ and $P : w_2$ and $w_1 \leq w_2$, then $P_{w_1}^{\mathcal{A}} = \mathcal{A}_{w_1} \cap P_{w_2}^{\mathcal{A}}$.

Let $(S, \leq, \Sigma, \Pi)$ be an order-sorted signature with predicates and $\mathcal{A}, \mathcal{A}'$ be $(S, \leq, \Sigma, \Pi)$-structures. Then, an $(S, \leq, \Sigma, \Pi)$-*homomorphism* $h : \mathcal{A} \to \mathcal{A}'$ is an $(S, \leq, \Sigma)$-homomorphism such that, for each $P : w$ in Π, if $(a_1, \ldots, a_n) \in P_w^{\mathcal{A}}$, then $h(a_1, \ldots, a_n) \in P_w^{\mathcal{A}'}$. Given an S-sorted *valuation mapping* $\alpha : \mathcal{X} \to \mathcal{A}$, the evaluation mapping $[\_]_{\mathcal{A}}^{\alpha} : \mathcal{T}_{\Sigma}(\mathcal{X}) \to \mathcal{A}$ is the unique $(S, \leq, \Sigma)$-homomorphism extending α [7]. Finally, $[\_]_{\mathcal{A}}^{\alpha} : Form_{\Sigma,\Pi} \to Bool$ is given by:

1. $[P(t_1, \ldots, t_k)]_{\mathcal{A}}^{\alpha} = $ true for $P : w$ and terms $t_1, \ldots, t_k$ if and only if $([t_1]_{\mathcal{A}}^{\alpha}, \ldots, [t_k]_{\mathcal{A}}^{\alpha}) \in P_w^{\mathcal{A}}$;
2. $[\neg\varphi]_{\mathcal{A}}^{\alpha} = $ true if and only if $[\varphi]_{\mathcal{A}}^{\alpha} = $ false;
3. $[\varphi \wedge \psi]_{\mathcal{A}}^{\alpha} = $ true if and only if $[\varphi]_{\mathcal{A}}^{\alpha} = $ true and $[\psi]_{\mathcal{A}}^{\alpha} = $ true;
4. $[(\forall x : s)\, \varphi]_{\mathcal{A}}^{\alpha} = $ true if and only if for all $a \in \mathcal{A}_s$, $[\varphi]_{\mathcal{A}}^{\alpha[x \mapsto a]} = $ true;

We say that $\mathcal{A}$ *satisfies* $\varphi \in Form_{\Sigma,\Pi}$ if there is $\alpha \in \mathcal{X} \to \mathcal{A}$ such that $[\varphi]_{\mathcal{A}}^{\alpha} = $ true. If $[\varphi]_{\mathcal{A}}^{\alpha} = $ true for *all* valuations α, we write $\mathcal{A} \models \varphi$ and say that $\mathcal{A}$ is a *model* of φ. Initial valuations are not relevant for establishing the satisfiability of *sentences*; thus, both notions coincide on them. We say that $\mathcal{A}$ is *a model of a set of sentences* $S \subseteq Form_{\Sigma,\Pi}$ (written $\mathcal{A} \models S$) if for all $\varphi \in S$, $\mathcal{A} \models \varphi$. And, given a sentence φ, we write $S \models \varphi$ if and only if for *all models* $\mathcal{A}$ of S, $\mathcal{A} \models \varphi$.

Sound logics guarantee that every provable sentence φ is true in *every model* of $\mathcal{S}$, i.e., $\mathcal{S} \vdash \varphi$ implies $\mathcal{S} \models \varphi$.

4 Interpreting Predicates Using Convex Domains

In [10] we have shown that convex domains [12] provide an appropriate basis to the *automatic* definition of algebras and structures that can be used in program analysis with order-sorted first-order specifications. In the following definition, vectors $\boldsymbol{x}, \boldsymbol{y} \in \mathbb{R}^n$ are *compared* using the *coordinate-wise* extension of the ordering $\geq$ among *numbers* which, by abuse, we denote using $\geq$ as well:

$$\boldsymbol{x} = (x_1, \ldots, x_n)^T \geq (y_1, \ldots, y_n)^T = \boldsymbol{y} \text{ iff } x_1 \geq y_1 \wedge \cdots \wedge x_n \geq y_n \tag{3}$$

Definition 2 [12, Definition 1]. *Given a matrix* $\mathsf{C} \in \mathbb{R}^{m \times n}$, *and* $\boldsymbol{b} \in \mathbb{R}^m$, *the set* $D(\mathsf{C}, \boldsymbol{b}) = \{\boldsymbol{x} \in \mathbb{R}^n \mid \mathsf{C}\boldsymbol{x} \geq \boldsymbol{b}\}$ *is called a* convex polytopic domain.

Sorts $s \in S$ are interpreted as convex domains $\mathcal{A}_s = D(\mathsf{C}^s, \boldsymbol{b}^s)$, where $\mathsf{C}^s \in \mathbb{R}^{m_s \times n_s}$ and $\boldsymbol{b}^s \in \mathbb{R}^{m_s}$ for some $m_s, n_s \in \mathbb{N}$. Thus, $\mathcal{A}_s \subseteq \mathbb{R}^{n_s}$. Function symbols $f : s_1 \cdots s_k \to s$ are interpreted by $F_1 x_1 + \cdots + F_k x_k + F_0$ where (1) for all i, $1 \leq i \leq k$, $F_i \in \mathbb{R}^{n_s \times n_{s_i}}$ are $n_s \times n_{s_i}$-matrices and x_i are variables ranging on $\mathbb{R}^{n_{s_i}}$, (2) $F_0 \in \mathbb{R}^{n_s}$, and (3) the following *algebraicity condition* holds:

$$\forall x_1 \in \mathbb{R}^{n_{s_1}}, \ldots \forall x_k \in \mathbb{R}^{n_{s_k}} \left(\bigwedge_{i=1}^k \mathsf{C}^{s_i} x_i \geq \boldsymbol{b}^{s_i} \Rightarrow \mathsf{C}^s (F_1 x_1 + \cdots + F_k x_k + F_0) \geq \boldsymbol{b}^s \right)$$

In [10] no procedure for the *automatic* generation of predicate interpretations was given. We solve this problem by providing (parametric) interpretations for predicate symbols P of *any* rank $w \in S^+$. Each predicate symbol $P \in \Pi_w$ with $w = s_1 \cdots s_k$ with $k > 0$ is given an expression

$$R_1 x_1 + \cdots + R_k x_k + R_0 \qquad \left(\text{or } \sum_{i=1}^k R_i x_i + R_0 \text{ for short}\right)$$

where (i) for all i, $1 \leq i \leq k$, $R_i \in \mathbb{R}^{m_P \times n_{s_i}}$ are $m_P \times n_{s_i}$-matrices for some $m_P > 0$ and x_i are variables ranging on $\mathbb{R}^{n_{s_i}}$ and (ii) $R_0 \in \mathbb{R}^{m_P}$. Then,

$$P_w^{\mathcal{A}} = \{(\boldsymbol{x}_1, \ldots, \boldsymbol{x}_k) \in \mathcal{A}_{s_1} \times \cdots \times \mathcal{A}_{s_k} \mid \sum_{i=1}^k R_i \boldsymbol{x}_i + R_0 \geq \boldsymbol{0}\}$$

or, in our specific setting,

$$P_w^{\mathcal{A}} = \{(\boldsymbol{x}_1, \ldots, \boldsymbol{x}_k) \in \mathbb{R}^{n_{s_1}} \times \cdots \times \mathbb{R}^{n_{s_k}} \mid \bigwedge_{i=1}^k \mathsf{C}^{s_i} \boldsymbol{x}_i \geq \boldsymbol{b}^{s_i} \wedge \sum_{i=1}^k R_i \boldsymbol{x}_i + R_0 \geq \boldsymbol{0}\}$$

Note that $P_w^{\mathcal{A}} \subseteq \mathcal{A}_w$, as required. As explained in [10, Sect. 4], the automatic generation of predicate interpretations is treated as done for sorts s and function symbols, i.e., by using *parametric entries* in the involved matrices and vectors that are given numeric values through constraint solving processes.

Example 2. 'Extreme' relations $P_w^{\mathcal{A}}$ associated to a predicate $P \in \Pi_w$ are obtained as follows: if $w = s_1 \cdots s_k$, let R_i be *null* $m_P \times n_{s_i}$-matrices for $i = 1, \ldots, k$.

- If $R_0 = (1, 0, \ldots, 0)^T$, then $P_w^{\mathcal{A}} = \varnothing$ (empty relation).
- If R_0 is a null vector, then $P_w^{\mathcal{A}} = \mathcal{A}_w$ (full relation).

Example 3 (Equality). Equality cannot be defined as such at the (first-order) logical level[1]. For this reason, the interpretation of an equality predicate $= \in \Pi_{ss}$ is explicitly required to be the *equality* relation $\{(x, x) \mid x \in \mathcal{A}_s\}$ in the domain $\mathcal{A}_s$ of sort s. Fortunately, we can easily obtain such an interpretation by using the generic method above. With $m_P = 2n_s$, $R_1, R_2 \in \mathbb{R}^{m_P \times n_s}$ given by

$$R_1 = \begin{bmatrix} I_{n_s} \\ -I_{n_s} \end{bmatrix} \text{ (for } I_{n_s} \text{ the } identity \text{ matrix of } n_s \times n_s \text{ entries) and } R_2 = -R_1,$$

respectively, and $R_0 = (0, \ldots, 0)^T \in \mathbb{R}^{m_P}$, we obtain the equality predicate on $\mathbb{R}^{n_s}$.

Example 4 (Orderings). The coordinate-wise extension (3) of $\geq$ to n-tuples $x, y \in \mathbb{R}^n$ is obtained if $R_1 = I_n$, $R_2 = -I_n$ and $R_0 = \boldsymbol{0}$. In particular, if $n = 1$, we obtain the usual ordering $\geq$ over the reals.

Definition 3 (Well-Founded Relation). *Consider a binary relation R on a set A, i.e., $R \subseteq A \times A$. We say that R is* well-founded *if there is no infinite sequence $a_1, a_2, \ldots$ such that for all $i \geq 1$, $a_i \in A$ and $a_i \, R \, a_{i+1}$.*

In the following, given $\delta > 0$, and $x, y \in \mathbb{R}$, we write $x >_\delta y$ iff $x - y \geq \delta$.

Example 5. (Well-Founded strict ordering). Borrowing [2], the following *strict* ordering on vectors in $\mathbb{R}^n$:

$$(x_1, \ldots, x_n)^T >_\delta (y_1, \ldots, y_n)^T \text{ iff } x_1 >_\delta y_1 \wedge (x_2, \ldots, x_n)^T \geq (y_2, \ldots, y_n)^T$$

is obtained if $R_1 = I_n$, $R_2 = -I_n$ and $R_0 = (-\delta, 0, \ldots, 0)^T$. In particular, if $n = 1$, we obtain the ordering $>_\delta$ over the reals which is well-founded on subsets A of real numbers which are *bounded from below*, i.e., such that $A \subseteq [\alpha, \infty)$ for some $\alpha \in \mathbb{R}$.

Example 6. For tuples of natural numbers the following *strict* ordering on vectors in $\mathbb{R}^n$ $x >_\Sigma^w y$ iff $x \geq y \wedge \sum_{i=1}^n x_i >_1 \sum_{i=1}^n y_i$, borrowed from the "*weak decrease + strict decrease in sum of components*" ordering over tuples of natural numbers in [17, Definition 3.1] is obtained if $m_P = n + 1$ (hence R_1, R_2 are $(n + 1) \times n$-matrices and $R_0 \in \mathbb{R}^{n+1}$) and we let

$$R_1 = \begin{bmatrix} \boldsymbol{1}^T \\ I_n \end{bmatrix} \qquad R_2 = -R_1 \qquad R_0 = (-\delta, 0, \ldots, 0)^T$$

for some $\delta > 0$, where $\boldsymbol{1}$ is the constant vector $(1, \ldots, 1)^T \in \mathbb{R}^n$.

---

[1] It is well-known that equality $x = y$ can be defined by the *second-order* expression $\forall P(P(x) \Leftrightarrow P(y))$.

5 Using the Removal Pair Processor

We can remove proof jumps $(A \Uparrow B_n)$ from OT problems $(\mathcal{S}, \mathcal{J})$ by using *removal pairs* $(\gtrsim, \sqsupset)$, where $\gtrsim$ and $\sqsupset$ are binary relations on $Form(\mathcal{S})$ such that $\sqsupset$ is *well-founded* and $\gtrsim \circ \sqsupset \subseteq \sqsupset$ or $\sqsupset \circ \gtrsim \subseteq \sqsupset$ (we say that $\gtrsim$ is *compatible* with $\sqsupset$) provided that the *hook* B_n is 'smaller' (w.r.t. $\sqsupset$) than the *head* A.

Definition 4 [14]. *Let $(\mathcal{S}, \mathcal{J}) \in OTP(\mathcal{L})$, $\psi : A \Uparrow B_n \in \mathcal{J}$, and $(\gtrsim, \sqsupset)$ be a removal pair. Then, $\mathsf{P}_{RP}(\mathcal{S}, \mathcal{J}) = \{(\mathcal{S}, \mathcal{J} - \{\psi\})\}$ if and only if*

1. *for all $C \Uparrow D_m \in \mathcal{J} - \{\psi\}$ and substitutions σ, if $\mathcal{S} \vdash \sigma(D_i)$ for all $1 \leq i < m$, then $\sigma(C) \gtrsim \sigma(D_m)$ or $\sigma(C) \sqsupset \sigma(D_m)$, and*
2. *for all substitutions σ, if $\mathcal{S} \vdash \sigma(B_i)$ for all $1 \leq i < n$, then $\sigma(A) \sqsupset \sigma(B_n)$.*

In order to *use* P_{RP}, we need to check conditions (1) and (2) in Definition 4. That is, given a proof jump $F \Uparrow E_p$ with $E_1, \ldots, E_p, F \in Form(\mathcal{S})$, and $\bowtie \in \{\gtrsim, \sqsupset\}$, we have to prove statements of the following form: for all substitutions σ,

$$\text{if } \mathcal{S} \vdash \sigma(F_i) \text{ for all } i, 1 \leq i < p, \text{ then } \sigma(E) \bowtie \sigma(F_p) \tag{4}$$

Although (4) is an "implication", the *provability statements* $\mathcal{S} \vdash \sigma(F_i)$, and the presence of symbols $\gtrsim$ and $\sqsupset$ (in statements $\sigma(E) \bowtie \sigma(F_p)$) which do *not* belong to the language of $\mathcal{S}$, prevents (4) from being an implication of the language of $\mathcal{S}$. We use theory transformations to overcome this problem.

Remark 3. Our approach leads to implementing P_{RP} when applied to an OT problem $\tau = (\mathcal{S}, \mathcal{J})$ as a *satisfiability* problem, i.e., the problem of finding a model $\mathcal{A}$ for a theory $\mathcal{S}_\tau$ which is obtained by extending $\mathcal{S}$ with appropriate sentences to represent the application of P_{RP} to τ (see Sect. 5.2).

5.1 Transforming Order-Sorted First-Order Theories

We define a transformation of order-sorted signatures with predicates as follows: given $\Omega = (S, \leq, \Sigma, \Pi)$, an Ω-theory $\mathcal{S}$ and an OT problem $\tau = (\mathcal{S}, \{A^i \Uparrow B_{n_i}^i \mid 1 \leq i \leq m\})$ where for all i, $1 \leq i \leq m$, A^i and $B_{n_i}^i$ are Ω-atoms, a new order-sorted signature with predicates $\Omega_\tau = (S_\tau, \leq_\tau, \Sigma_\tau, \Pi_\tau)$ is defined, where, if we let $\Psi_\tau = \{pred(A^i) \mid 1 \leq i \leq m\} \cup \{pred(B_{n_i}^i) \mid 1 \leq i \leq m\}$, then

- $S_\tau = S \cup \{s_\tau\}$ where s_τ is a fresh sort symbol.
- $\leq_\tau$ extends $\leq$ by defining $s_\tau \leq_\tau s_\tau$, and for all $s, s' \in S$, $s \leq_\tau s'$ iff $s \leq s'$. Note that we do *not* assume any subsort relation between s_τ and sorts $s \in S$.
- $\Sigma_\tau = \Sigma \cup \{f_P : w \to s_\tau \mid w \in S^+, P \in \Psi_\tau \cap \Pi_w\}$, i.e., each (overloaded version of a) predicate symbol P in Ψ_τ with input sorts w is given a new function symbol $f_P : w \to s_\tau$ with input sorts w and output sort s_τ.
- $\Pi_\tau = \Pi \cup \Pi_{s_\tau s_\tau}$ where $\Pi_{s_\tau s_\tau} = \{\pi_\gtrsim, \pi_\sqsupset\}$ for new binary (infix) predicate symbols $\pi_\gtrsim$ and $\pi_\sqsupset$.

Since Ω_τ is an extension of Ω, every Σ_τ, Π_τ-structure $\mathcal{A}$ is also a Σ, Π-structure. Given an atom $P(t_1, \ldots, t_n)$ with $P \in \Psi_\tau \cap \Pi_{s_1 \cdots s_n}$ and terms $t_i \in \mathcal{T}_\Sigma(\mathcal{X})_{s_i}$, for $1 \leq i \leq n$, the transformation $\_^\downarrow$ from atoms in Ω to *terms* in Ω_τ is obtained by replacing P by $f_P \in \Sigma_\tau$: $P(t_1, \ldots, t_n)^\downarrow = f_P(t_1, \ldots, t_n)$. We can use Ω_τ-structures $\mathcal{A}$ to define binary relations on Ω-formulas.

Definition 5. *Let Ω be an order-sorted signature with predicates, τ be an OT-problem, and $\mathcal{A}$ be an Ω_τ-structure. Given $\pi_{\bowtie} \in \Pi_{s_\tau s_\tau}$, we define a relation $\bowtie$ on Ω-formulas as follows: for all Ω-formulas A and B $A \bowtie B$ iff $\mathcal{A} \models A^{\downarrow} \pi_{\bowtie} B^{\downarrow}$.*

Now, we can recast (4) as a logic formula:

$$\forall \boldsymbol{x}(F_1 \wedge \cdots \wedge F_{p-1} \Rightarrow E^{\downarrow} \pi_{\bowtie} F_p^{\downarrow}) \tag{5}$$

Theorem 3. *Let Ω be an order-sorted signature with predicates, $\tau = E \Uparrow F_p$ be an OT-problem, $\mathcal{A}$ be an Ω_τ-structure such that $\mathcal{A} \models \mathcal{S}$, $\pi_{\bowtie} \in \Pi_{s_\tau s_\tau}$, and σ be a substitution. If for all i, $1 \leq i < p$, $\mathcal{S} \vdash \sigma(F_i)$ holds and $\mathcal{A} \models \forall \boldsymbol{x}(F_1 \wedge \cdots \wedge F_{p-1} \Rightarrow E^{\downarrow} \pi_{\bowtie} F_p^{\downarrow})$, then (4) holds for $\bowtie$ as in Definition 5.*

Proof. Since for all i, $1 \leq i < p$, $\mathcal{S} \vdash \sigma(F_i)$ holds and $\mathcal{A} \models \mathcal{S}$, by soundness we have $\mathcal{A} \models \sigma(F_i)$ for all i, $1 \leq i < p$. Now, since $\mathcal{A} \models \forall \boldsymbol{x}(F_1 \wedge \cdots \wedge F_{p-1} \Rightarrow E^{\downarrow} \pi_{\bowtie} F_p^{\downarrow})$, we have that $\mathcal{A} \models \sigma(E^{\downarrow} \pi_{\bowtie} F_p^{\downarrow})$ holds, i.e., $\mathcal{A} \models \sigma(E)^{\downarrow} \pi_{\bowtie} \sigma(F_p)^{\downarrow}$ holds. Thus, by Definition 5, we have $\sigma(E) \bowtie \sigma(F_p)$ as desired. ∎

Compatibility. Component $\gtrsim$ of a removal pair $(\gtrsim, \sqsupset)$ must be *compatible* with $\sqsupset$. This can be guaranteed at the *logical level* by the following Ω_τ-sentence:

$$(\forall xyz : s_\tau(x \pi_{\gtrsim} y \wedge y \pi_{\sqsupset} z \Rightarrow x \pi_{\sqsupset} z)) \vee (\forall xyz : s_\tau(x \pi_{\sqsupset} y \wedge y \pi_{\gtrsim} z \Rightarrow x \pi_{\sqsupset} z))$$

Well-Foundedness. We also need to guarantee *well-foundedness* of $\sqsupset$. Unfortunately, the well-foundedness of a relation $P^{\mathcal{A}}$ interpreting a binary predicate symbol P can *not* be characterized at once in first-order logic [18, Sect. 5.1.4]. We can guarantee well-foundedness of $\sqsupset$, though, at the *semantic* level by interpreting $\pi_{\sqsupset}$ as a well-founded relation $\pi_{\sqsupset}^{\mathcal{A}}$ in the Ω_τ-structure $\mathcal{A}$.

Proposition 1. *Let Ω be an order-sorted signature with predicates, τ be an OT problem, and $\mathcal{A}$ be a Ω_τ-structure. If $\pi_{\sqsupset}^{\mathcal{A}}$ is a well-founded relation on $\mathcal{A}_{s_\tau}$, then $\sqsupset$ as in Definition 5 is a well-founded relation on Ω-formulas.*

Proof. By contradiction. If there is an infinite sequence $(A_i)_{i \geq 1}$ of Ω-formulas such that for all $i \geq 1$ $A_i \sqsupset A_{i+1}$, then, by Definition 5, for all $i \geq 1$ we have $\mathcal{A} \models A_i^{\downarrow} \pi_{\sqsupset} A_{i+1}^{\downarrow}$, i.e., for all valuations α, $([A_i^{\downarrow}]_{\mathcal{A}}^{\alpha}, [A_{i+1}^{\downarrow}]_{\mathcal{A}}^{\alpha}) \in \pi_{\sqsupset}^{\mathcal{A}}$. Therefore, there is an infinite sequence $([A_i^{\downarrow}]_{\mathcal{A}}^{\alpha})_{i \geq 1}$ for some valuation α that contradicts well-foundedness of $\pi_{\sqsupset}^{\mathcal{A}}$. ∎

5.2   A Semantic Version of the Removal Pair Processor

We can provide the following *semantic version* of the removal pair processor.

Definition 6 (Semantic Version of P_{RP}). *Let $\mathcal{L}$ be an OS-FOL with order-sorted signature with predicates Ω, $\tau = (\mathcal{S}, \mathcal{J}) \in OTP(\mathcal{L})$, $\mathcal{A}$ be an Ω_τ-structure, and $\psi : A \Uparrow B_n \in \mathcal{J}$. Then, $\mathsf{P}_{RP}(\mathcal{S}, \mathcal{J}) = \{(\mathcal{S}, \mathcal{J} - \{\psi\})\}$ if $\mathcal{A} \models \mathcal{S}$, and the following conditions hold:*

1. *if* $\mathcal{J} - \{\psi\} \neq \varnothing$, *then*

$$\mathcal{A} \models (\forall xyz : s_\tau(x\, \pi_{\gtrsim}\, y \wedge y\, \pi_\sqsupset\, z \Rightarrow x\, \pi_\sqsupset\, z)) \vee (\forall xyz : s_\tau(x\, \pi_\sqsupset\, y \wedge y\, \pi_{\gtrsim}\, z \Rightarrow x\, \pi_\sqsupset\, z))$$

2. *for each* $C \Uparrow D_m \in \mathcal{J} - \{\psi\}$, *there is* $\pi_{\bowtie} \in \{\pi_{\gtrsim}, \pi_\sqsupset\}$ *such that*
   $\mathcal{A} \models \bigwedge_{i=1}^{m-1} D_i \Rightarrow C^{\downarrow}\, \pi_{\bowtie}\, D_m^{\downarrow}$.
3. $\pi_\sqsupset^{\mathcal{A}}$ *is well-founded and* $\mathcal{A} \models \bigwedge_{i=1}^{n-1} B_i \Rightarrow A^{\downarrow}\, \pi_\sqsupset\, B_n^{\downarrow}$

Definition 6 transforms the application of P_{RP} to $(\mathcal{S}, \mathcal{J})$ into the problem of *finding a model* $\mathcal{A}$ of $\mathcal{S}$ which satisfies the following formulas (where J is the number of proof jumps in $\mathcal{J}$):

1. φ^1 (for the modeling condition (1) in Definition 6; only required if $J > 1$),
2. $\varphi_1^2, \ldots, \varphi_{J-1}^2$ (where, for all j, $1 \leq j < J$, φ_j^2 is a disjunction of two formulas due to condition (2)) and
3. φ^3 (the formula in the *removal* condition (3)).

Remark 4 (Finding Models ·to Implement P_{RP}). Let $\mathcal{S}_\tau = \mathcal{S} \cup \{\varphi^1, \varphi_1^2, \ldots, \varphi_{J-1}^2, \varphi^3\}$. We can use the theory in [10] and Sect. 4 to obtain a model $\mathcal{A}$ such that $\mathcal{A} \models \mathcal{S}_\tau$ holds. Then, if $\pi_\sqsupset^{\mathcal{A}}$ is *well-founded*, we can remove the targetted proof jump ψ from $\mathcal{J}$ in τ.

We still need to envisage a method to guarantee that $\pi_\sqsupset^{\mathcal{A}}$ is *well-founded*. In the following section, we show how to guarantee that binary relations synthesized as part of a model as explained in Sect. 4 are well-founded.

5.3   Well-Foundedness of Relations Defined on Convex Domains

The following result provides a sufficient condition to guarantee *well-foundedness* of a binary relation R on a subset $A \subseteq \mathbb{R}^n$ defined as explained in Sect. 4. It is based on generalizing the fact that the relation $>_\delta$ over real numbers given by $x >_\delta y$ iff $x - y \geq \delta$ is *well-founded* on subsets $A \subseteq \mathbb{R}$ of real numbers which are *bounded from below* (i.e., $A \subseteq [\alpha, +\infty)$ for some $\alpha \in \mathbb{R}$) whenever $\delta > 0$ [9].

Theorem 4. *Let* $R_1, R_2 \in \mathbb{R}^{m \times n}$ *and* $R_0 \in \mathbb{R}^m$ *for some* $m, n > 0$, *and* R *be a binary relation on* $A \subseteq \mathbb{R}^n$ *as follows: for all* $x, y \in A$, $x\, R\, y$ *if and only if* $R_1 x + R_2 y + R_0 \geq 0$. *If there is* $i \in \{1, \ldots, n\}$ *such that*

1. $(R_2)_{i\cdot} = -(R_1)_{i\cdot}$, *i.e., the* i-th *row of* R_2 *is obtained from the* i-th *row of* R_1 *by negating all components,*
2. *There is* $\alpha \in \mathbb{R}$ *such that for all* $x \in A$, $(R_1)_{i\cdot} x \geq \alpha$, *and*
3. $(R_0)_i < 0$,

then R *is well-founded.*

Proof. By contradiction. If R is not well-founded, then there is an infinite sequence $x_1, \ldots, x_n, \ldots$ of vectors in $\mathbb{R}^n$ such that, for all $j \geq 1$, $x_j\, R\, x_{j+1}$. By (1), we have that, for all $j \geq 1$, $(R_1)_{i\cdot} x_j - (R_1)_{i\cdot} x_{j+1} + (R_0)_i \geq 0$. For all $p > 0$,

$$\sum_{j=1}^{p} (R_1)_i.\boldsymbol{x}_j - (R_1)_i.\boldsymbol{x}_{j+1} + (R_0)_i = (R_1)_i.\boldsymbol{x}_1 - (R_1)_i.\boldsymbol{x}_{p+1} + p(R_0)_i \geq 0$$

By (2), there is $\alpha \in \mathbb{R}$ such that for all $p > 0$, $(R_1)_i.\boldsymbol{x}_p \geq \alpha$. Therefore, for all $p > 0$, $(R_1)_i.\boldsymbol{x}_1 - \alpha \geq (R_1)_i.\boldsymbol{x}_1 - (R_1)_i.\boldsymbol{x}_{p+1}$, and then $(R_1)_i.\boldsymbol{x}_1 - \alpha + p(R_0)_i \geq 0$. By (3), $(R_0)_i < 0$; let $r = -(R_0)_i$. Note that $r > 0$. Then, for all $p > 0$, $(R_1)_i.\boldsymbol{x}_1 \geq \alpha + pr$, leading to a contradiction because $\alpha + pr$ tends to infinite as p grows to infinite, but $(R_1)_i.\boldsymbol{x}_1 \in \mathbb{R}$ is fixed.

Example 7. Theorem 4 applies to $>_\delta$ and $>_\Sigma^w$ defined on $\mathcal{A}_s$ as follows:

1. For $>_\delta$, take $A \subseteq [\alpha, +\infty) \times \mathbb{R}^{n-1}$, for some $\alpha \in \mathbb{R}$ and $i = 1$ in Theorem 4 with the corresponding R_1, R_2, and R_0 to prove $>_\delta$ well-founded on A.
2. For $>_\Sigma^w$, take $A \subseteq [\alpha, +\infty)^n$, for some $\alpha \geq 0$ and $i = 1$ with the corresponding R_1, R_2, and R_0 to prove $>_\Sigma^w$ well-founded on A.

Note that we can use Theorem 4 to prove well-foundedness of relations R defined on domains $\mathcal{A}$ which are *not* bounded from below.

Example 8. Consider $\mathsf{C} = \begin{bmatrix} 1 & 0 \\ -1 & 0 \end{bmatrix}$ and $\boldsymbol{b} = (0, -2)^T$. Then, $\mathcal{A} = D(\mathsf{C}, \boldsymbol{b}) = [0, 2] \times \mathbb{R}$ is *not* bounded from below in the sense that there is no $\alpha \in \mathbb{R}$ such that $\mathcal{A} \subseteq [\alpha, +\infty)^2$. The relation R on $\mathcal{A}$ defined by $R_1 = \begin{bmatrix} 1 & 0 \\ 1 & 1 \end{bmatrix}$, $R_2 = \begin{bmatrix} -1 & 0 \\ 0 & 1 \end{bmatrix}$ and $R_0 = (-1, 0)$ is well-founded as it satisfies the conditions of Theorem 4.

6   Operational Termination of PATH in the OT-Framework

The set $\mathcal{J}_{\mathsf{PATH}}$ of proof jumps for $\mathcal{I}(\mathsf{PATH})$ has 43 elements. A powerful processor to *reduce* the size of an OT problem $(\mathcal{S}, \mathcal{J})$ is the *SCC processor* [14]. The so-called *estimated proof graph* $\mathsf{EPG}(\mathcal{S}, \mathcal{J})$ for $(\mathcal{S}, \mathcal{J})$ has $\mathcal{J}$ as set of *nodes*; and there is an *arc* from $\psi : (A \Uparrow \boldsymbol{B}_m)$ to $\psi' : (A' \Uparrow \boldsymbol{B}'_n)$ iff $\sigma(B_m) = \sigma(A')$ for some substitution σ. The *Strongly Connected Components* (SCCs) of a graph are its *maximal* cycles, i.e., those cycles that are not part of other cycles. The *SCC Processor* (P_{SCC}) is given by

$$\mathsf{P}_{SCC}(\mathcal{S}, \mathcal{J}) = \{(\mathcal{S}, \mathcal{J}') \mid \mathcal{J}' \text{ is an SCC in } \mathsf{EPG}(\mathcal{S}, \mathcal{J})\}$$

This is a sound and complete processor.

Example 9. Although $\mathsf{EPG}(\mathsf{PATH}, \mathcal{J}_{\mathsf{PATH}})$ is huge and we do not display it here, the SCCs are displayed in Fig. 2. The involved proof jumps are made explicit in Fig. 3 to ease our further developments. We use P_{SCC} to transform the *initial* OT problem $\tau_{\mathsf{PATH}} = (\mathsf{PATH}, \mathcal{J}_{\mathsf{PATH}})$ by $\mathsf{P}_{SCC}(\tau_{\mathsf{PATH}}) = \{\tau_1, \ldots, \tau_9\}$ where

$\tau_1 = (\mathsf{PATH}, \{[SR_N]^2\})$ $\tau_2 = (\mathsf{PATH}, \{[SR_E]^2\})$ $\tau_3 = (\mathsf{PATH}, \{[SR_P]^2\})$

$\tau_4 = (\mathsf{PATH}, \{[T_N]^2\})$ $\tau_5 = (\mathsf{PATH}, \{[T_P]^2\})$ $\tau_6 = (\mathsf{PATH}, \{[C_{\mathsf{sq}_1}]^1\})$

$\tau_7 = (\mathsf{PATH}, \{[C_{\mathsf{sq}_2}]^1\})$ $\tau_8 = (\mathsf{PATH}, \{[M1_{\dots}]^2\})$ $\tau_9 = (\mathsf{PATH}, \{[T_T]^2\})$

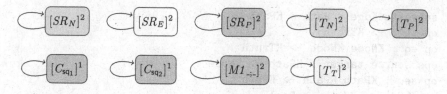

Fig. 2. SCCs of the estimated dependency graph of PATH

$[SR_N]^2$ $t : Node \Uparrow t \rightarrow_{[Node]} u \quad u : Node$

$[SR_E]^2$ $t : Edge \Uparrow t \rightarrow_{[Path]} u \quad u : Edge$

$[SR_P]^2$ $t : Path \Uparrow t \rightarrow_{[Path]} u \quad u : Path$

$[T_N]^2$ $t \rightarrow^*_{[Node]} v \Uparrow t \rightarrow_{[Node]} u \quad\quad u \rightarrow^*_{[Node]} v$

$[T_P]^2$ $t \rightarrow^*_{[Path]} v \Uparrow t \rightarrow_{[Path]} u \quad\quad u \rightarrow^*_{[Path]} v$

$[T_T]^2$ $t \rightarrow^*_{[Truth]} v \Uparrow t \rightarrow_{[Truth]} u \quad\quad u \rightarrow^*_{[Truth]} v$

$[C_{sq_1}]^1$ $t ; v \rightarrow_{[Path]} u ; v \Uparrow t \rightarrow_{[Path]} u$

$[C_{sq_2}]^1$ $v ; t \rightarrow_{[Path]} v ; u \Uparrow t \rightarrow_{[Path]} u$

$[M1_{\_;\_}]^2$ $E ; P :: Path \Uparrow E :: Edge \quad P :: Path$

Fig. 3. Proof jumps of the SCCs in Fig. 2

Any further use of P_{SCC} on $\tau_1, \ldots, \tau_9$ is hopeless. Note that $\tau_1, \ldots, \tau_9$ all consist of a *single* proof jump, i.e., $\tau_i = (\text{PATH}, \{\psi_i\})$ for $1 \leq i \leq 9$. With P_{RP} we prove them finite, thus obtaining a proof of operational termination of PATH.

6.1 Using P_{RP} to Prove τ_{PATH} finite

Following the approach in Sect. 5.2 (see Remark 4), for each OT problem τ_i we need to find a appropriate model $\mathcal{A}_i$ to *remove* ψ_i from τ_i thus obtaining the *empty* OT problem $(\text{PATH}, \varnothing)$ which is trivially finite. For this purpose, we use the tool AGES to automatically generate models for order-sorted first-order theories [8]. The tool provides an implementation of the techniques introduced in [10] and also in this paper (Sects. 4 and 5.3).

First we express the *order-sorted first-order signature with predicates* that corresponds to PATH as a Maude module as follows:

```
mod PATH_OSSig is
  sorts KTruth .
  sorts Node KNode .
  sorts Edge Path KPath .
  subsorts Node < KNode .
```

```
    subsorts Edge < Path < KPath .
    op tt : -> KTruth .
    op eq : KNode KNode -> KTruth .
    ops source target : KPath -> KNode .
    op seq : KPath KPath -> KPath .
    op mbEdge : KPath -> Bool .
    op mbNode : KNode -> Bool .
    op mbPath : KPath -> Bool .
    op redN : KNode KNode -> Bool .
    op redsN : KNode KNode -> Bool .
    op redP : KPath KPath -> Bool .
    op redsP : KPath KPath -> Bool .
    op redT : KTruth KTruth -> Bool .
    op redsT : KTruth KTruth -> Bool .
endm
```

where

1. KNode, KPath, and KTruth represent *kinds* [Node], [Path], and [Truth] of the
   MEL specification of PATH and have the expected *subsort* relation with the
   corresponding sorts in the kind.
2. We use the function seq instead of the infix operator _;_.
3. We are using *predicates* (encoded here as *boolean functions*, as Maude has
   no specific notation for predicates) mbEdge, mbNode, and mbEdge instead of
   _ : *Edge*, _ : *Node* and _ : *Path*.
4. Similarly, we use redN, redsN, redP, redsP, redT, and redsT instead of
   $\rightarrow_{[Node]}$, $\rightarrow^*_{[Node]}$, $\rightarrow_{[Path]}$, $\rightarrow^*_{[Path]}$, $\rightarrow_{[Truth]}$, and $\rightarrow^*_{[Truth]}$, respectively.

The OS-FOL *theory* $\mathcal{S}^{\text{PATH}}$ consists of the sentences obtained from $\mathcal{I}(\text{PATH})$ in
Fig. 1 when each rule $\frac{B_1\cdots B_n}{A}$ (with variables $x_1,\ldots,x_m$ of sorts $s_1,\ldots,s_m$) is
interpreted as a sentence $\forall x_1 : s_1 \cdots x_m : s_m (B_1 \wedge \cdots \wedge B_n \Rightarrow A)$ and written
by using the symbols in PATH_OSSig. For instance, rule (SR_N) becomes

```
    redN(t:KNode,u:KNode) /\ mbNode(u:KNode) => mbNode(t:KNode)
```

in the notation used in AGES, where each variable bears its sort, and universal
quantification is assumed.

For the sake of brevity, rather than computing a model $\mathcal{A}_i$ for each OT
problem τ_i, $1 \leq i \leq 9$, we proceed in *three* steps by computing models for
different *clusters* of OT Problems.

- For OT problems $\tau_1,\ldots,\tau_5$, we compute a model $\mathcal{A}$ of $\mathcal{S} \cup \{\varphi_1^3,\ldots,\varphi_5^3\}$ being
  φ_i^3 for $1 \leq i \leq 5$ the specific formula φ^3 in Sect. 5.2 particularized to ψ_i.
- For OT problems $\tau_6,\ldots,\tau_8$, we compute a model $\mathcal{A}'$ of $\mathcal{S} \cup \{\varphi_6^3,\ldots,\varphi_8^3\}$.
- For τ_9, we compute a model $\mathcal{A}''$ of $\mathcal{S} \cup \{\varphi_9^3\}$.

Obviously, each computed structure can be used with each *individual* OT problem τ_i in its cluster to remove the corresponding proof jump. Note that, since

each OT problem τ_i contains a single proof jump, we do not pay attention to the component $\gtrsim_i$ of the removal pair. Hence, no instance of formulas φ^1 and φ^2 in Sect. 5.2 is required in the extensions of $\mathcal{S}$.

OT Problems $\tau_1, \ldots, \tau_5$. We extend PATH_OSSig with new sorts, functions and predicate symbols due to the transformation described in Sect. 5.1:

```
mod PATH-tau1to5 is
    sorts Top1 Top2 Top3 Top4 Top5 .
    op fmbNode : KNode -> Top1 .
    op wfr1 : Top1 Top1 -> Bool [wellfounded] .
    op fisEdge : KPath -> Top2 .
    op wfr2 : Top2 Top2 -> Bool [wellfounded] .
    op fisPath : KPath -> Top3 .
    op wfr3 : Top3 Top3 -> Bool [wellfounded] .
    op fredsN : KNode KNode -> Top4 .
    op wfr4 : Top4 Top4 -> Bool [wellfounded] .
    op fredsP : KPath KPath -> Top5 .
    op wfr5 : Top5 Top5 -> Bool [wellfounded] .
endm
```

In AGES we can impose that the relations interpreting binary predicates wfr1,...,wfr5 (representing the well-founded components $\sqsupset_i$ of the removal pair which is used in the application of P_{RP} to τ_i for $1 \leq i \leq 5$) be *well-founded*[2]. AGES uses Theorem 4 to ensure this. Then, we obtain a new theory $\mathcal{S}_{1..5}^{\text{PATH}}$ by adding new sentences $\varphi_1^3, \ldots, \varphi_5^3$ corresponding to the proof jumps in $\tau_1, \ldots, \tau_5$ to $\mathcal{S}^{\text{PATH}}$; in AGES notation:

```
redN(tN:KNode,uN:KNode) =>
   wfr1(fmbNode(tN:KNode),fmbNode(uN:KNode))
redP(tP:KPath,uP:KPath) =>
   wfr2(fisEdge(tP:KPath),fisEdge(uP:KPath))
redP(tP:KPath,uP:KPath) =>
   wfr3(fisPath(tP:KPath),fisPath(uP:KPath))
redN(tN:KNode,uN:KNode) =>
   wfr4(fredsN(tN:KNode,vN:KNode),fredsN(uN:KNode,vN:KNode))
redP(tP:KPath,uP:KPath) =>
   wfr5(fredsP(tP:KPath,vP:KPath),fredsP(uP:KPath,vP:KPath))
```

AGES obtains the following model $\mathcal{A}$ for $\mathcal{S}_{1..5}^{\text{PATH}}$:

1. Interpretation of sorts:

$$\begin{aligned}
\mathcal{A}_{\text{KTruth}} &= [-1, +\infty) & \mathcal{A}_{\text{Node}} &= [-1, 0] & \mathcal{A}_{\text{KNode}} &= [-1, 0] \\
\mathcal{A}_{\text{Edge}} &= \{-1\} & \mathcal{A}_{\text{Path}} &= \{-1\} & \mathcal{A}_{\text{KPath}} &= [-1, 0] \\
\mathcal{A}_{\text{Top1}} &= [0, +\infty) & \mathcal{A}_{\text{Top2}} &= [-1, +\infty) & \mathcal{A}_{\text{Top3}} &= [0, +\infty) \\
\mathcal{A}_{\text{Top4}} &= [0, +\infty) & \mathcal{A}_{\text{Top5}} &= [-1, 0]
\end{aligned}$$

---

[2] We have enriched the syntax of Maude modules to specifiy this requirement.

2. Interpretation of function symbols (with argument variables taking values in the corresponding sort):

$$eq^{\mathcal{A}}(x,y) = y - x \qquad seq^{\mathcal{A}}(x,y) = -1 - y \qquad source^{\mathcal{A}}(x) = 0$$
$$target^{\mathcal{A}}(x) = -1 \qquad\qquad tt^{\mathcal{A}} = 0$$

$$fisEdge^{\mathcal{A}}(x) = 1 + x \qquad fisPath^{\mathcal{A}}(x) = 2 + x \qquad fmbNode^{\mathcal{A}}(x) = 2 + x$$
$$fredsN^{\mathcal{A}}(x,y) = 4 + x + y \qquad fredsP^{\mathcal{A}}(x,y) = 0$$

3. Interpretation of predicate symbols (as characteristic predicates):

$$mbEdge^{\mathcal{A}}(x) \Leftrightarrow x \in [-1,0] \qquad mbNode^{\mathcal{A}}(x) \Leftrightarrow x \in [-1,0]$$
$$mbPath^{\mathcal{A}}(x) \Leftrightarrow x \in [-1,0] \qquad redN^{\mathcal{A}}(x,y) \Leftrightarrow \textit{false}$$
$$redP^{\mathcal{A}}(x,y) \Leftrightarrow \textit{false} \qquad redT^{\mathcal{A}}(x,y) \Leftrightarrow x,y \in [-1,+\infty) \wedge y \geq x$$
$$redsN^{\mathcal{A}}(x,y) \Leftrightarrow x,y \in [-1,0] \qquad redsP^{\mathcal{A}}(x,y) \Leftrightarrow x,y \in [-1,0] \wedge x \geq y$$
$$redsT^{\mathcal{A}}(x,y) \Leftrightarrow x,y \in [-1,+\infty) \wedge y \geq x$$

$$wfr1^{\mathcal{A}}(x,y) \Leftrightarrow x,y \in [0,+\infty) \wedge x >_1 y$$
$$wfr2^{\mathcal{A}}(x,y) \Leftrightarrow x,y \in [0,+\infty) \wedge x >_1 y$$
$$wfr3^{\mathcal{A}}(x,y) \Leftrightarrow x,y \in [0,+\infty) \wedge x >_1 y$$
$$wfr4^{\mathcal{A}}(x,y) \Leftrightarrow \textit{false}$$
$$wfr5^{\mathcal{A}}(x,y) \Leftrightarrow x,y \in [-1,0] \wedge y >_1 x$$

Note that $redN^{\mathcal{A}}$ and $redP^{\mathcal{A}}$ are *empty* relations. Actually, this is enough to guarantee that conditions $\varphi_1^3, \ldots, \varphi_5^3$ for the proof jumps at stake hold, thus enabling their removal from the corresponding OT problem.

OT Problems $\tau_6, \ldots, \tau_8$. We extend now PATH_OSSig with the following:

```
mod PATH-tau6to8 is
  sorts Top6 Top7 Top8 .
  op fredP : KPath KPath -> Top6 .
  op wfr6 : Top6 Top6 -> Bool [wellfounded] .
  op fredP : KPath KPath -> Top7 .
  op wfr7 : Top7 Top7 -> Bool [wellfounded] .
  op fisPath : KPath -> Top8 .
  op wfr8 : Top8 Top8 -> Bool [wellfounded] .
endm
```

The new theory $\mathcal{S}_{6..8}^{PATH}$ extends $\mathcal{S}^{PATH}$ with $\varphi_6^3, \ldots, \varphi_6^3$, i.e.,

```
wfr6(fredP(seq(tP:KPath,vP:KPath),seq(uP:KPath,vP:KPath)),
    fredP(tP:KPath,uP:KPath))
wfr7(fredP(seq(vP:KPath,tP:KPath),seq(vP:KPath,uP:KPath)),
    fredP(tP:KPath,uP:KPath))
EP:KPath :: Edge =>
    wfr8(fisPath(seq(EP:KPath,PP:KPath)),fisPath(PP:KPath))
```

AGES computes the following model $\mathcal{A}'$ of $\mathcal{S}_{6..8}^{PATH}$:

1. Interpretation of sorts:

$$\mathcal{A}'_{\text{KTruth}} = [-1, +\infty) \quad \mathcal{A}'_{\text{Node}} = [0, +\infty) \quad \mathcal{A}'_{\text{KNode}} = [0, +\infty)$$
$$\mathcal{A}'_{\text{Edge}} = \{1\} \quad \mathcal{A}'_{\text{Path}} = [1, +\infty) \quad \mathcal{A}'_{\text{KPath}} = [1, +\infty)$$
$$\mathcal{A}'_{\text{Top6}} = [0, +\infty) \quad \mathcal{A}'_{\text{Top7}} = [0, +\infty) \quad \mathcal{A}'_{\text{Top8}} = [0, +\infty)$$

2. Interpretation of function symbols:

$$\text{eq}^{\mathcal{A}'}(x, y) = x + y - 1 \quad \text{seq}^{\mathcal{A}'}(x, y) = x + y \quad \text{source}^{\mathcal{A}'}(x) = x - 1$$
$$\text{target}^{\mathcal{A}'}(x) = 0 \quad \text{tt}^{\mathcal{A}'} = 0$$
$$\text{fisPath}^{\mathcal{A}'}(x) = 1 + x \quad \text{fredP}^{\mathcal{A}'}(x, y) = y - 1$$

3. Interpretation of predicate symbols:

$$\text{mbEdge}^{\mathcal{A}'}(x) \Leftrightarrow x \in [1, +\infty) \quad \text{mbNode}^{\mathcal{A}'}(x) \Leftrightarrow x \in [0, +\infty)$$
$$\text{mbPath}^{\mathcal{A}'}(x) \Leftrightarrow x \in [1, +\infty) \quad \text{redN}^{\mathcal{A}'}(x, y) \Leftrightarrow x, y \in [0, +\infty) \wedge x \geq y$$
$$\text{redT}^{\mathcal{A}'}(x, y) \Leftrightarrow x, y \in [-1, +\infty) \quad \text{redP}^{\mathcal{A}'}(x, y) \Leftrightarrow x, y \in [1, +\infty) \wedge x \geq y$$
$$\text{redsN}^{\mathcal{A}'}(x, y) \Leftrightarrow x, y \in [0, +\infty) \quad \text{redsP}^{\mathcal{A}'}(x, y) \Leftrightarrow x, y \in [1, +\infty)$$
$$\text{redsT}^{\mathcal{A}'}(x, y) \Leftrightarrow x, y \in [-1, +\infty)$$

$$\text{wfr6}^{\mathcal{A}'}(x, y) \Leftrightarrow x, y \in [0, +\infty) \wedge x >_1 y$$
$$\text{wfr7}^{\mathcal{A}'}(x, y) \Leftrightarrow x, y \in [0, +\infty) \wedge x >_1 y$$
$$\text{wfr8}^{\mathcal{A}'}(x, y) \Leftrightarrow x, y \in [0, +\infty) \wedge x >_1 y$$

Note that $\text{wfr6}^{\mathcal{A}'}$, $\text{wfr7}^{\mathcal{A}'}$, and $\text{wfr8}^{\mathcal{A}'}$ coincide with the ordering $>_1$ on $[0, +\infty)$ which is clearly well-founded.

OT Problem τ_9. We extend PATH_OSSig with:

```
mod PATH-tau9 is
  sorts Top9 .
  op fredsT : KTruth KTruth -> Top9 .
  op wfr9 : Top9 Top9 -> Bool [wellfounded] .
endm
```

We obtain a new theory $\mathcal{S}_9^{\text{PATH}}$ by adding the sentence φ_9^3:

$$\text{wfr9}(\text{fredsT}(\text{tT:KTruth}, \text{vT:KTruth}), \text{fredsT}(\text{uT:KTruth}, \text{vT:KTruth}))$$

corresponding to the proof jumps in τ_9 to $\mathcal{S}^{\text{PATH}}$. We obtain a model $\mathcal{A}''$ of $\mathcal{S}_9^{\text{PATH}}$:

1. Interpretation of sorts:

$$\mathcal{A}''_{\text{KTruth}} = [-1, +\infty) \quad \mathcal{A}''_{\text{Node}} = [-1, 1] \quad \mathcal{A}''_{\text{KNode}} = [-1, 1]$$
$$\mathcal{A}''_{\text{Edge}} = \{-1\} \quad \mathcal{A}''_{\text{Path}} = \{-1\} \quad \mathcal{A}''_{\text{KPath}} = [-1, 0] \quad \mathcal{A}''_{\text{Top9}} = [-1, +\infty)$$

2. Interpretation of function symbols:

$$\text{eq}^{\mathcal{A}''}(x, y) = x - y + 1 \quad \text{seq}^{\mathcal{A}''}(x, y) = 0 \quad \text{source}^{\mathcal{A}''}(x) = -x$$
$$\text{target}^{\mathcal{A}''}(x) = -1 \quad \text{tt}^{\mathcal{A}''} = 0 \quad \text{fredsT}^{\mathcal{A}''}(x, y) = x$$

3. Interpretation of predicate symbols:

$$\texttt{mbEdge}^{\mathcal{A}''}(x) \Leftrightarrow x \in [-1,0] \qquad \texttt{mbNode}^{\mathcal{A}''}(x) \Leftrightarrow x \in [-1,1]$$

$$\texttt{mbPath}^{\mathcal{A}''}(x) \Leftrightarrow x \in [-1,0] \qquad \texttt{redN}^{\mathcal{A}''}(x,y) \Leftrightarrow \textit{false}$$

$$\texttt{redP}^{\mathcal{A}''}(x,y) \Leftrightarrow \textit{false} \qquad \texttt{redT}^{\mathcal{A}''}(x,y) \Leftrightarrow x,y \in [-1,+\infty) \wedge x >_1 y$$

$$\texttt{redsN}^{\mathcal{A}''}(x,y) \Leftrightarrow x,y \in [-1,1] \qquad \texttt{redsP}^{\mathcal{A}''}(x,y) \Leftrightarrow x,y \in [-1,0] \wedge x \geq y$$

$$\texttt{redsT}^{\mathcal{A}''}(x,y) \Leftrightarrow x,y \in [-1,+\infty) \wedge x \geq y$$

$$\texttt{wfr9}^{\mathcal{A}''}(x,y) \Leftrightarrow x,y \in [-1,+\infty) \wedge x >_1 y$$

6.2   Proof of Operational Termination of PATH

Putting all together, we have the following OT-Tree for the proof:

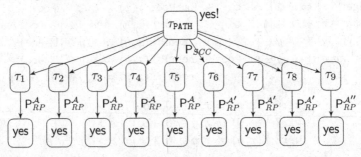

We label the application of P_{RP} with symbols $\mathcal{A}$, $\mathcal{A}'$, and $\mathcal{A}''$ to highlight the *different ways* to apply it. By Theorem 2, PATH is operationally terminating.

7   Conclusions

The use of logical models in proofs of operational termination in the OT Framework was suggested in [14] as an possible approach to implement the new processor P_{RP} introduced in the paper. This observation was a main motivation to develop the idea of convex polytopic domain [12] as a sufficiently simple but flexible approach to obtain a variety of domains that can be used in proofs of termination and which are amenable for automation [10]. The research in this paper closes some gaps left during these developments and provides a basis for the implementation of P_{RP} in the OT Framework by means of the automatic generation of logical models for order-sorted first-order theories.

We have extended the work in [10] to achieve the automatic generation of interpretations for *predicate symbols* using *convex polytopic domains*. These results are the basis of the implementation of the tool AGES for the automatic generation of models for OS-FOL theories. To our knowledge, no systematic treatment of the generation of (homogeneous or *heterogeneous*, i.e., with arguments in different sorts) *predicate interpretations* has been attempted to date. We have also shown how to *mechanize* the use of P_{RP} in the OT Framework for proving operational termination of declarative programs by recasting it as the problem of *finding a model* through appropriate transformations.

We believe that the research in this paper is an important step towards the practical use of logical models in proofs of operational termination of programs and hence towards the implementation of a tool for automatically proving operational termination of declarative programs based on the OT Framework in [14]. This is a subject for future work.

Acknowledgments. I thank Raúl Gutiérrez for implementing the results of Sects. 4 and 5.3 in AGES.

References

1. Alarcón, B., Gutiérrez, R., Lucas, S., Navarro-Marset, R.: Proving termination properties with MU-TERM. In: Johnson, M., Pavlovic, D. (eds.) AMAST 2010. LNCS, vol. 6486, pp. 201–208. Springer, Heidelberg (2011)
2. Alarcón, B., Lucas, S., Navarro-Marset, R.: Using matrix interpretations over the reals in proofs of termination. In: Lucio, F., Moreno, G., Peña, R.. (eds.) Proceedings of the IX Jornadas Sobre Programación y Lenguajes, PROLE 2009, pp. 255–264, September 2009
3. Clavel, M., Durán, F., Eker, S., Lincoln, P., Martí-Oliet, N., Meseguer, J., Talcott, C.: All About Maude - A High-Performance Logical Framework. LNCS, vol. 4350. Springer, Heidelberg (2007)
4. Cook, B., Rybalchenko, A., Podelski, A.: Proving program termination. Commun. ACM **54**(5), 88–98 (2011)
5. Durán, F., Lucas, S., Marché, C., Meseguer, J., Urbain, X.: Proving operational termination of membership equational programs. High.-Order Symbolic Comput. **21**(1–2), 59–88 (2008)
6. Goguen, J., Meseguer, J.: Models and equality for logical programming. In: Ehrig, H., Kowalsky, R.A., Levi, G., Montanari, U. (eds.) TAPSOFT 1987. LNCS, vol. 250, pp. 1–22. Springer, Heidelberg (1987)
7. Goguen, J., Meseguer, J.: Order-sorted algebra I: equational deduction for multiple inheritance, overloading, exceptions and partial operations. Theor. Comput. Sci. **105**, 217–273 (1992)
8. Gutiérrez, R., Lucas, S., Reinoso, P.: A tool for the automatic generation of logical models of order-sorted first-order theories (Submitted). http://zenon.dsic.upv.es/ages/
9. Lucas, S.: Polynomials over the reals in proofs of termination: from theory to practice. RAIRO Theor. Inform. Appl. **39**(3), 547–586 (2005)
10. Lucas, S.: Synthesis of models for order-sorted first-order theories using linear algebra and constraint solving. Electron. Proc. Theor. Comput. Sci. **200**, 32–47 (2015)
11. Lucas, S., Marché, C., Meseguer, J.: Operational termination of conditional term rewriting systems. Inform. Proc. Lett. **95**, 446–453 (2005)
12. Lucas, S., Meseguer, J.: Models for logics and conditional constraints in automated proofs of termination. In: Aranda-Corral, G.A., Calmet, J., Martín-Mateos, F.J. (eds.) AISC 2014. LNCS (LNAI), vol. 8884, pp. 7–18. Springer, Heidelberg (2014)
13. Lucas, S., Meseguer, J.: Operational termination of membership equational programs: the order-sorted way. In: Rosu, G. (ed.) Proceedings of the 7th International Workshop on Rewriting Logic and its Applications, WRLA 2008. Electronic Notes in Theoretical Computer Science, vol. 238, pp. 207–225 (2009)

14. Lucas, S., Meseguer, J.: Proving operational termination of declarative programs in general logics. In: Danvy, O. (ed.) Proceedings of the 16th International Symposium on Principles and Practice of Declarative Programming, PPDP 2014, pp. 111–122. ACM Digital Library (2014)
15. Meseguer, J.: General logics. In: Ebbinghaus, H.-D., et al. (eds.) Logic Colloquium 1987, pp. 275–329, North-Holland (1989)
16. Meseguer, J.: Membership algebra as a logical framework for equational specification. In: Parisi-Presicce, F. (ed.) WADT 1997. LNCS, vol. 1376, pp. 18–61. Springer, Heidelberg (1998)
17. Neurauter, F., Middeldorp, A.: Revisiting matrix interpretations for proving termination of term rewriting. In: Schmidt-Schauss, M. (ed.) Proceedings of the 22nd International Conference on Rewriting Techniques and Applications, RTA 2011. LIPICS, vol. 10, pp. 251–266 (2011)
18. Shapiro, S.: Foundations without Foundationalism: A Case for Second-Order Logic. Clarendon Press, Oxford (1991)

A Maude Framework for Cache Coherent Multicore Architectures

Shiji Bijo[(✉)], Einar Broch Johnsen, Ka I Pun, and Silvia Lizeth Tapia Tarifa

Department of Informatics, University of Oslo, Oslo, Norway
{shijib,einarj,violet,sltarifa}@ifi.uio.no

Abstract. On shared memory multicore architectures, cache memory is used to accelerate program execution by providing quick access to recently used data, but enables multiple copies of data to co-exist during execution. Although cache coherence protocols ensure that cores do not access stale data, the organisation of data in memory and the scheduling of tasks may significantly influence the performance of a parallel program in this setting. As a step towards understanding how the data organisation impacts the performance of a given parallel program using shared memory, this paper proposes a framework defined in Maude for the executable modelling of program execution on cache coherent multicore architectures, formalising the interactions between cores executing tasks, their caches, and main memory. The framework allows the specification and comparison of program execution with different design choices for the underlying hardware architecture, such as the number of cores, the data layout in main memory, and the cache associativity.

1 Introduction

Program execution on multicore architectures can be accelerated by cache memory, which provides quick access to recently used data but allows multiple copies of data to co-exist during execution. Cache coherence protocols ensure that the data in the caches is consistent and that cores never access stale data from the caches. Requested data which has become stale or which is not in the cache, leads to a so-called *cache miss*; the requested data needs to be loaded into the cache before it can be accessed, resulting in a performance penalty. With the current dominating position of multicore architectures in hardware design, we believe that language designers may benefit from a better understanding and ability to reason about interactions between cores executing tasks, their caches, and main memory. For this purpose we need clear and precise operational models which allow us to reason about such interactions. However, work on operational semantics for parallel programs generally abstracts from the caches of multicore architectures, and assumes that there are only single copies of data in memory

This work is partly funded by the EU research project FP7-612985 *UpScale: From Inherent Concurrency to Massive Parallelism Through Type-Based Optimisations* (www.upscale-project.eu).

D. Lucanu (Ed.): WRLA 2016, LNCS 9942, pp. 47–63, 2016.
DOI: 10.1007/978-3-319-44802-2_3

(i.e., memory is directly accessed from threads). As a consequence, these semantic models provide little guidance for language designers in making efficient use of cache memory.

Maude has been proposed as a unifying framework for language semantics which supports a wide range of definitional styles (e.g., [22,30]). Its usefulness as a semantic framework has been widely demonstrated, including low-level and highly complex languages such as C [13]. In this paper, we develop a Maude framework for modelling execution on cache consistent multicore architectures, capturing how data movement between cores and main memory is triggered by the execution of program tasks on the different cores. Our purpose is not to evaluate the specifics of a concrete cache coherence protocol, but rather to capture program execution on shared data at locations with coherent caches in a formal yet highly configurable way. We let the Maude specification keep track of the cache hit/miss ratio per core as a way to evaluate the performance of an execution path. This allows runtime design choices for programs to be compared by means of Maude's analysis techniques. We illustrate how models of multicore architectures can be configured and compared with some small examples.

Related Work. Previous work by the authors developed an SOS for cache coherent multicore architectures using multi-set label synchronisation on transitions to model parallel instantaneous broadcast, and proved that this semantics guaranteed properties such as data race free access to data and no access to stale data [2]. This paper extends the previous work in several ways: (1) it makes the source-level programming language more expressive by supporting loops, choice, and dynamic task creation, (2) it allows the modeller to configure the cache associativity of the architecture, and (3) it refines the abstracted declarative definitions of the previous work, resulting in an executable semantics in Maude. Rewriting logic has previously been used to specify and analyse interaction between a single microprocessor and its cache [1,14], and to model and analyse memory safety and garbage collection for hardware architectures [24,29].

Other approaches to the analysis of multicore architectures include on the one hand simulators for evaluating the efficiency of specific cache coherence protocols and on the other hand formal techniques for proving their correctness. Simulation tools allow cache coherence protocols to be specified in order to evaluate their performance on different architectures (e.g., gems [19] and gem5 [3]). These tools run benchmark programs written as low-level read and write instructions to memory and perform measurements, e.g., the cache hit/miss ratio. Advanced simulators such as Graphite [23] and Sniper [5] can handle multicore architectures with thousands of cores by running on distributed clusters. A framework, proposed in [17], statically estimates the worst-case response times for concurrent applications running on multiple cores with shared cache.

Both operational and axiomatic formal models have been used to describe the effect of parallel executions on shared memory under relaxed memory models, including abstract calculi [7], memory models for programming languages such as Java [16], and machine-level instruction sets for concrete processors such as POWER [18,31] and x86 [32]. The behaviour of programs executing under total store order (TSO) architectures is studied in [12,33]. However, work on weak memory models abstracts from caches, and is as such largely orthogonal to our work which does not consider the reordering of source-level syntax. Cache coherence protocols can be formally specified as automata and verified by (parametrised) model checking (e.g., [9,25,27]) in terms of operational formalisations which abstract from the specific number of cores to prove the correctness of the protocols (e.g., [10,11,34]). For example, Maude's model checker has recently been used to verify the correctness of configurations of the MSI and ESI protocols [20,28]. In contrast, our work, which also uses MSI, focuses on specifying the abstract interactions between caches and shared memory for parallel programs executing on a multicore architecture.

Paper Overview. Section 2 reviews background concepts on rewriting logic and Maude, and on multicore architectures, Sect. 3 presents our abstract model of cache coherent multicore architectures, Sect. 4 details the Maude model, Sect. 5 presents examples with different configurations, and Sect. 6 concludes the paper.

2 Preliminaries

2.1 Maude

The semantics of our framework is defined in Maude [6], a specification and analysis system based on rewriting logic (RL) [21]. In a rewrite theory (Σ, E, R), the signature Σ defines the ground terms, E equations between terms, and R a set of labelled rewrite rules. Rewrite rules apply to terms of given sorts, specified in (membership) equational logic (Σ, E). When modelling computational systems, different system components are typically modelled by terms of suitable sorts and the global state configuration is represented as a multi-set of these terms. RL extends algebraic specification techniques with transition rules which capture the dynamic behaviour of a system. *Conditional rewrite rules* on the form `crl [label]:` $t \longrightarrow t'$ `if` *cond* transform an instance of the pattern t into the corresponding instance of the pattern t', where the condition *cond* is a conjunction of rewriting conditions and equalities that must hold for the rule to apply (the `label` identifies the rule). When auxiliary functions are needed, these can be defined in equational logic, and thus evaluated in between the state transitions [21]. In a *conditional equation* `ceq` $t = t'$ `if` *cond*, the condition must similarly hold for the equation to apply. Unconditional rewrite rules and equations are denoted by the keywords `rl` and `eq`, respectively.

To structure specifications in Maude, equations and rewrite rules can be scoped in modules which may be parameterised. In particular, Maude supports the modelling of systems as multi-sets of objects in a standardised format, with suitable communication mechanisms. The pre-defined Maude module CONFIGURATION provides a notation for object syntax. An object in a given state has the form $\langle$ O `:C|` $a_1: v_1, \ldots, a_n: v_n \rangle$, where C is the class name and O the object identifier, and there is a set of attributes with identifiers a_i

which have corresponding values v_i in the current state. Given an initial config-uration, Maude supports simulation and breadth-first search through reachable states, and model checking of systems with a finite number of reachable states. In this paper, Maude is used to implement executable operational semantics of a framework to experiment with architectural models.

2.2 Overview of Multicore Architectures

Processing units, or *cores*, in modern multicore architectures use *caches* to store their most recently accessed data. Caches are usually small and fast compared to *main memory*, and they can be either private to one core or shared among multiple cores. Main memory in general consists of *blocks*, each with a unique *address*. Each block is organised in multiple continuous *words*, and each word is associated to a *memory reference*. Cache memory, on the other hand, consists of *cache lines*, each of which may contain several words. In general, a cache line can contain at least as many words as one memory block.

A cache *hit* refers to the case that the desired data is found in the cache, the other case is called a cache *miss*. In the case of a miss, the cache fetches data from the next levels in the memory hierarchy (e.g., main memory). The fetched data, which includes the requested data, consists of consecutive words starting at the beginning of a memory block and corresponds in size to a cache line. Since caches are small in size compared to main memory, fetching data from main memory to caches may require the eviction of existing cache lines. The choice of cache lines to evict depends on the organisation of the cache lines, the so-called *cache associativity*, and on the *replacement policy*. In *k*-way *set associative caches*, the cache lines are grouped as sets with *k* cache lines and the fetched data can go anywhere in a particular set. *Direct mapped caches* have one-way set associativity as these caches are organised in single-line sets. In *fully associative caches*, the entire cache is considered as a single set and the fetched data can be placed anywhere in the cache. The modulo operation $n\%c$ calculates the index of the cache set to which the fetched data starting at the block with address n should be placed, where c is the number of sets per cache. Replacement policies select the line to evict from a specific cache set when the fetched data is placed into that set, e.g., random, FIFO, LRU (Least Recently Used).

Since multiple copies of data may be stored in different local caches and in main memory, cache coherence protocols are used to keep all copies consistent. In particular, *invalidation-based protocols* broadcast invalidation messages when a particular core requires write access to a memory address. Typical invalidation protocols are MSI and its extensions (e.g., MESI and MOESI). In MSI, a cache line can be in one of three states: Modified, Shared, and Invalid. A line in *modified* state indicates that it is the most updated copy and that all other copies in the system are *invalid*, whereas a line in *shared* state implies that all copies in the system are consistent. A cache has a miss when the requested line is either invalid or is not present in the cache; in this case, the cache broadcasts a request. Upon receiving this request, the cache which has the modified copy of the relevant cache line flushes the cache line to the main memory. The state of the cache line will then be updated to shared in both the cache and the main memory. An invalidation message will be broadcast in the system before writing in a cache line. The state of the cache line will be updated to modified if the write operation succeeds. Upon the arrival of an invalidation message, a cache will invalidate its shared copy. For more details on variations of multicore architectures, coherence protocols, and memory consistency, the reader may consult, e.g., [8,15,26].

3   An Abstract Model of Execution on Cache Coherent Multicore Architectures

This section outlines an abstract model of execution for parallel programs running on multicore architectures. We first explain the source-level language that the model executes, then the abstract model of the hardware architecture, and finally how the relation between these two is captured by the execution model.

The Source-Level Language. Programs are written in a source-level input language with the following syntax, where r is a memory reference and T a task name:

$$LLP ::= \overline{Task}\ \mathbf{main}\{sst\}$$
$$Task ::= \mathbf{task}\ T\{sst\}$$
$$sst ::= \varepsilon \mid sst; sst \mid \mathbf{PrRd}(r) \mid \mathbf{PrWr}(r) \mid \mathbf{commit}(r) \mid sst \sqcap sst \mid sst^* \mid \mathbf{Spawn}\ T$$

A (low-level) program LLP consists of a set of tasks, denoted by the overbar $\overline{Task}$, and a main block. Each task $\mathbf{task}\ T\{sst\}$ has a name T and a body with statements sst. Statements include $\mathbf{PrRd}(r)$ for reading the word from main memory reference r, $\mathbf{PrWr}(r)$ for writing to r, $\mathbf{commit}(r)$ for flushing the content of the cache line with reference r to main memory, and $\mathbf{Spawn}\ T$ to dynamically create a task T. In addition, there are standard operators for sequential composition $sst; sst$, non-deterministic choice $sst \sqcap sst$, and repetition sst^*.

Example 1. Let r_0, r_1, r_2, and r_3 be references inside memory blocks. This is a simple example of a low-level program:
     $\mathbf{task}\ T_1\{\mathbf{PrRd}(r_0); \mathbf{PrWr}(r_1)\}$
     $\mathbf{task}\ T_2\{\mathbf{PrRd}(r_2); \mathbf{PrWr}(r_3)\}$
     $\mathbf{main}\{\mathbf{Spawn}\ T_1; \mathbf{Spawn}\ T_2\}$ □

The Hardware Architecture. As depicted in Fig. 1, our hardware architecture model consists of multiple cores with shared memory, where each core has a *private one-level* cache. Communications between different components are through messages. Cores are responsible for sending messages to other components in the architecture, if needed. The exchange of messages between different cores and main memory is captured by a *communication medium*, which abstracts from different concrete topologies such as bus, ring, or mesh. Observe that the communication medium needs to arbitrate between requests from different cores (e.g., to exclude conflicting invalidation messages). We here abstract from how this

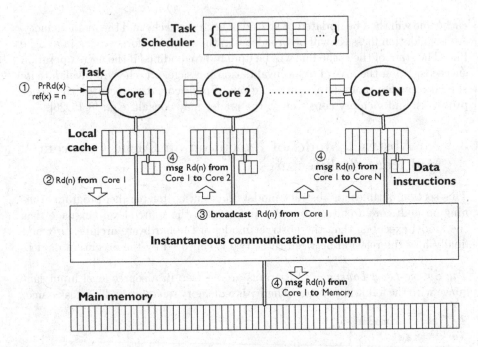

Fig. 1. Abstract model of multicore architecture (illustration). Here we let circled numbers ① – ④ suggest the ordering of communication events.

arbitration is realised by a specific communication medium by modelling the communication as *instantaneous*. For simplicity, we ignore the data contained in memory blocks and cache lines. We further assume that the size of a cache line is same as the size of a memory block, and data move from one core to another one indirectly via the main memory. Our model includes an abstract version of the MSI protocol.

The Execution Model. A runtime configuration consists of several components: the cores with their associated cache, where each cache has its own associativity relation, a main memory, a scheduler with a global pool of dynamically created tasks that are waiting to be executed, a task lookup table $[T \mapsto sst]$ mapping task names to bodies, and a reference lookup table $[r \mapsto n]$ binding references to block addresses.

To execute *LLP* programs, new tasks are scheduled on the idle cores in the abstract model. Cores execute *runtime statements* rst by interacting with their local caches. Runtime statements include the *source-level statements* sst and statements **PrRdBl**(r), **PrWrBl**(r) and **commit**. Statements such as **PrRd**(r) and **PrWr**(r) may trigger data movement between the cache and main memory. Such data movements are captured by *data instructions* **fetch**(n) and **flush**(n), where n is the address of the memory block in which the word with reference r resides. A task executing on a core may be *blocked* waiting for data to be fetched, which is captured by statements **PrRdBl**(r) and **PrWrBl**(r). To ensure that modified data is stored in main memory before another task is scheduled, we use **commit** to force all modified lines in the cache to be flushed after the execution of a task. In an *initial state*, all memory blocks in the main memory have status shared, the task pool contains a main block *sst* generated from **main**$\{sst\}$, and each core has an empty cache, no data instructions and no executing task.

To illustrate a behaviour in our model, let a reference r map to a memory address n, and consider a core which does not have the memory block n available in the local cache and attempts to access n by executing a statement **PrRd**(r) (or **PrWr**(r)). To retrieve the memory block, the core first broadcasts the request as messages to other cores and main memory through the communication medium. Messages include requests for *read* and *read exclusive* (for write operation) access to memory address n, which are of the form $Rd(n)$ and $RdX(n)$, respectively. Once the message is broadcast, the execution of the task in the core will be blocked by a **PrRdBl**(r) (or **PrWrBl**(r)) statement and a **fetch**(n) instruction is added to the data instructions. The request will be instantaneously broadcast to the other cores and to main memory (thereby mimicking the use of label synchronisation in SOS such as [2]). If the requested cache line is modified in another cache, the protocol ensures that the line in the other cache is first *flushed* to main memory. The requesting core can then proceed to *fetch* the memory block n from main memory after the **flush**(n) instruction, and continue with the execution of its task. Note that a request message for read exclusive access will invalidate all copies of the relevant block in the other caches as well as in main memory. Consequently, data race freedom and the consistency of copies of data in different caches in this model are maintained by an abstracted version of the basic coherence protocol MSI.

4 Formalising Multicore Architectures in Maude

We formalise the abstract model presented in Sect. 3 as an object-oriented specification in Maude [6], and focus the presentation on the main parts of this specification. Section 4.1 explains the main sorts and signatures of the model, Sect. 4.2 focuses on a subset of the rewriting rules which capture task execution and Sect. 4.3 on a subset of the equations and rewriting rules for coordination and communication between cores and main memory using message passing[1].

4.1 Sorts and Signatures of the Model

Figure 2 shows the main sorts and objects used in our model. The components (e.g., cores, memory, and scheduler) are modelled as Maude objects floating in a global configuration. A system wide operator $\{\_\}$ is used to wrap complete

---

[1] The complete Maude model is available from http://folk.uio.no/~shijib/ wrla2016maude.zip.

```
op {_} : Configuration → GlobalSystem [ctor] .
op ref : Int → Reference [ctor] .
op Assoc : Int → MapPolicy [ctor] .

op CR : → Cid [ctor format(n d)] .
op CM:_ : Cache{Int, MemoryMap} → Attribute [ctor] .
op Rst:_ : stList → Attribute [ctor] .
op D:_ : stList → Attribute [ctor] .
op Miss:_ : Int → Attribute [ctor] .
op Hit:_ : Int → Attribute [ctor] .
op CacheSz:_ : Int → Attribute [ctor] .
op ~:_ : MapPolicy → Attribute [ctor] .

op ⟨_: MM|M:_, fetchCount:_⟩ : Oid MemoryMap Int → Object [ctor] .
op ⟨_: Task|Data:_⟩ : Oid task{Qid, stList} → Object [ctor] .
op ⟨_: Qu|TidSet:_⟩ : Oid Set{Qid} → Object [ctor] .
op ⟨_: TBL|Addr:_⟩ : Oid Tbl{Reference, Address} → Object [ctor] .
```

Fig. 2. Runtime syntax: relevant sorts and object representation in Maude

configurations into the sort GlobalSystem, and ensures that communication messages are correctly propagated to every part of the system. Each memory block has an address of sort Address and may contain multiple words. The operator ref(r) of sort Reference means the reference r to a word in a memory block. Observe that multiple references can be mapped to the same block address, which gives us flexibility to specify the size of memory blocks and cache lines. The Assoc operator of sort MapPolicy takes an integer k as parameter to specify that each cache set has k cache lines. As shown in Fig. 2, the object MM models the main memory. The attribute M is a map of sort MemoryMap that binds Address to Status, which can be modified mo, shared sh or invalid inv, as in the MSI protocol. The attribute fetchCount logs the total number of *fetch* operations which have been used in the whole configuration during an execution.

Cores are modelled by a class identifier CR and a number of attributes, such as CM stores the cache memory, Rst the task to be executed, D the data instructions (fetch and flush), CacheSz the size of the cache, ~ the cache associativity, Miss the number of local cache misses, and Hit the number of local cache hits. As the core object has a number of attributes, we model it using the pre-defined object syntax from the CONFIGURATION module, which introduces an object format with a set of attributes. This allows a compact presentation format for the rewrite rules as a variable Atts of sort AttributeSet can be used to replace all attributes which are not important for a specific rule as shown later in Fig. 3. The cache memory CM of sort Cache{Int, MemoryMap} is a collection of cache sets where each set has an integer index as the identifier. Similar to the attribute M, a cache set is also of sort MemoryMap, which maps each cache line in the set to its status. The sort stList refers to the sequence of statements to be executed in both Rst and D.

Object Task models a task lookup table which binds task Qid to sequences of statements (for dynamic task allocation). The scheduler is modelled by the object Qu, which selects a task id from its pool and allocates the sequence of statements (using the object Task) to an idle core. Object TBL models the reference lookup table by mapping each reference r to a word in the main memory to the address of the memory block where the word resides.

4.2   Rewriting Rules for Task Execution

Rewriting rules are used to capture the execution of parallel tasks in the multicore hardware architecture. For brevity in the presented rules, we omit the static table TBL and use addr[ref(r)] to denote the block address of a memory reference r. Figure 3 contains the subset of rules that are explained in this section, gray boxes are used to highlight the evolving patterns in each rule.

Rule *PrRd1* describes the case when a read statement PrRd(r) proceeds with a cache hit, because the block N (= addr[ref(r)]) is either in status mo or sh in the cache. To simplify the presentation of the rules, we let σ denote the frequently recurring expression selectStatus(*mapPol, Ca, size*, addr[ref(r)]), where *mapPol, Ca, size*, and r are the parameters which respectively refer to the cache associativity $\sim$, the cache memory, the number of cache lines and references. The function returns the status of block N; if N is not present in the cache, it returns unknown. In the case of a cache miss, rule *PrRd2* adds a fetch-instruction to the data instructions D, (which will later fetch data from the main memory) and replaces the read statement by a blocking statement PrRdBl(r) to indicate that the core is waiting for the memory block to be fetched. To request block N, rule *PrRd2* broadcasts a read request Rd(N) to the communication medium from which all other cores instantaneously receive the request; upon receipt, a core which has a modified copy of the requested block will make a flush. For each cache hit and cache miss, the related local counters are incremented.

A write statement PrWr(r) is treated as a hit if the status of the relevant block N is mo, where the corresponding rule is similar to the rule *PrRd1* (and therefore omitted here). In case block N is in sh status, which is also counted as a cache hit, the core needs to broadcast an invalidation message RdX(N) to ensure exclusive access to the block N, captured by rule *PrWr2*. Upon receiving the invalidation message, all other cores and the main memory will instantaneously invalidate their shared copy of block N. In the case of a cache miss, the core first requests the block by sending a read request Rd(N), as captured by rule *PrWr3*, and the write statement is replaced by a blocked statement PrWrBl(r), indicating that the core is waiting for the block to be fetched. Once the block is fetched, the core will request exclusive access to N, similar to rule *PrWr2*. Observe that before requesting exclusive access, the cache line may get invalidated by a RdX(N) message from another core in the configuration. In this situation, the core has to broadcast the Rd(N) message again as in rule *PrWr3*. Rule *PrWrBlock2* captures this situation; here, the occurs operation avoids repeated execution of the same rule by checking whether the fetch instruction for the requested block is already added to the data instructions D or not. Rule *Commit1* forces a core to flush the modified copy of a particular memory block to main memory.

```
crl [PrRd1] :
⟨C1: CR | CM: Ca, Rst:(PrRd(r);rst), Hit:h, CacheSz: size,~: mapPol,Atts⟩
⟶
⟨C1: CR | CM: Ca, Rst:rst, Hit:(h+1), CacheSz: size, ~: mapPol, Atts⟩
if σ = sh or σ = mo .


crl [PrRd2] :
⟨C1: CR | CM: Ca, Rst:(PrRd(r);rst), D:d, Miss:m, CacheSz: size,~: mapPol,Atts⟩
⟶
⟨C1: CR | CM: Ca, Rst:(PrRdBl(r);rst), D:(d;fetch(addr[ref(r)])), Miss:(m + 1),
CacheSz: size,~: mapPol,Atts⟩ (broadcast Rd(addr[ref(r)]) from C1)
if σ = inv or σ = unknown .


crl [PrWr2] :
⟨C1: CR | CM: Ca, Rst:(PrWr(r);rst), Hit:h, CacheSz: size,~: mapPol,Atts⟩
⟶
⟨C1: CR | CM: Ca, Rst:(PrWrBl(r);rst), Hit:(h+1), CacheSz: size,~: mapPol,
Atts⟩ (broadcast RdX(addr[ref(r)]) from C1)
if σ = sh .


crl [PrWr3] :
⟨C1: CR | CM: Ca, Rst:(PrWr(r);rst), D:d, Miss:m, CacheSz: size,~: mapPol,Hit: h⟩
⟶
⟨C1: CR | CM: Ca, Rst:(PrWrBl(r);rst), D:(d;fetch(addr[ref(r)])), Miss:(m+1),
CacheSz: size,~: mapPol,Hit:h ⟩ (broadcast Rd(addr[ref(r)]) from C1)
if σ = inv or σ = unknown .


crl [PrWrBlock2] :
⟨C1: CR | CM: Ca, Rst:(PrWrBl(r);rst), D:d, CacheSz: size,~: mapPol,Atts⟩
⟶
⟨C1: CR | CM: Ca, Rst:(PrWrBl(r);rst), D:(d;fetch(addr[ref(r)])),~: mapPol,
CacheSz: size,Atts ⟩ (broadcast Rd(addr[ref(r)]) from C1)
if( σ = inv or σ = unknown) and (occurs(fetch(addr[ref(r)]),d) = false) .


crl [Commit1] :
⟨C1: CR | CM: Ca, Rst:(commit(r);rst), D:d, CacheSz: size,~: mapPol,Atts⟩
⟶
⟨C1: CR | CM: Ca, Rst:rst, D:(d;flush(addr[ref(r)])), CacheSz: size,~: mapPol,
Atts⟩ if σ = mo .


crl [Fetch1] :
⟨C1: CR | CM:Ca, D:(fetch(N);d), CacheSz: size, ~: mapPol,Atts⟩
⟨Me: MM | M: mapSet, fetchCount: x' ⟩
⟶
⟨C1: CR | CM:fetchUpdateLine(Ca,size,N,sh,mapPol), D:d, CacheSz: size,
~: mapPol, Atts⟩ ⟨Me: MM | M: mapSet, fetchCount:(x'+1)⟩
if allModified(cacheLineSet(Ca,size,N,mapPol),mapPol) = false and
selectStatus(mapSet, N) = sh .


crl [Flush1] :
⟨Me: MM | M:mapSet, fetchCount: x⟩
⟨C1: CR | CM:Ca, D:(flush(N);d), CacheSz: size,~: mapPol,Atts⟩
⟶
⟨Me: MM | M:updateLine(mapSet,N,inv), fetchCount: x⟩
⟨C1: CR | CM:updateLine(mapPol,Ca,size,N,sh,mo), D:d, CacheSz: size,
~: mapPol,Atts ⟩ if σ = mo .
```

Fig. 3. Subset of rewriting rules in Maude (part 1)

Only memory blocks with status `sh` can be fetched from main memory. Otherwise, the fetch instruction is blocked until the data is flushed from another cache. In the rule *Fetch1*, the `allModified` function returns `true` if the cache set in which the memory block should be placed is full with modified cache lines. This function returns `false` if there is vacant space in the set or all cache lines in the set are not modified (resulting in an *eviction* without flushing). Apart from fetching the cache line, this rule uses `fetchUpdateLine` to update the status of the fetched block to `sh`. The global counter `fetchCount` is used to log the total number of fetch operations. As explained in rule *PrWrBlock2*, executing one read (or write) statement may entail multiple fetch operations, and therefore the value of `fetchCount` can be greater than the sum of local cache misses from all cores. Rule *Flush1* stores a modified cache line in main memory, setting its status to `sh` both in the cache and main memory. The rules for the remaining statements (e.g., spawn, choice, repetition) are standard.

4.3 Synchronisation Through Message Passing

Figure 4 contains the main equations used to coordinate the accesses to memory blocks. To access a memory block N, a core broadcasts a read request Rd(N) to get the most recent copy of N or a write request RdX(N) to get exclusive access to N. Each broadcast request is of the form **broadcast** Re **from** C1, where Re denotes the read or write request and C1 the identity of the sender. As the requests are broadcast to all the other cores and to the main memory, each broadcast request is recursively transformed into individual messages of the form **msg** Re **from** C1 **to** C2 where Re is the request and C1 and C2 are the sender and receiver, respectively. The function `objectIds` collects the identities of objects from the configuration REST.

Upon receiving a read request Rd(N), if the core has the requested block N in its cache with status `mo`, the block will be flushed to the main memory. This

```
eq {(broadcast Re from C1) REST} =
    {(multicast Re from C1 to objectIds(REST)) REST} .
eq multicast Re from C1 to none = none .
eq multicast Re from C1 to C2 ; ReSet = (msg Re from C1 to C2)
                                  (multicast Re from C1 to ReSet) .

ceq (msg RdX(N) from C2 to C1)
⟨C1 : CR | CM: Ca, CacheSz: size, ~: mapPol, Atts ⟩
=
⟨C1: CR | CM: updateLine(mapPol,Ca,size,N,inv,sh), CacheSz: size,~: mapPol,
Atts⟩ if σ = sh and C2 ≠ C1 .

ceq (msg Rd(N) from C2 to C1)
⟨C1 : CR | CM: Ca, D: d, CacheSz: size, ~: mapPol, Atts ⟩
=
⟨C1 : CR | CM: Ca, D: (flush(N) ; d), CacheSz: size,~: mapPol,Atts⟩
if σ = mo .
```

Fig. 4. Subset of rewriting rules and equations in Maude (part 2)

allows the core sending the request to eventually get access to the most recent copy of N. If a core receives a read request about a block that is not locally modified, the message is ignored. Note that the main memory will discard all messages with a read request. When receiving a write request RdX(N), the main memory and all cores with a local copy of N (except the sender) will update the status of the relevant block to inv by the function updateLine. If the sender and the receiver are the same core, it indicates that exclusive access to the relevant block is granted to that core. In this case, the status of the block is updated from sh to mo. Note that the rewriting rules for write operations ensure that a write request can only be sent when the block is in sh status.

5   Examples

The presented Maude specification constitutes a highly configurable modelling framework for programs executing on cache coherent multicore architectures. In this section we consider small examples to show how the cache associativity relation, cache size, and memory layout can be configured in concrete models, and how these parameters can influence the *cache hit/miss ratio*. In addition, we consider search conditions to check the correctness of concrete instances of our modelling framework. Maude's **search** command evaluates all reachable states from a given initial configuration with respect to a given condition. Out of these reachable states of the execution of terminating *LLP*s, we are interested in the *worst case scenarios*, that is, states which give the highest number of cache misses or the worst hit/miss ratios.

Below, we present the execution paths which give the highest number of total cache misses. To observe differences in the status of cache lines and memory blocks in main memory, we inspect the state where all the tasks have been executed, but before the cache is flushed (using the commit[2] statement). We refer to this state as the *observing state* of the execution path.

Example 2. In this example we illustrate the effect of changing the cache size and cache associativity. Consider an initial configuration config0 consisting of one core C1 with a cache of size five, CacheSz: 5, and with direct map associativity ~: Assoc(1). The size of a memory block is one word and the reference table TBL maps exactly one memory reference to each block. Assume that a program which consists of a main block that spawns a task executes in this configuration:

```
eq config0 =
⟨C1: CR | M: empty,Rst: nil,D: nil,Miss: 0,Hit: 0,CacheSz: 5,~: Assoc(1)⟩
⟨M: MM | M:  0↦sh,  1↦sh,  2↦sh,3↦sh,  4↦sh,  5↦sh,  fetchCount: 0⟩
⟨Sch: Qu | TidSet: ('main)⟩
⟨Tbl: TBL | Addr: ref(0)↦0,ref(1)↦1,ref(2)↦2,ref(3)↦3,ref(4)↦4,ref(5)↦5⟩
⟨Ta: Task | Data: 'main↦Spawn('T1),  'T1↦(PrWr(0);PrWr(5);PrWr(0))⟩  .
```

---

[2] Recall that the commit statement forces the flushing of all modified cache lines, which does not affect the number of cache misses.

In the following observing state (which omits the static tables TBL and Task), observe that due to the cache size and associativity, memory blocks with addresses 0 and 5 will compete for the same cache line with index 0. All the statements in task 'T1 entail a cache miss, which gives the global counter fetchCount: 3 in the main memory and the local counter Miss: 3 in the cache:

```
⟨c1: CR | M: 0↦(0↦mo),Rst: commit,D:nil,Miss: 3,Hit: 0,CacheSz: 5,~: Assoc(1)⟩
⟨m: MM | M:  0↦inv, 1↦sh, 2↦sh, 3↦sh, 4↦sh, 5↦sh, fetchCount: 3⟩
⟨sch: Qu | TidSet: empty⟩
...
```

Let us change the cache size to CacheSz: 10 and cache associativity to ~: Assoc(2), which means that each cache set has two cache lines. In this setting, there is enough space for two memory blocks 0 and 5 to be in the same cache set with index 0 at the same time:

```
⟨C1: CR | M: 0  ↦(0↦mo,5↦mo),Rst: commit,D: nil,Miss: 2,
          Hit: 1,CacheSz: 10,~:  Assoc(2)⟩
⟨M: MM | M:  0↦inv, 1↦sh, 2↦sh, 3↦sh, 4↦sh, 5↦inv, fetchCount: 2⟩
⟨sch: Qu | TidSet:  empty⟩
...
```

Observe that the same program executing in this configuration has only two cache misses in the observing state.   □

Example 3. In this example we illustrate the effect of changing the main memory organisation. Consider an initial configuration config1 consisting of two cores C1 and C2 with caches of size five, CacheSz: 5, and with direct map associativity ~: Assoc(1). The size of a memory block is four words, so the reference table TBL maps four different memory references to one block. Consider the program in Example 1, which consists of tasks trying to concurrently access the memory block 0, executes in this configuration:

```
eq config1 =
⟨C1: CR | M: empty,Rst: nil,D: nil,Miss: 0,Hit: 0,CacheSz: 5,~: Assoc(1)⟩
⟨C2: CR | M: empty,Rst: nil,D: nil,Miss: 0,Hit: 0,CacheSz: 5,~: Assoc(1)⟩
⟨M: MM | M:  0↦sh, 1↦sh, 2↦sh, 3↦sh, 4↦sh, fetchCount: 0⟩
⟨Sch: Qu | TidSet: ('main)⟩
⟨Tbl: TBL | Addr:  ref(0)↦0, ref(1)↦0, ref(2)↦0, ref(3)↦0,
                   ref(4)↦1, ref(5)↦1, ref(6)↦1, ref(7)↦1⟩
⟨Ta: Task | Data: 'main↦(Spawn('T1);Spawn('T2)), 'T1↦(PrRd(0);PrWr(1)),
                  'T2↦(PrRd(2);PrWr(3))⟩ .
```

Observe that in a possible path: C1 executes the main block and then spawns two tasks where C2 executes 'T1 and later C1 executes 'T2. The concurrent execution of 'T1 and 'T2 may lead to the mutual invalidation of memory block 0 in both caches due to the presence of the so-called *false sharing* pattern in which parallel cores operate on independent words located in the same memory block. This pattern causes mutual cache invalidations as if cores were truly using shared memory block, which increases the number of cache misses. For this configuration, the total number of cache misses is three in the observing state:

```
⟨C1: CR | M: 0↦(0↦inv),Rst: commit,D: nil,Miss: 1,Hit: 1,CacheSz: 5,~: Assoc(1)⟩
⟨C2: CR | M: 0↦(0↦mo),Rst: commit,D: nil,Miss: 2,Hits:1,CacheSz: 5,~: Assoc(1)⟩
```

```
⟨M: MM | M:  0↦inv, 1↦sh, 2↦sh, 3↦sh, 4↦sh, fetchCount: 3⟩
⟨sch: Qu | TidSet: empty⟩
...
```

Let `config2` be a variant of `config1`, where the main memory layout in the `TBL` object is organised such that `'T1` and `'T2` access different memory blocks, preventing the false sharing pattern. In this case, the observing state is:

```
⟨C1: CR | M: 0↦(0↦mo),Rst: commit,D: nil,Miss: 1,Hit: 1,CacheSz: 5,~: Assoc(1)⟩
⟨C2: CR | M: 1↦(1↦mo),Rst: commit,D: nil,Miss: 1,Hit: 1,CacheSz: 5,~: Assoc(1)⟩
⟨M: MM | M:  0↦inv, 1↦inv, 2↦sh, 3↦sh, 4↦sh, fetchCount: 2⟩
⟨sch: Qu | TidSet: empty⟩
⟨Tbl: TBL | Addr:  ref(0)↦0, ref(1)↦0, ref(4)↦0, ref(5)↦0,
                   ref(2)↦1, ref(3)↦1, ref(6)↦1, ref(7)↦1⟩
...
```

Observe that the highest number of total cache misses is two from this initial configuration, which reorganises the memory layout in the `TBL` object.   □

We now consider *search* conditions to show a *correctness property* for concrete instances of our modelling framework with respect to data race freedom. Consider the initial configuration `config1` in Example 3. We consider a search condition stating that after a core executes a `PrWr(n)` statement, only that core has the modified copy of n, while all other copies are invalid. This property, for which Maude's search finds no reachable states, can be formulated as follows:

```
search {config1} ⟶ *{C: Configuration
⟨C1: Oid: CR | CM: (x: Int↦(y: Address↦stA: Status),CaA: Cache{Int,MemoryMap}),
Atts: AttributeSet⟩
⟨C2: Oid: CR | CM: (x: Int↦(y: Address↦stB: Status),CaB: Cache{Int,MemoryMap}),
Atts': AttributeSet⟩
 ⟨O: Oid: MM  | M: (y:  Address↦ stM:  Status D: MemoryMap),fetchCount N: Int⟩
 } such that ((stM: Status  = sh) and (stA: Status  = mo)) or
            ((stA: Status  = mo) and (stB: Status  = mo)) or
            ((stA: Status  = mo) and (stB: Status  = sh)) .
```

We can similarly verify the absence of deadlock and livelock which result in statements or data instructions to be remained in the final state.

```
search {config1} ⟶ ! {C: Configuration
⟨A: Oid : CR | Rst: rstA: stList,D: dA: stList,Atts: AttributeSet ⟩
 } such that (rstA: stList ≠ nil) or (dA: stList ≠ nil) .
```

6   Conclusions

This paper has presented a Maude framework for modelling programs executing on cache coherent multicore architectures. The framework formalises in a highly configurable way how task execution on cores with explicit caches triggers interactions between the different caches and between the caches and main memory in cache coherent multicore architectures. The framework allows the specification and comparison of program execution with different design choices for the underlying hardware architecture, such as the number of cores, the data layout in main memory and the cache associativity. We have illustrated by examples that the presented framework may be used to help us understand how the data organisation and the properties of the caches influence the performance of parallel programs executing on shared memory.

There are several interesting possible extensions of the presented work. At the level of the presented model, ongoing work considers the inclusion of multi-level caches and abstract notions of data locality. It is also interesting to see how models such as the one presented in this paper can be used to understand real programs, for example by extracting LLP programs from real code; here we run into the problem of optimisations and instruction reordering which could perhaps be addressed by extracting worst-case LLP representations. In the context of the actor-based programming language Encore [4], we plan in future work to try that approach and use the presented framework to study the effects of program specific optimisations of data layout and scheduling derived by, e.g., locking disciplines, annotations such as behavioural type systems, or static analyses.

Acknowledgments. We are grateful to the anonymous reviewers for their very thorough reviews and for giving helpful and critical feedback.

References

1. Ayala-Rincón, M., Neto, R.M., Jacobi, R.P., Llanos, C.H., Hartenstein, R.W.: Applying ELAN strategies in simulating processors over simple architectures. Electron. Notes Theor. Comput. Sci. **70**(6), 84–99 (2002)
2. Bijo, S., Johnsen, E.B., Pun, K.I, Tapia Tarifa, S.L.: An operational semantics of cache coherent multicore architectures. In: Proceedings of the 31st Annual ACM Symposium on Applied Computing (SAC 2016). ACM (2016)
3. Binkert, N.L., Beckmann, B.M., Black, G., Reinhardt, S.K., Saidi, A.G., Basu, A., Hestness, J., Hower, D., Krishna, T., Sardashti, S., Sen, R., Sewell, K., Shoaib, M., Vaish, N., Hill, M.D., Wood, D.A.: The gem5 simulator. SIGARCH Comput. Archit. News **39**(2), 1–7 (2011)
4. Brandauer, S., et al.: Parallel objects for multicores: a glimpse at the parallel language Encore. In: Bernardo, M., Johnsen, E.B. (eds.) Formal Methods for Multicore Programming. LNCS, vol. 9104, pp. 1–56. Springer, Heidelberg (2015)
5. Carlson, T., Heirman, W., Eeckhout, L.: Sniper: exploring the level of abstraction for scalable and accurate parallel multi-core simulation. In: International Conference on High Performance Computing, Networking, Storage and Analysis (SC 2011), pp. 1–12 (2011)
6. Clavel, M., Durán, F., Eker, S., Lincoln, P., Martí-Oliet, N., Meseguer, J., Talcott, C.L.: All About Maude - A High-Performance Logical Framework, How to Specify, Program and Verify Systems in Rewriting Logic. LNCS, vol. 4350. Springer, Heidelberg (2007)
7. Crary, K., Sullivan, M.J.: A calculus for relaxed memory. In: Proceedings of the 42nd Annual ACM Symposium on Principles of Programming Languages (POPL 2015), pp. 623–636. ACM (2015)
8. Culler, D.E., Gupta, A., Singh, J.P.: Parallel Computer Architecture: A Hardware/Software Approach. Morgan Kaufmann Publishers Inc., Burlington (1997)

9. Delzanno, G.: Constraint-based verification of parameterized cache coherence protocols. Formal Methods Syst. Des. **23**(3), 257–301 (2003)
10. Dill, D.L., Drexler, A.J., Hu, A.J., Yang, C.H.: Protocol verification as a hardware design aid. In: Proceedings of the International Conference on Computer Design: VLSI in Computer and Processors (ICCD 1992), pp. 522–525. IEEE Computer Society (1992)
11. Dill, D.L., Park, S., Nowatzyk, A.G.: Formal specification of abstract memory models. In: Proceedings of the Symposium on Research on Integrated Systems, pp. 38–52. MIT Press (1993)
12. Dongol, B., Travkin, O., Derrick, J., Wehrheim, H.: A high-level semantics for program execution under total store order memory. In: Liu, Z., Woodcock, J., Zhu, H. (eds.) ICTAC 2013. LNCS, vol. 8049, pp. 177–194. Springer, Heidelberg (2013)
13. Ellison, C., Rosu, G.: An executable formal semantics of C with applications. In: Proceedings of the 39th ACM SIGPLAN-SIGACT Symposium on Principles of Programming Languages (POPL 2012), pp. 533–544. ACM (2012)
14. Harman, N.A.: Verifying a simple pipelined microprocessor using Maude. In: Cerioli, M., Reggio, G. (eds.) WADT 2001 and CoFI WG Meeting 2001. LNCS, vol. 2267, p. 128. Springer, Heidelberg (2002)
15. Hennessy, J.L., Patterson, D.A.: Computer Architecture: A Quantitative Approach. Morgan Kaufmann Publishers Inc., Burlington (2011)
16. Jagadeesan, R., Pitcher, C., Riely, J.: Generative operational semantics for relaxed memory models. In: Gordon, A.D. (ed.) ESOP 2010. LNCS, vol. 6012, pp. 307–326. Springer, Heidelberg (2010)
17. Li, Y., Suhendra, V., Liang, Y., Mitra, T., Roychoudhury, A.: Timing analysis of concurrent programs running on shared cache multi-cores. In: Real-Time Systems Symposium (RTSS 2009), pp. 57–67. IEEE Computer Society, December 2009
18. Mador-Haim, S., et al.: An axiomatic memory model for POWER multiprocessors. In: Madhusudan, P., Seshia, S.A. (eds.) CAV 2012. LNCS, vol. 7358, pp. 495–512. Springer, Heidelberg (2012)
19. Martin, M.M.K., Sorin, D.J., Beckmann, B.M., Marty, M.R., Xu, M., Alameldeen, A.R., Moore, K.E., Hill, M.D., Wood, D.A.: Multifacet's general execution-driven multiprocessor simulator (GEMS) toolset. SIGARCH Comput. Archit. News **33**(4), 92–99 (2005)
20. Martín, Ó., Verdejo, A., Martí-Oliet, N.: Model checking TLR* guarantee formulas on infinite systems. In: Iida, S., Meseguer, J., Ogata, K. (eds.) Specification, Algebra, and Software. LNCS, vol. 8373, pp. 129–150. Springer, Heidelberg (2014)
21. Meseguer, J.: Conditional rewriting logic as a unified model of concurrency. Theor. Comput. Sci. **96**, 73–155 (1992)
22. Meseguer, J., Rosu, G.: The rewriting logic semantics project: a progress report. Inf. Comput. **231**, 38–69 (2013)
23. Miller, J.E., Kasture, H., Kurian, G., Gruenwald III, C., Beckmann, N., Celio, C., Eastep, J., Agarwal, A.: Graphite: a distributed parallel simulator for multicores. In: 16th International Conference on High-Performance Computer Architecture (HPCA-16), pp. 1–12. IEEE Computer Society (2010)
24. Morrisett, G., Felleisen, M., Harper, R.: Abstract models of memory management. In: Proceedings of the 7th International Conference on Functional Programming Languages and Computer Architecture, FPCA 1995, pp. 66–77. ACM (1995)
25. Pang, J., Fokkink, W., Hofman, R.F.H., Veldema, R.: Model checking a cache coherence protocol of a Java DSM implementation. J. Logic Algebraic Program. **71**(1), 1–43 (2007)

26. Patterson, D.A., Hennessy, J.L.: Computer Organization and Design: The Hardware/Software Interface. Morgan Kaufmann Publishers Inc., Burlington (2013)
27. Pong, F., Dubois, M.: Verification techniques for cache coherence protocols. ACM Comput. Surv. **29**(1), 82–126 (1997)
28. Ramirez, S., Rocha, C.: Formal verification of safety properties for a cache coherence protocol. In: 10th Colombian Computing Conference (10CCC), pp. 9–16. IEEE (2015)
29. Roşu, G., Schulte, W., Şerbănuţă, T.F.: Runtime verification of C memory safety. In: Bensalem, S., Peled, D.A. (eds.) RV 2009. LNCS, vol. 5779, pp. 132–151. Springer, Heidelberg (2009)
30. Rusu, V., Lucanu, D., Serbanuta, T., Arusoaie, A., Stefanescu, A., Rosu, G.: Language definitions as rewrite theories. J. Log. Algebr. Meth. Program. **85**(1), 98–120 (2016)
31. Sarkar, S., Sewell, P., Alglave, J., Maranget, L., Williams, D.: Understanding POWER multiprocessors. In: Proceedings of the 32nd ACM SIGPLAN Conference on Programming Language Design and Implementation (PLDI 2011), pp. 175–186. ACM (2011)
32. Sewell, P., Sarkar, S., Owens, S., Nardelli, F.Z., Myreen, M.O.: X86-TSO: a rigorous and usable programmer's model for x86 multiprocessors. Commun. ACM **53**(7), 89–97 (2010)
33. Smith, G., Derrick, J., Dongol, B.: Admit your weakness: verifying correctness on TSO architectures. In: Lanese, I., Madelaine, E. (eds.) FACS 2014. LNCS, vol. 8997, pp. 364–383. Springer, Heidelberg (2015)
34. Yu, X., Vijayaraghavan, M., Devadas, S.: A proof of correctness for the Tardis cache coherence protocol (2015). arXiv preprint arXiv:1505.06459

Synchronized Tree Languages for Reachability in Non-right-linear Term Rewrite Systems

Yohan Boichut, Vivien Pelletier[✉], and Pierre Réty

LIFO - Université d'Orléans, B.P. 6759, 45067 Orléans cedex 2, France
{yohan.boichut,vivien.pelletier,pierre.rety}@univ-orleans.fr

Abstract. Over-approximating the descendants (successors) of an initial set of terms under a rewrite system is used in reachability analysis. The success of such methods depends on the quality of the approximation. Regular approximations (i.e. those using finite tree automata) have been successfully applied to protocol verification and Java program analysis. In [2,10], non-regular approximations have been shown more precise than regular ones. In [3] (fixed version of [2]), we have shown that sound over-approximations using synchronized tree languages can be computed for left-and-right-linear term rewriting systems (TRS). In this paper, we present two new contributions extending [3]. Firstly, we show how to compute at least all innermost descendants for any left-linear TRS. Secondly, a procedure is introduced for computing over-approximations independently of the applied rewrite strategy for any left-linear TRS.

Keywords: Term rewriting · Tree languages · Reachability analysis

1 Introduction

The reachability problem $R^*(I) \cap Bad \overset{?}{=} \emptyset$ is a well-known undecidable problem, where I is an initial set of terms, Bad is a set of *forbidden* terms and $R^*(I)$ denotes the terms issued from I using the rewrite system R. Some techniques compute regular over-approximations of $R^*(I)$ in order to show that no term of Bad is reachable from I [1,4,6,7]. [8] introduce regular over-approximations of $R^*(I)$ using innermost strategy.

In [5], we have defined a reachability problem for which none of those techniques works. In [3] (corrected version of [2]), we have described a technique for computing non-regular approximations using synchronized tree languages. This technique can handle the reachability problem of [5]. These synchronized tree languages [9,11] are recognized using CS-programs [12], i.e. a particular class of Horn clauses. From an initial CS-program *Prog* and a linear term rewrite system (TRS) R, another CS-program *Prog'* is computed in such a way that its *language* represents an over-approximation of the set of terms (called descendants) reachable by rewriting using R, from the terms of the language of *Prog*. This algorithm is called completion.

In this paper, we present two new results that hold even if the TRS is not right-linear:

© Springer International Publishing Switzerland 2016
D. Lucanu (Ed.): WRLA 2016, LNCS 9942, pp. 64–81, 2016.
DOI: 10.1007/978-3-319-44802-2_4

1. We show that a slight modification of completion gives an over-approximation of the descendants obtained with an innermost strategy (see Sect. 3).
2. We introduce a technique for over-approximating[1] copying[2] clauses by non-copying ones, so that all descendants (not only the innermost ones) are obtained (see Sect. 4).

2   Preliminaries

Consider two disjoint sets, Σ a *finite ranked alphabet* and *Var* a set of variables. Each symbol $f \in \Sigma$ has a unique arity, denoted by $ar(f)$. The notions of *first-order term*, *position* and *substitution* are defined as usual. Given two substitutions σ and σ', $\sigma \circ \sigma'$ denotes the substitution such that for any variable x, $\sigma \circ \sigma'(x) = \sigma(\sigma'(x))$. T_Σ denotes the set of ground terms (without variables) over Σ. For a term t, $Var(t)$ is the set of variables of t, $Pos(t)$ is the set of positions of t. For $p \in Pos(t)$, $t(p)$ is the symbol of $\Sigma \cup Var$ occurring at position p in t, and $t|_p$ is the subterm of t at position p. The term t is *linear* if each variable of t occurs only once in t. The term $t[t']_p$ is obtained from t by replacing the subterm at position p by t'. $PosVar(t) = \{p \in Pos(t) \mid t(p) \in Var\}$, $PosNonVar(t) = \{p \in Pos(t) \mid t(p) \notin Var\}$.

A *rewrite rule* is an oriented pair of terms, written $l \rightarrow r$. We always assume that l is not a variable, and $Var(r) \subseteq Var(l)$. A *rewrite system R* is a finite set of rewrite rules. *lhs* stands for left-hand-side, *rhs* for right-hand-side. The rewrite relation $\rightarrow_R$ is defined as follows: $t \rightarrow_R t'$ if there exist a position $p \in PosNonVar(t)$, a rule $l \rightarrow r \in R$, and a substitution θ s.t. $t|_p = \theta(l)$ and $t' = t[\theta(r)]_p$. $\rightarrow_R^*$ denotes the reflexive-transitive closure of $\rightarrow_R$. t' is a *descendant* of t if $t \rightarrow_R^* t'$. If E is a set of ground terms, $R^*(E)$ denotes the set of descendants of elements of E. The rewrite rule $l \rightarrow r$ is *left (resp. right) linear* if l (resp. r) is linear. R is *left (resp. right) linear* if all its rewrite rules are left (resp. right) linear. R is *linear* if R is both left and right linear.

2.1   CS-Program

In the following, we consider the framework of *pure logic programming*, and the class of synchronized tree-tuple languages defined by CS-clauses [12,13]. Given a set *Pred* of *predicate* symbols; *atoms*, *goals*, *bodies* and *Horn-clauses* are defined as usual. Note that both *goals* and *bodies* are sequences of atoms. We will use letters G or B for sequences of atoms, and A for atoms. Given a goal $G = A_1, \ldots, A_k$ and positive integers i, j, we define $G|_i = A_i$ and $G|_{i.j} = (A_i)|_j = t_j$ where $A_i = P(t_1, \ldots, t_n)$.

---

[1] This approximation is often exact, but not always. This is due to the fact that a tree language expressed by a copying CS-program cannot always be expressed by a non-copying one.
[2] I.e. clause heads are not linear.

Definition 1. *Let B be a sequence of atoms.*
B *is* flat *if for each atom $P(t_1, \ldots, t_n)$ of B, all terms $t_1, \ldots, t_n$ are variables.*
B *is* linear *if each variable occurring in B (possibly at sub-term position) occurs only once in B. So the empty sequence of atoms (denoted by $\emptyset$) is flat and linear.*

A CS-clause[3] *is a Horn-clause $H \leftarrow B$ s.t. B is flat and linear. A CS-program Prog is a logic program composed of CS-clauses. Variables contained in a CS-Clause have to occur only in this clause. $Pred(Prog)$ denotes the set of predicate symbols of Prog. Given a predicate symbol P of arity n, the tree-(tuple) language generated by P is $L_{Prog}(P) = \{t \in (T_\Sigma)^n \mid P(t) \in Mod(Prog)\}$, where T_Σ is the set of ground terms over the signature Σ and $Mod(Prog)$ is the least Herbrand model of Prog. $L_{Prog}(P)$ is called* synchronized language.

The following definition describes syntactic properties over CS-clauses.

Definition 2. *A CS-clause $P(t_1, \ldots, t_n) \leftarrow B$ is :*

- empty *if $\forall i \in \{1, \ldots, n\}$, t_i is a variable.*
- normalized *if $\forall i \in \{1, \ldots, n\}$, t_i is a variable or contains only one occurrence of function-symbol.*
- non-copying *if $P(t_1, \ldots, t_n)$ is linear.*
- synchronizing *if B is composed of only one atom.*

A CS-program is normalized *and* non-copying *if all its clauses are.*

Example 1. Let x, y, z be variables. $P(x) \leftarrow Q(f(x))$ is not a CS-clause.
$P(x, y, z) \leftarrow Q(x, y, z)$ *is a CS-clause, and is empty, normalized, non-copying and synchronizing.*
The CS-clause $P(f(x), y, g(x, z)) \leftarrow Q_1(x), Q_2(y, z)$ is normalized and copying.
$P(f(g(x)), y) \leftarrow Q(x)$ *is not normalized.*

Given a CS-program, we focus on two kinds of derivations.

Definition 3. *Given a logic program Prog and a sequence of atoms G,*

- G *derives into G' by a* resolution *step if there exist a clause $H \leftarrow B$ in Prog and an atom $A \in G$ such that A and H are unifiable by the most general unifier σ (then $\sigma(A) = \sigma(H)$) and $G' = \sigma(G)[\sigma(A) \leftarrow \sigma(B)]$. It is written $G \leadsto_\sigma G'$.*
- G *rewrites into G' if there exist a clause $H \leftarrow B$ in Prog, an atom $A \in G$, and a substitution σ, such that $A = \sigma(H)$ (A is not instantiated by σ) and $G' = G[A \leftarrow \sigma(B)]$. It is written $G \rightarrow_\sigma G'$.*

Sometimes, we will write $G \leadsto_{[H \leftarrow B, \sigma]} G'$ or $G \rightarrow_{[H \leftarrow B, \sigma]} G'$ to indicate the clause used by the step.

Example 2. $Prog = \{P(x_1, g(x_2)) \leftarrow P'(x_1, x_2). \ P(f(x_1), x_2) \leftarrow P''(x_1, x_2).\}$, and consider $G = P(f(x), y)$. Thus, $P(f(x), y) \leadsto_{\sigma_1} P'(f(x), x_2)$ with $\sigma_1 = [x_1/f(x), y/g(x_2)]$ and $P(f(x), y) \rightarrow_{\sigma_2} P''(x, y)$ with $\sigma_2 = [x_1/x, x_2/y]$.

---

[3] In former papers, synchronized tree-tuple languages were defined thanks to sorts of grammars, called constraint systems. Thus "CS" stands for Constraint System.

Note that for any atom A, if $A \to B$ then $A \rightsquigarrow B$. On the other hand, $A \rightsquigarrow_\sigma B$ implies $\sigma(A) \to B$. Consequently, if A is ground, $A \rightsquigarrow B$ implies $A \to B$.

We note the transitive closure $\rightsquigarrow^+$ and the reflexive-transitive closure $\rightsquigarrow^*$ of $\rightsquigarrow$.

For both derivations, given a logic program $Prog$ and three sequences of atoms G_1, G_2 and G_3 :

- if $G_1 \rightsquigarrow_{\sigma_1} G_2$ and $G_2 \rightsquigarrow_{\sigma_2} G_3$ then one has $G_1 \rightsquigarrow^*_{\sigma_2 \circ \sigma_1} G_3$;
- if $G_1 \to_{\sigma_1} G_2$ and $G_2 \to_{\sigma_2} G_3$ then one has $G_1 \to^*_{\sigma_2 \circ \sigma_1} G_3$.

In the remainder of the paper, given a set of CS-clauses $Prog$ and two sequences of atoms G_1 and G_2, $G_1 \rightsquigarrow^*_{Prog} G_2$ (resp. $G_1 \to^*_{Prog} G_2$) also denotes that G_2 can be derived (resp. rewritten) from G_1 using clauses of $Prog$.

It is well known that resolution is complete.

Theorem 1. *Let A be a ground atom. $A \in Mod(Prog)$ iff $A \rightsquigarrow^*_{Prog} \emptyset$.*

2.2 Computing Descendants

Figure 1 summarizes the procedure introduced in [2] (corrected by [3]) and formally reminded in Definition 8. This procedure always terminates and computes an over-approximation of the descendants obtained by a linear rewrite system, using synchronized tree-(tuple) languages expressed by logic programs.

The notion of critical pair (Definition 4) is at the heart of the technique. Given an CS-program $Prog$, a predicate symbol P and a rewrite rule $l \to r$, a critical pair is a way to detect a possible rewriting by $l \to r$ for a term t in a tuple of $L_{Prog}(P)$. A convergent critical pair means that the rewrite step is already handled i.e. if $t \to_{l \to r} s$ then s is in a tuple of $L_{Prog}(P)$. Consequently, the language of a normalized CS-program involving only convergent critical pairs is closed by rewriting.

For short, a non-convergent critical pair gives rise to a CS-clause. Adding this CS-clause to the current CS-program makes the critical pair convergent. However, this new clause may not be normalized. This is why we apply a normalization step (Definition 7). The function removeCycles has been introduced in [2] to ensure that every finite set of CS-clauses generates finitely many critical pairs.

Critical Pairs. The notion of critical pair allows to add CS-clauses into the current CS-program in order to cover rewriting steps. It is described below.

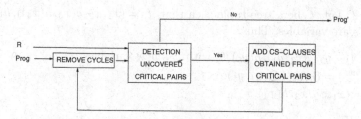

Fig. 1. An overview of completion technique

Definition 4 [2]. *Let Prog be a CS-program and $l \to r$ be a left-linear rewrite rule. Let $x_1, \ldots, x_n$ be distinct variables s.t. $\{x_1, \ldots, x_n\} \cap Var(l) = \emptyset$. If there are P and k s.t. $P(x_1, \ldots, x_{k-1}, l, x_{k+1}, \ldots, x_n) \rightsquigarrow_\theta^+ G$ where resolution is applied only on non-flat atoms, G is flat, and the clause $P(t_1, \ldots, t_n) \leftarrow B$ used during the first step of this derivation satisfies t_k is not a variable[4], then the clause $\theta(P(x_1, \ldots, x_{k-1}, r, x_{k+1}, \ldots, x_n)) \leftarrow G$ is called* critical pair.*

Critical pairs that are already covered by the current CS-program are said to be convergent.

Definition 5 [2]. *A critical pair $H \leftarrow B$ is said* convergent *if $H \to_{Prog}^* B$.*

Example 3. Let *Prog* be the normalized and non-copying CS-program defined by $Prog = \{P(c(x), y) \leftarrow Q(x, y).\ Q(h(x), y) \leftarrow Q(x, y).\ Q(c(x), y) \leftarrow Q(x, y).\ Q(a, b) \leftarrow .\}$ and consider the left-linear rewrite rule $c(c(x')) \to h(h(x'))$. It generates 2 critical pairs, $P(h(h(x')), y) \leftarrow Q(x', y)$ which is not convergent and $Q(h(h(x')), y) \leftarrow Q(x', y)$ which is convergent.

Normalizing CS-Clause. Since rewriting is done only at root position in clauses, we need a normalized CS-Program. But in general, critical pairs are not normalized. Normalization is achieved thanks to Function norm (Definition 7). We first need some technical definitions.

Definition 6 [2]. *Consider a tree-tuple $\overrightarrow{t} = (t_1, \ldots, t_n)$. We define :*

- $\overrightarrow{t}^{cut} = (t_1^{cut}, \ldots, t_n^{cut})$, *where* $t_i^{cut} = \begin{vmatrix} x'_{i,1} & \textit{if } t_i \textit{ is a variable} \\ t_i & \textit{if } t_i \textit{ is a constant} \\ t_i(\epsilon)(x'_{i,1}, \ldots, x'_{i,ar(t_i(\epsilon))}) & \textit{otherwise} \end{vmatrix}$

  and variables $x'_{i,k}$ are new variables that do not occur in $\overrightarrow{t}$.
- *for each i, $\overrightarrow{Var(t_i^{cut})}$ is the (possibly empty) tuple composed of the variables of t_i^{cut} (taken in the left-right order).*
- $\overrightarrow{Var(\overrightarrow{t}^{cut})} = \overrightarrow{Var(t_1^{cut})} \ldots \overrightarrow{Var(t_n^{cut})}$ *(concatenation of tuples).*
- *for each i, t_i^{rest} is the tree-tuple* $t_i^{rest} = \begin{vmatrix} (t_i) & \textit{if } t_i \textit{ is a variable} \\ \textit{the empty tuple if } t_i \textit{ is a constant} \\ (t_i|_1, \ldots, t_i|_{ar(t_i(\epsilon))}) & \textit{otherwise} \end{vmatrix}$
- $\overrightarrow{t}^{rest} = (t_1^{rest} \ldots t_n^{rest})$ *(concatenation of tuples).*

Example 4. Let $\overrightarrow{t}$ be a tree-tuple such that $\overrightarrow{t} = (x_1, x_2, g(x_3, h(x_4)), h(x_5), b)$ where x_i's are variables. Thus,

- $\overrightarrow{t}^{cut} = (y_1, y_2, g(y_3, y_4), h(y_5), b)$ with y_i's new variables;
- $\overrightarrow{Var(\overrightarrow{t}^{cut})} = (y_1, y_2, y_3, y_4, y_5)$;
- $\overrightarrow{t}^{rest} = (x_1, x_2, x_3, h(x_4), x_5)$.

---

[4] In other words, the overlap of l on the clause head $P(t_1, \ldots, t_n)$ is done at a non-variable position.

Note that $\overrightarrow{t}^{cut}$ is normalized, $\overrightarrow{Var}(\overrightarrow{t}^{cut})$ is linear, $\overrightarrow{Var}(\overrightarrow{t}^{cut})$ and $\overrightarrow{t}^{rest}$ have the same arity.

Adding a critical pair (after normalizing it) into the CS-program may create new critical pairs, and the completion process may not terminate. To force termination, two bounds *predicate-limit* and *arity-limit* are fixed. If *predicate-limit* is reached, Function norm should re-use existing predicate symbols instead of creating new ones. On the other hand, if a new predicate symbol is created whose arity[5] is greater than *arity-limit*, then this predicate has to be split by Function norm into several predicates whose arities do not exceed *arity-limit*.

Definition 7 (norm [2]). *Let Prog be a normalized CS-program.*
Let Pred be the set of predicate symbols of Prog, and for each positive integer
i, let $Pred_i = \{P \in Pred \mid ar(P) = i\}$ where ar means arity.
Let arity-limit and predicate-limit be positive integers s.t. $\forall P \in Pred$, $arity(P) \leq$
arity-limit, and $\forall i \in \{1, \dots, arity\text{-}limit\}$, $card(Pred_i) \leq predicate\text{-}limit$. Let
$H \leftarrow B$ be a CS-clause.
Function $\mathsf{norm}_{Prog}(H \leftarrow B)$
$Res = Prog$
If $H \leftarrow B$ is normalized
then $Res = Res \cup \{H \leftarrow B\}$
else If $H \rightarrow_{Res} A$ by a synchronizing and non-empty clause
    then *(note that A is an atom)* $Res = \mathsf{norm}_{Res}(A \leftarrow B)$ (*)
    else *let us write* $H = P(\overrightarrow{t})$
        If $ar(\overrightarrow{Var}(\overrightarrow{t}^{cut})) \leq arity\text{-}limit$
        then *let c' be the clause* $P(\overrightarrow{t}^{cut}) \leftarrow P'(\overrightarrow{Var}(\overrightarrow{t}^{cut}))$
           where P' is a new or an existing predicate symbol[6]
           $Res = \mathsf{norm}_{Res \cup \{c'\}}(P'(\overrightarrow{t}^{rest}) \leftarrow B)$
        else *choose tuples* $\overrightarrow{vt_1}, \dots, \overrightarrow{vt_k}$ *and tuples* $\overrightarrow{tt_1}, \dots, \overrightarrow{tt_k}$ *s.t.*
           $\overrightarrow{vt_1} \dots \overrightarrow{vt_k} = \overrightarrow{Var}(\overrightarrow{t}^{cut})$ *and* $\overrightarrow{tt_1} \dots \overrightarrow{tt_k} = \overrightarrow{t}^{rest}$,
           and for all j, $ar(\overrightarrow{vt_j}) = ar(\overrightarrow{tt_j})$ and $ar(\overrightarrow{vt_j}) \leq arity\text{-}limit$
           let c' be the clause $P(\overrightarrow{t}^{cut}) \leftarrow P_1'(\overrightarrow{vt_1}), \dots, P_k'(\overrightarrow{vt_k})$
           where $P_1', \dots, P_k'$ are new or existing predicate symbols[7]
           $Res = Res \cup \{c'\}$
              For $j=1$ to k **do** $Res = \mathsf{norm}_{Res}(P_j'(\overrightarrow{tt_j}) \leftarrow B)$ **EndFor**
        EndIf
    EndIf
EndIf
return Res

(*) Before normalizing a critical pair $H \leftarrow B$ (more precisely at the beginning of Function norm), for efficiency we first try to reduce H using the CS-clauses of

---

[5] The number of arguments.
[6] If $card(Pred_{ar(\overrightarrow{Var}(\overrightarrow{t}^{cut}))}(Res)) < predicate\text{-}limit$, then P' is new, otherwise P' is chosen in $Pred_{ar(\overrightarrow{Var}(\overrightarrow{t}^{cut}))}(Res)$.
[7] For all j, P_j' is new iff $card(Pred_{ar(\overrightarrow{vt_j})}(Res)) + j - 1 < predicate\text{-}limit$.

Prog. This mechanism is called *by-pass.* An example of normalization is given in Example 5.

Completion

Definition 8 [3]. *Let arity-limit and predicate-limit be positive integers. Let R be a linear rewrite system, and Prog be a finite, normalized and non-copying CS-program. The completion process is defined by:*
Function $\text{comp}_R(Prog)$

> *Prog* = removeCycles(*Prog*)
> **while** *there exists a non-convergent critical pair* $H \leftarrow B$ *in Prog* **do**
> > *Prog* = removeCycles($Prog \cup \text{norm}_{Prog}(H \leftarrow B)$)
> **end while**
> **return** *Prog*

For a given CS-program, the number of critical pairs may be infinite. Function removeCycles modifies some clauses so that the number of critical pairs is finite. Due to the lack of space, we do not give this mechanism here. See [2] for a formal description.

Given a rewrite system R and CS-program *Prog*, if every critical pair that can be detected is convergent, then for any set of terms I such that $I \subseteq Mod(Prog)$, $Mod(Prog)$ is an over-approximation of the set of terms reachable by R from I.

Theorem 2 [3]. *Let R be a left-linear[8] rewrite system and Prog be a normalized non-copying CS-program.*
If all critical pairs are convergent, then Mod(Prog) is closed under rewriting by R, i.e. $(A \in Mod(Prog) \wedge A \rightarrow^*_R A') \implies A' \in Mod(Prog)$.

Theorem 3 [3]. *Let R be a linear rewrite system and Prog be a normalized non-copying CS-program. Function* comp *always terminates, and all critical pairs are convergent in* $\text{comp}_R(Prog)$. *Thus* $R^*(Mod(Prog)) \subseteq Mod(\text{comp}_R(Prog))$.

Example 5. Let $I = \{f(a,a)\}$, and $R = \{f(x,y) \rightarrow u(f(v(x), w(y)))\}$. Intuitively, the exact set of descendants is $R^*(I) = \{u^n(f(v^n(a), w^n(a))) \mid n \in \mathbb{N}\}$. We define $Prog = \{P_0(f(x,y)) \leftarrow P_1(x), P_1(y). \ P_1(a) \leftarrow .\}$. We choose *predicate-limit* = 4 and *arity-limit* = 2.

The following critical pair is detected: $P_0(u(f(v(x), w(y)))) \leftarrow P_1(x), P_1(y)$. The normalization produces $P_0(u(x)) \leftarrow P_2(x)$. $P_2(f(x,y)) \leftarrow P_3(x,y)$ and $P_3(v(x), w(y)) \leftarrow P_1(x), P_1(y)$. Adding these three CS-clauses into *Prog* produces the new critical pair $P_2(u(f(v(x), w(y)))) \leftarrow P_3(x,y)$. It can be normalized without exceeding *predicate-limit* $P_2(u(x)) \leftarrow P_4(x)$. $P_4(f(x,y)) \leftarrow P_5(x,y)$. and $P_5(v(x), w(y)) \leftarrow P_3(x,y)$.

Once again, a new critical pair has been introduced: $P_4(u(f(v(x), w(y)))) \leftarrow P_5(x,y)$. Note that, from now, we are not allowed to introduce any new predicate

---

[8] From a theoretical point of view, left-linearity is sufficient when every critical pair is convergent. However, to make every critical pair convergent by completion, full linearity is necessary (see Theorem 3).

of arity 1. Let us proceed the normalization of $P_4(u(f(v(x), w(y)))) \leftarrow P_5(x, y)$ step by step. We choose to re-use the predicate P_4. Thus, we first generate the following CS-clause: $P_4(u(x)) \leftarrow P_4(x)$. So, we have to normalize now $P_4(f(v(x), w(y))) \leftarrow P_5(x, y)$. Note that $P_4(f(v(x), w(y))) \rightarrow^+_{Prog} P_3(x, y)$. Consequently, the CS-clause $P_3(x, y) \leftarrow P_5(x, y)$ is added into $Prog$.

Note that there is no critical pair anymore.

To summarize, we obtain the final CS-program $Prog_f$ composed of the following CS-clauses:

$Prog_f =$

$$\left\{ \begin{array}{lll} P_0(f(x, y)) \leftarrow P_1(x), P_1(y). & P_1(a) \leftarrow . & P_0(u(x)) \leftarrow P_2(x) \\ P_3(v(x), w(y)) \leftarrow P_1(x), P_1(y). & P_2(f(x, y)) \leftarrow P_3(x, y). & P_2(u(x)) \leftarrow P_4(x). \\ P_5(v(x), w(y)) \leftarrow P_3(x, y). & P_4(f(x, y)) \leftarrow P_5(x, y). & P_4(u(x)) \leftarrow P_4(x). \\ P_3(x, y) \leftarrow P_5(x, y) & & \end{array} \right\}$$

For $Prog_f$, note that $L(P_0) = \{u^n(f(v^m(a), w^m(a))) \mid n, m \in \mathbb{N}\}$ and $R^*(I) \subseteq L(P_0)$.

3 Computing Innermost Descendants

Starting from a non-copying program $Prog$ and given a left-linear TRS R, using the completion algorithm presented in the previous section we may obtain a copying final program $Prog'$. Consequently, the language accepted by $Prog'$ may not be closed under rewriting i.e. $Prog'$ may not recognize an over-approximation of the descendants. Example 6 illustrates this problem.

Example 6. Let $Prog = \{P(g(x)) \leftarrow Q(x). \ Q(a) \leftarrow\}$ and $R = \{a \rightarrow b, \ g(x) \rightarrow f(x, x)\}$. Performing the completion algorithm detailed in Definition 8 returns $\text{comp}_R(Prog) = \{P(g(x)) \leftarrow Q(x). \ P(f(x, x)) \leftarrow Q(x). \ Q(a) \leftarrow . \ Q(b) \leftarrow\}$. Note that $P(f(a, b)) \notin Mod(\text{comp}_R(Prog))$ although $P(g(a)) \in Mod(Prog)$ and $P(g(a)) \rightarrow^*_R P(f(a, b))$.

Thus, some descendants of $Mod(Prog)$ are missing in $Mod(\text{comp}_R(Prog))$. However, all descendants obtained by innermost rewriting (subterms are rewritten at first) are in $Mod(\text{comp}_R(Prog))$, since the only innermost rewrite derivation issued from $g(a)$ is $g(a) \rightarrow^{in}_R g(b) \rightarrow^{in}_R f(b, b)$.

In this section, we show that with a slight modification of [3], if the initial CS-program $Prog$ is non-copying and R is left-linear (and not necessarily right-linear), we can perform reachability analysis for innermost rewriting. Theorem 5 shows that, in that case, we compute at least all the descendants obtained by innermost rewriting. To get this result, it has been necessary to prove a result about closure under innermost rewriting (Theorem 4).

To prove these results, additional definitions are needed. Indeed, to perform innermost rewriting, the rewrite steps are done on terms whose subterms are irreducible (cannot be rewritten). However, for a given TRS, the property of irreducibility is not preserved by instantiation, i.e. if a term t and a substitution θ are irreducible, then θt is not necessarily irreducible. This is why we need to consider a stronger property.

Definition 9. *Let R be a TRS. A term t is* strongly irreducible *(by R) if for all $p \in PosNonVar(t)$, for all $l \to r \in R$, $t|_p$ and l are not unifiable. A substitution θ is* strongly irreducible *if for all $x \in Var$, θx is strongly irreducible.*

Lemma 1. *If t is strongly irreducible, then t is irreducible.*

Proof. By contrapositive. If $t \to_{[p,l \to r,\sigma]} t'$, then $t|_p = \sigma l$. Since it is assumed that $Var(t) \cap Var(l) = \emptyset$, then $t|_p$ and l are unifiable by σ.

Lemma 2. *If t is strongly irreducible, then for all $p \in Pos(t)$, $t|_p$ is strongly irreducible.*
For a substitution θ, if θt is strongly irreducible, then for all $x \in Var(t)$, θx is strongly irreducible (but t is not necessarily strongly irreducible).

Proof. Obvious.

Example 7. Let $t = f(x)$, $\theta = (x/a)$, $R = \{f(b) \to b\}$. Thus $\theta t = f(a)$ is strongly irreducible whereas t is not.

Corollary 1. *For substitutions α, θ, if $\alpha.\theta$ is strongly irreducible, then α is strongly irreducible.*

Note that the previous definitions and lemmas trivially extend to atoms and atom sequences.

Lemma 3 *(Closure by Instantiation).* *If t is strongly irreducible and θ is irreducible, then θt is irreducible.*

Proof. By contrapositive. If $\theta t \to_{[p,l \to r,\sigma]} t'$, then $(\theta t)|_p = \sigma l$.

- If $p \notin PosNonVar(t)$, then there exist a variable x and a position p' s.t. $(\theta x)|_{p'} = \sigma l$. Then θ is reducible.
- Otherwise, $\theta(t|_p) = \sigma l$. Then $t|_p$ and l are unifiable, hence t is not strongly irreducible.

Example 8. Let $t = f(x)$, $\theta = (x/g(y))$, and $R = \{g(a) \to b\}$. Thus t is strongly irreducible, θ is irreducible, and $\theta t = f(g(y))$ is irreducible. Note that θt is not strongly irreducible.

Before introducing two families of derivations, we show in Example 9 that performing the completion, as presented in Sect. 2.2, with a non-right-linear TRS may add copying clauses, and some innermost descendants may be missing.

Example 9. Let $R = \{f(x) \to g(h(x), h(x)), \; i(x) \to g(x,x), \; h(a) \to b\}$, and $Prog$ be the initial non-copying program:
$Prog = \{P(i(x)) \leftarrow Q_1(x). \; Q_1(a) \leftarrow . \; P(f(x)) \leftarrow Q_2(x). \; Q_2(a) \leftarrow\}$. We start with $Prog' = \emptyset$. The completion procedure computes the critical pairs:

1. $P(g(x,x)) \leftarrow Q_1(x)$ and add it into $Prog'$,
2. $P(g(h(x),h(x))) \leftarrow Q_2(x)$, which could be by-passed into:
   $Q_1(h(x)) \leftarrow Q_2(x)$, which is added into $Prog'$,
3. $Q_1(b) \leftarrow$, which is added into $Prog'$.

No more critical pairs are detected, thus all critical pairs are convergent in $Prog'' = Prog \cup Prog'$. However $P(f(a)) \rightarrow_R P(g(h(a),h(a))) \rightarrow_R P(g(b,h(a)))$ by an innermost derivation, whereas $P(f(a)) \in Mod(Prog)$ and $P(g(b,h(a))) \notin Mod(Prog'')$.

Actually, the clause $P(g(x,x)) \leftarrow Q_1(x)$ prevents the reduction of $P(g(b,h(a)))$ and consequently, it is impossible to get the set of all innermost-descendants up to now. Now, we introduce two families of derivations, i.e. NC and SNC, which allow us to compute every innermost descendant. For an atom H, $Var^{mult}(H)$ denotes the set of the variables that occur several times in H. For instance, $Var^{mult}(P(f(x,y),x,z)) = \{x\}$.

Definition 10. *Let A be an atom (A may contain variables).*
The step $A \rightsquigarrow_{[H \leftarrow B, \sigma]} G$ is NC (resp. SNC[9]) if for all $x \in Var^{mult}(H)$, σx is irreducible (resp. strongly irreducible) by R.
A derivation is NC (resp. SNC) if all its steps are.

Remark 1. SNC implies NC and if the clause $H \leftarrow B$ is non-copying, then the step $A \rightsquigarrow_{[H \leftarrow B, \sigma]} G$ is SNC (and NC).

Example 10. Consider the clause $P(g(x,x)) \leftarrow Q(x)$ and $R = \{h(a) \rightarrow b\}$. The step $P(g(h(y),h(y))) \rightsquigarrow_{[(x/h(y))]} Q(h(y))$ is NC ($h(y)$ is irreducible), but it is not SNC ($h(y)$ is not strongly irreducible).

Lemma 4. *If $A \rightarrow_{[H \leftarrow B, \sigma]} G$ is SNC and $\forall x \in Var^{mult}(H)$, $\forall y \in Var(\sigma(x))$, θy is irreducible, then $\theta A \rightarrow_{[H \leftarrow B, \theta.\sigma]} \theta G$ is NC.*

Proof. Let $x \in Var^{mult}(H)$. Then σx is strongly irreducible. From Lemma 3, $\theta.\sigma(x)$ is irreducible. Therefore $\theta A \rightarrow_{[H \leftarrow B, \theta.\sigma]} \theta G$ is NC.

Lemma 5. *If $\sigma' A \rightsquigarrow_{[H \leftarrow B, \gamma]} G$ is NC, then $A \rightsquigarrow_{[H \leftarrow B, \theta]} G'$ is NC and there exists a substitution α s.t. $\alpha G' = G$ and $\alpha.\theta = \gamma.\sigma'$.*

Proof. From the well-known resolution properties, we get $A \rightsquigarrow_{[H \leftarrow B, \theta]} G'$ and there exists a substitution α s.t. $\alpha G' = G$ and $\alpha.\theta = \gamma.\sigma'$.
Now, if $A \rightsquigarrow_{[H \leftarrow B, \theta]} G'$ is not NC, then there exists $x \in Var^{mult}(H)$ s.t. θx is reducible. Then $\gamma x = \gamma.\sigma'(x) = \alpha.\theta(x)$ is reducible. Therefore $\sigma' A \rightsquigarrow_{[H \leftarrow B, \gamma]} G$ is not NC, which is impossible.

Let us now define a subset of $Mod(Prog)$.

Definition 11. *Let $Prog$ be a CS-program and R be a rewrite system.*
$Mod^R_{NC}(Prog)$ *is composed of the ground atoms A such that there exists a NC derivation $A \rightsquigarrow^* \emptyset$.*

---

[9] NC stands for Non-Copying. SNC stands for Strongly Non-Copying.

Remark 2. $Mod_{NC}^R(Prog) \subseteq Mod(Prog)$ and if $Prog$ is non-copying, then $Mod_{NC}^R(Prog) = Mod(Prog)$.

Example 11. Let $Prog = \{P(f(x), f(x)) \leftarrow Q(x). \; Q(a) \leftarrow . \; Q(b) \leftarrow .\}$ and $R = \{a \to b\}$. $P(f(a), f(a)) \notin Mod_{NC}^R(Prog)$, hence $Mod_{NC}^R(Prog) \neq Mod(Prog)$.

Theorem 4. *Let $Prog$ be a normalized CS-program and R be a left-linear rewrite system. If all critical pairs are convergent by SNC derivations, $Mod_{NC}^R(Prog)$ is closed under innermost rewriting by R, i.e.*

$$(A \in Mod_{NC}^R(Prog) \wedge A \to_R^{in,*} A') \implies A' \in Mod_{NC}^R(Prog)$$

Proof. Let $A \in Mod_{NC}^R(Prog)$ s.t. $A \to_{l \to r}^{in} A'$. Then $A|_i = C[\sigma(l)]$ for some $i \in \mathbb{N}$, σ is irreducible, and $A' = A[i \leftarrow C[\sigma(r)]]$.

Since $A \in Mod_{NC}^R(Prog)$, $A \rightsquigarrow^* \emptyset$ by a NC derivation. Since $Prog$ is normalized, resolution consumes symbols in C one by one, thus $G_0''=A \rightsquigarrow^* G_k'' \rightsquigarrow^* \emptyset$ by a NC derivation, and there exists an atom $A'' = P(t_1, \ldots, t_n)$ in G_k'' and j s.t. $t_j = \sigma(l)$ and the top symbol of t_j is consumed (or t_j disappears) during the step $G_k'' \rightsquigarrow G_{k+1}''$.

Since t_j is reducible by R and $A \in Mod_{NC}^R(Prog)$, $t_j = \sigma(l)$ admits only one antecedent in A. Then $A' \rightsquigarrow^* G_k''[A'' \leftarrow P(t_1, \ldots, \sigma(r), \ldots, t_n)]$ by a NC derivation (I).

Consider new variables $x_1, \ldots, x_n$ s.t. $\{x_1, \ldots, x_n\} \cap Var(l) = \emptyset$, and let us define the substitution σ' by $\forall i, \sigma'(x_i) = t_i$ and $\forall x \in Var(l), \sigma'(x) = \sigma(x)$. Then $\sigma'(P(x_1, \ldots, x_{j-1}, l, x_{j+1}, \ldots, x_n)) = A''$.

From $G_k'' \rightsquigarrow^* \emptyset$ we can extract the sub-derivation $G_k = A'' \rightsquigarrow_{\gamma_k} G_{k+1} \rightsquigarrow_{\gamma_{k+1}} G_{k+2} \rightsquigarrow^* \emptyset$, which is NC. From Lemma 5, there exist a positive integer $u > k$, a NC derivation $G_k' = P(x_1, \ldots, l, \ldots, x_n) \rightsquigarrow_\theta^* G_u'$, and a substitution α s.t. $\alpha G_u' = G_u$, $\alpha.\theta = \gamma_{u-1}. \ldots .\gamma_k.\sigma'$, G_u' is flat, and for all i, $k < i < u$ implies G_i' is not flat. In other words, there is a critical pair, which is assumed to be convergent by a SNC derivation. Therefore $\theta(G_k'[l \leftarrow r]) \to^* G_u'$ by a SNC derivation.

Let us write $\gamma = \gamma_{u-1}. \ldots .\gamma_k$. If there exist a clause $H \leftarrow B$ used in this derivation, and $x \in Var^{mult}(H)$ s.t. $\alpha.\theta(x)$ is reducible, then there exist i and p s.t. $\alpha.\theta(x) = \gamma.\sigma'(x) = \gamma(t_i|_p)$ (because σ is irreducible). Note that γ is a unifier, then $\gamma x = \gamma(t_i|_p)$. Therefore $\gamma x = \gamma(t_i|_p) = \gamma.\sigma'(x) = \alpha.\theta(x)$, which is reducible. This is impossible because $x \in Var^{mult}(H)$ and $G_k \rightsquigarrow_\gamma^* G_u$ is a NC derivation.

Consequently, from Lemma 4, $\alpha.\theta(G_k'[l \leftarrow r]) \to^* \alpha(G_u') = G_u \rightsquigarrow^* \emptyset$ by a NC derivation. Note that $\alpha.\theta(G_k'[l \leftarrow r]) = \gamma.\sigma'(P(x_1, \ldots, r, \ldots, x_n)) = \gamma(P(t_1, \ldots, \sigma(r), \ldots, t_n))$. Then $\gamma(P(t_1, \ldots, \sigma(r), \ldots, t_n)) \rightsquigarrow^* \emptyset$ by a NC derivation. From Lemma 5 we get: $P(t_1, \ldots, \sigma(r), \ldots, t_n) \rightsquigarrow^* \emptyset$ by a NC derivation. Considering Derivation (I) again, we get $A' \rightsquigarrow^* G_k''[A'' \leftarrow P(t_1, \ldots, \sigma(r), \ldots, t_n)] \rightsquigarrow^* \emptyset$ by a NC derivation. In other words, $A' \in Mod_{NC}^R(Prog)$.

By trivial induction, the proof can be extended to the case of several rewrite steps.

In the following result, we consider an initial non-copying CS-program $Prog$, and a possibly copying program $Prog'$ composed of the CS-clauses added by the completion process. The normalization function norm makes critical pairs convergent by SNC derivations, provided by-pass step is achieved only if the clause used to rewrite is SNC.

Theorem 5. *Let R be a left-linear rewrite system and $Prog'' = Prog \cup Prog'$ be a normalized CS-program s.t. $Prog$ is non-copying and all critical pairs of $Prog''$ are convergent by SNC derivations. If $A \in Mod(Prog)$ and $A \rightarrow_R^* A'$ with an innermost strategy, then $A' \in Mod(Prog'')$.*

Proof. Since $Prog$ is non-copying, $Mod(Prog) = Mod_{NC}^R(Prog)$. Then $A \in Mod_{NC}^R(Prog)$, and since $Prog \subseteq Prog''$ we have $A \in Mod_{NC}^R(Prog'')$. From Theorem 4, $A' \in Mod_{NC}^R(Prog'')$, and since $Mod_{NC}^R(Prog'') \subseteq Mod(Prog'')$, we get $A' \in Mod(Prog'')$.

Example 12. Let us focus on the critical pair given in Example 9 Item 2 i.e. $P(g(h(x), h(x))) \leftarrow Q_2(x)$. Adding the clause $Q_1(h(x)) \leftarrow Q_2(x)$ makes the clause convergent in $Prog''$ (in Example 9), but not convergent by a SNC derivation. Indeed (just here, we add primes to avoid conflict of variables): $P(g(h(x'), h(x'))) \leadsto_{[x/h(x')]} Q_1(h(x')) \leadsto_{[x/x']} Q_2(x')$. But the following step $P(g(h(x'), h(x'))) \leadsto_{[x/h(x')]} Q_1(h(x'))$ is not SNC. Consequently, one has to normalize $P(g(h(x), h(x))) \leftarrow Q_2(x)$ in an SNC way.
For instance, $P(g(h(x), h(x))) \leftarrow Q_2(x)$ can be normalized into the following clauses: $P(g(x, y)) \leftarrow Q_3(x, y).\ Q_3(h(x), h(x)) \leftarrow Q_2(x)$. After adding these clauses, new critical pairs are detected, and the clauses $Q_3(b, h(x)) \leftarrow Q_2(x).\ Q_3(h(x), b) \leftarrow Q_2(x).\ Q_3(b, b) \leftarrow$. will be added. So, the final CS-program is $Prog'' = Prog \cup$
$\{P(g(x, x)) \leftarrow Q_1(x).\ Q_3(b, b) \leftarrow.\ P(g(x, y)) \leftarrow Q_3(x, y).\ Q_3(h(x), h(x)) \leftarrow Q_2(x).\ Q_3(b, h(x)) \leftarrow Q_2(x).\ Q_3(h(x), b) \leftarrow Q_2(x).\ \}$.
Thus $P(g(b, h(a))) \in Mod(Prog'')$.

One can apply this approach to a well-known problem: the Post Correspondence Problem.

Example 13. Consider the instance of the Post Correspondence Problem (PCP) composed of the pairs (ab, aa) and (bba, bb). To encode it by tree languages, we see a and b as unary symbols, and introduce a constant 0. Let $R = \{Test(x) \rightarrow g(x, x), g(0, 0) \rightarrow True, g(a(b(x)), a(a(y))) \rightarrow g(x, y), g(b(b(a(x))), b(b(y))) \rightarrow g(x, y)\}$, and let $I = \{Test(t) \mid t \in T_{\{a,b,0\}}, t \neq 0\}$ be the initial language generated by P_0 in $Prog = \{P_0(Test(z)) \leftarrow P_1(z).\ P_1(a(z)) \leftarrow P_2(z).\ P_1(b(z)) \leftarrow P_2(z).\ P_2(a(z)) \leftarrow P_2(z).\ P_2(b(z)) \leftarrow P_2(z).\ P_2(0) \leftarrow\}$.
Thus, this instance of PCP has at least one solution iff $True$ is reachable by R from I. Note that R is not right-linear. However, each descendant is innermost, and from Theorem 5 it is recognized by the CS-program obtained by completion:

$\text{comp}_R(Prog) = Prog \; \cup$

$$\left\{ \begin{array}{l} P_0(g(x,x)) \leftarrow P_1(x). \quad P_0(g(x,y)) \leftarrow P_4(x,y). \; P_4(x,a(x)) \leftarrow P_2(x). \\ P_0(g(x,y)) \leftarrow P_5(x,y). \; P_5(x,b(x)) \leftarrow P_2(x). \quad P_0(g(x,y)) \leftarrow P_6(x,y). \\ P_6(x,b(y)) \leftarrow P_7(x,y). \; P_7(x,a(x)) \leftarrow P_2(x). \end{array} \right\}$$

Note that $P_0(True) \notin Mod(\text{comp}_R(Prog))$, which proves that this instance of PCP has no solution.

4 Getting Rid of Copying Clauses

In this section, we propose a process (see Definition 16) that transforms a copying CS-clause into a set of non-copying ones. In a second part we introduce a way to force termination of this process by over-approximating the generated language. In that way, even if the TRS is not right-linear and consequently copying clauses may be generated during the completion process, we can get rid of them as soon as they appear. Thus, the final CS-program is non-copying, and Theorem 2 applies. Therefore, an over-approximation of the set of all descendants can be computed.

For instance, let $Prog = \{P(f(x,x)) \leftarrow Q(x). \; Q(s(x)) \leftarrow Q(x). \; Q(a) \leftarrow\}$. Note that the language generated by P is $\{f(s^n(a), s^n(a)) \mid n \in \mathbb{N}\}$. We introduce a new binary predicate symbol Q^2 that generates the language $\{(t,t) \mid Q(t) \in Mod(Prog)\}$, and we transform the copying clause $P(f(x,x)) \leftarrow Q(x)$ into a non-copying one as follows: $P(f(x,y)) \leftarrow Q^2(x,y)$. Now Q^2 can be defined by the clauses $Q^2(s(x), s(x)) \leftarrow Q(x)$ and $Q^2(a,a) \leftarrow$. Unfortunately $Q^2(s(x), s(x)) \leftarrow Q(x)$ is copying. Then using the same idea again, we transform it into the non-copying clause $Q^2(s(x), s(y)) \leftarrow Q^2(x,y)$. The body of this clause uses Q^2, which is already defined. Thus the process terminates with $Prog' = \{P(f(x,y)) \leftarrow Q^2(x,y). \; Q^2(s(x), s(y)) \leftarrow Q^2(x,y). \; Q^2(a,a) \leftarrow . \; Q(s(x)) \leftarrow Q(x). \; Q(a) \leftarrow\}$. Note that $Prog'$ is non-copying and generates the same language as $Prog$. The clauses that define Q are useless in $Prog'$, but in general it is necessary to keep them.

Let us formalize the general process.

Definition 12 (expand). *Let $P(x_1, \ldots, x_k)$ be a linear atom, $x_1, \ldots, x_k$ be variables and n be a number.*

$$\text{expand}(P(x_1, \ldots, x_k), n) = \begin{cases} P^n(x_1^1, \ldots, x_k^1, \ldots, x_1^n, \ldots, x_k^n) & \text{if } n > 1 \\ P(\overrightarrow{t}) & \text{Otherwise.} \end{cases}$$

Definition 13 (copy). *Let $P(\overrightarrow{t})$ be an atom and n be a number.*

$$\text{copy}(P(\overrightarrow{t}), n) = \begin{cases} P^n(\underbrace{\overrightarrow{t}, \ldots, \overrightarrow{t}}_{n \; times}) & \text{if } n > 1 \\ P(\overrightarrow{t}) & \text{Otherwise.} \end{cases}$$

Definition 14 (clauses^{new}). *Let Prog be a set of CS-clauses. Let $Q^n(\overrightarrow{t})$ be an atom where Q is a predicate symbol occuring in Prog and n is an integer with $n > 1$.*

$$\text{clauses}^{new}(Q^n(\overrightarrow{t}), Prog) = \{\text{copy}(Q(\overrightarrow{t}), n) \leftarrow B \mid Q(\overrightarrow{t}) \leftarrow B \in Prog\}.$$

Definition 15 (uncopy$_{Prog}^{one}$). *Let Prog be a set of normalized CS-clauses. Let $P(\overrightarrow{t}) \leftarrow Q_1, \ldots, Q_n$ be a copying clause such that $P(\overrightarrow{t}) \leftarrow Q_1, \ldots, Q_n \notin Prog$. Let $Var(\overrightarrow{t}) = \{x_1, \ldots, x_k\}$ be the set of variables occurring in $\overrightarrow{t}$. Let $m_1, \ldots, m_k \in \mathbb{N}$ be integers such that x_i occurs exactly m_i times in $\overrightarrow{t}$.*

$$\text{uncopy}_{Prog}^{one}(P(\overrightarrow{t}) \leftarrow Q_1, \ldots, Q_n) = \{P(\overrightarrow{t'}) \leftarrow Q_1', \ldots, Q_n'\} \cup$$
$$\bigcup_{Q_i' \neq Q_i}(\text{clauses}^{new}(Q_i', Prog'))$$

where $Prog' = Prog \cup \{P(\overrightarrow{t'}) \leftarrow Q_1', \ldots, Q_n'\}$, $\overrightarrow{t'}$ is obtained from $\overrightarrow{t}$ by replacing for each $j \in \{1, \ldots, k\}$, the different occurrences of x_j by $x_j^1, \ldots, x_j^{m_j}$ and $Q_i' = \text{expand}(Q_i, max_i)$ with $max_i = \left(\underset{x_i \in Var(Q_i)}{Max}\{m_i\}\right)$ when $max_i > 1$.

Definition 16 (uncopying($Prog$)). *Let Prog be a set of normalized CS-clauses.*

$$\text{uncopying}(Prog) = \begin{cases} \text{uncopying}(\text{uncopy}_{Rem}^{one}(H \leftarrow B) \cup Rem) \ if \ COND \\ Prog \qquad\qquad\qquad\qquad\qquad\qquad\qquad\qquad Otherwise. \end{cases}$$

where COND is $Prog = \{H \leftarrow B\} \cup Rem$ and $H \leftarrow B$ is copying.

Let us illustrate the previous definitions in Example 14.

Example 14. Let *Prog* be a normalized copying CS-Program such that $Prog = \{P(f(x)) \leftarrow Q_1(x). \ Q_1(a) \leftarrow . \ Q_1(b) \leftarrow . \ P(g(x,x) \leftarrow Q_1(x)\}$. Thus, according to Definition 16, one has

$$\text{uncopying}(Prog) = \text{uncopying}(\text{uncopy}_{Rem}^{one}(P(g(x,x)) \leftarrow Q_1(x)) \cup Rem) \quad (1)$$

where $Rem = \{P(f(x)) \leftarrow Q_1(x). \ Q_1(a) \leftarrow . \ Q_1(b) \leftarrow .\}$.

Applying Definition 15, uncopy$_{Rem}^{one}(P(g(x,x)) \leftarrow Q_1(x)) = \{P(g(x^1,x^2)) \leftarrow \text{expand}(Q_1(x),2)\} \cup \text{clauses}^{new}(Q_1^2(x^1,x^2), Rem \cup \{P(g(x^1,x^2)) \leftarrow \text{expand}(Q_1(x), 2)\})$ since $\text{expand}(Q_1(x),2) = Q_1^2(x^1,x^2)$ according to Definition 12. So, for now, one has uncopy$_{Rem}^{one}(P(g(x,x)) \leftarrow Q_1(x)) = \{P(g(x^1,x^2)) \leftarrow Q_1^2(x^1,x^2)\} \cup \text{clauses}^{new}(Q_1^2(x^1,x^2), Rem \cup \{P(g(x^1,x^2)) \leftarrow Q_1^2(x^1,x^2)\})$.

So, applying Definition 14, one obtains that clauses$^{new}(Q_1^2(x^1,x^2), Rem \cup \{P(g(x^1,x^2)) \leftarrow Q_1^2(x^1,x^2)\}) = \{\text{copy}(Q_1(a),2) \leftarrow .\} \cup \{\text{copy}(Q_1(b),2) \leftarrow .\}$. Consequently, according to Definition 13, one has clauses$^{new}(Q_1^2(x^1,x^2), Rem \cup \{P(g(x^1,x^2)) \leftarrow Q_1^2(x^1,x^2)\}) = \{Q_1^2(a,a) \leftarrow . \ Q_1^2(b,b) \leftarrow .\}$. Thus, one has: $Prog' = \text{uncopy}_{Rem}^{one}(P(g(x,x)) \leftarrow Q_1(x)) = \{P(g(x^1,x^2)) \leftarrow Q_1^2(x^1,x^2). \ Q_1^2(a,a) \leftarrow . \ Q_1^2(b,b) \leftarrow .\}$. Using Eq. (1), one obtains uncopying($Prog$)

$= \mathsf{uncopying}(Prog') \cup \{P(f(x)) \leftarrow Q_1(x). \; Q_1(a) \leftarrow . \; Q_1(b) \leftarrow .\}$. Moreover, $Prog'$ is a non-copying normalized CS-program. So, $\mathsf{uncopying}(Prog') = Prog'$ according to Definition 16.

Let $Prog_f$ be the set of CS-clause resulting from $\mathsf{uncopying}(Prog)$. One can note that $Prog_f$ is a normalized CS-Program and $Prog_f$ generates the same language as $Prog$.

Lemma 6. *If algorithm (Definition 16) terminates, then for all copying clauses $P(\overrightarrow{t}) \leftarrow B \in Prog$, $L_{\mathsf{uncopying}(Prog)}(P) = L_{Prog}(P)$.*

It comes from the fact that if Q_i has p arguments, then $Q_i^{max_i}$ has $max_i \times p$

arguments, and $L(Q_i^{max_i}) = \left\{ \underbrace{\overrightarrow{t} \ldots \overrightarrow{t}}_{max_i \text{ times}} \mid \overrightarrow{t} \in L(Q_i) \right\}$.

Then $L(Q_i^1) = L(Q_i)$ and [10] $L((Q_i^x)^y) = L(Q_i^{x \times y})$. Thus we will confuse Q_i^1 with Q_i, and $(Q_i^x)^y$ with $Q_i^{x \times y}$.

Now, we give some examples of completion (Definition 8) supplied with uncopying.

Example 15. Let $R = \{f(x) \rightarrow g(x,x), \; a \rightarrow b\}$, $Prog_0 = \{P(f(x)) \leftarrow Q_1(x). \; Q_1(a) \leftarrow\}$. $Prog_0$ is a normalized non-copying CS-Program and R is a non-right-linear rewrite system. There are 2 critical pairs, $P(g(x,x)) \leftarrow Q_1(x).$ and $Q_1(b) \leftarrow$. To make the critical pairs convergent, we add them into the program and we get

$Prog_1 = Prog_0 \cup \{P(g(x,x)) \leftarrow Q_1(x). \; Q_1(b) \leftarrow\}$

$Prog_1$ contains the copying clause $P(g(x,x)) \leftarrow Q_1(x)$ and is exactly $Prog$ used in Example 14. So, $\mathsf{uncopying}(Prog_1) = Prog_0 \cup \{Q_1(b) \leftarrow . \; P(g(x^1, x^2)) \leftarrow Q_1^2(x^1, x^2). \; Q_1^2(a,a) \leftarrow . \; Q_1^2(b,b) \leftarrow\}$.

Let $Prog_2 = \mathsf{uncopying}(Prog_1)$. Now, there are 2 non-convergent critical pairs, $Q_1^2(a,b) \leftarrow$ and $Q_1^2(b,a) \leftarrow$. If we add them to $Prog_2$, we get a normalized non-copying CS-Program, all critical pairs are convergent. Applying Theorem 2, $Mod(Prog_2)$ is closed by rewriting.

Remark 3. If at least one $Q_i^{max_i}$ is not defined and there is a clause $Q_i(\overrightarrow{t_j}) \leftarrow B_j$ in $Prog$ such that $\overrightarrow{t_j}$ is not ground, then the algorithm will generate new copying clauses.

Unfortunately, this algorithm does not terminate in general case. For instance, the example below does not.

Example 16. Let $Prog = \{P(c(x,x)) \leftarrow P(x).(1) \; P(a) \leftarrow .(2)\}$. $Prog$ is a normalized, copying CS-Program. Clause (1) is copying, we apply uncopying and add $\{P(c(x,x')) \leftarrow P^2(x,x').(3) \; P^2(a,a) \leftarrow .(4) \; P^2(c(x,x'),c(x,x')) \leftarrow P^2(x,x').(5)\}$ to $Prog$. Clause (5) is copying. Thus, the same process

---

[10] If the loop while is run several times, predicate symbols of the form $(Q_i^x)^y$ may appear.

is performed and the clauses $\{P^2(c(x_1, x_1'), c(x_2, x_2')) \leftarrow P^4(x_1, x_1', x_2,$ $x_2').(6) \quad P^4(a, a, a, a) \leftarrow .(7) \quad P^4(c(x_1, x_1'), c(x_2, x_2'), c(x_1, x_1'), c(x_2, x_2')) \leftarrow$ $P^4(x_1, x_1', x_2, x_2').(8)\}$ are added to $Prog$. Unfortunately Clause (8) is copying. The process does not terminate, consequently we will never get a program without copying clauses.

To force termination while getting rid of all copying clauses, we fix a positive integer $UncopyingLimit$. If we need to generate a predicate Q^x where $x > UncopyingLimit$ we cut Q^x into $Q^{x_1}, \ldots, Q^{x_n}$ with $\sum_{i \in [1,n]} x_i = x$, which leads to an over-approximation since

$$L(Q^x) = \left\{ \underbrace{\vec{t} \ldots \vec{t}}_{x \text{ times}} \mid \vec{t} \in L(Q) \right\} \subseteq L(Q^{x_1}) \times \ldots \times L(Q^{x_n})$$

Example 17. Consider Example 16 again, and let $UncopyingLimit = 4$. Clause (8) is copying. Applying the process would generate the clause

$$P^4(c(x_1, x_1'), c(x_2, x_2'), c(x_3, x_3'), c(x_4, x_4')) \leftarrow P^8(x_1, x_1', x_2, x_2', x_3, x_3', x_4, x_4')$$

However $UncopyingLimit$ is exceeded. So, we cut P^8 and obtain

$$P^4(c(x_1, x_1'), c(x_2, x_2'), c(x_3, x_3'), c(x_4, x_4'))$$
$$\leftarrow P^4(x_1, x_1', x_2, x_2'), P^2(x_3, x_3'), P^2(x_4, x_4').(9)$$

Predicates P^4 and P^2 have been defined previously in $Prog$, so we do not need to add more clauses to do it.

Finally, the CS-program uncopying($Prog$) includes the uncopying clauses (2), (3), (4), (6), (7) and (9). Recall that $L(P^8)$ is supposed to be defined so that $L(P^8) = \{\underbrace{\vec{t} \ldots \vec{t}}_{8 \text{ times}} \mid \vec{t} \in L(P)\}$. Then replacing $P^8(x_1, x_1', x_2, x_2', x_3, x_3', x_4, x_4')$ by $P^4(x_1, x_1', x_2, x_2'), P^2(x_3, x_3'), P^2(x_4, x_4')$ in the clause-body generates the set $\{\underbrace{\vec{t} \ldots \vec{t}}_{4 \text{ times}} .\vec{t'}.\vec{t'}.\vec{t''}.\vec{t''} \mid \vec{t}, \vec{t'}, \vec{t''} \in L(P)\} \subset L(P^8)$, which leads to an over-approximation. For example $P^4(c(a, a), c(a, a), c(c(a, a), c(a, a)), c(a, a))$ is in $Mod(\text{uncopying}(Prog))$ but not in $Mod(Prog)$.

Now, we give a simple example of completion (Definition 8) supplied with uncopying.

Example 18. Let $R = \{f(x) \rightarrow g(x, x), a \rightarrow b\}$, $Prog_0 = \{P(f(x)) \leftarrow Q_1(x). \; Q_1(a) \leftarrow\}$. $Prog_0$ is a normalized non-copying CS-Program and R is a non-right-linear rewrite system. There are 2 critical pairs, $P(g(x_1, x_1)) \leftarrow Q_1(x_1)$. and $Q_1(b) \leftarrow$. To make the critical pairs convergent, we add them into the program and we get

$$Prog_1 = Prog_0 \cup \{P(g(x_1, x_1)) \leftarrow Q_1(x_1). \; Q_1(b) \leftarrow\}$$

$Prog_1$ contains the copying clause $P(g(x_1, x_1)) \leftarrow Q_1(x_1)$. So, Definition 16 has to be applied on $Prog_1$. From $P(g(x_1, x_1)) \leftarrow Q_1(x_1)$, one obtains the clause $P(g(x_1^1, x_1^2)) \leftarrow Q_1^2(x_1^1, x_1^2)$ by applying applying Definition 15. Thus, in the same time, one has to compute clauses$^{new}(Q_1^2(x_1^1, x_1^2), Prog_1)$. From $Q_1(a) \leftarrow$ and $Q_1(b) \leftarrow$ we get respectively $Q_1^2(a, a) \leftarrow$ and $Q_1^2(b, b) \leftarrow$ using Definition 14. Finally uncopying($Prog_1$) = $Prog_0 \cup \{Q_1(b) \leftarrow . \ P(g(x_1^1, x_1^2)) \leftarrow Q_1^2(x_1^1, x_1^2). \ Q_1^2(a, a) \leftarrow . \ Q_1^2(b, b) \leftarrow\}$. So, uncopying($Prog_1$) is a normalized non-copying CS-Program.

Let $Prog_2$ = uncopying($Prog_1$). Now, there are 2 non-convergent critical pairs, $Q_1^2(a, b) \leftarrow$ and $Q_1^2(b, a) \leftarrow$. If we add them to $Prog_2$, we get a normalized non-copying CS-Program, all critical pairs are convergent. Applying Theorem 2, $Mod(Prog_2)$ is closed by rewriting.

5 Further Work

In this paper, we have shown that the non-regular approximation technique by means of CS-programs can also deal with left-linear non-right-linear rewrite systems. Naturally, the question that still arises is: can this technique be extended to non-left-linear rewrite systems. From a theoretical point of view, applying a non-left-linear rewrite rule amounts to compute the intersection of several languages of sub-terms, i.e. the intersection of CS-programs. Unfortunately, it is known that the class of synchronized tree languages (i.e. the languages recognized by CS-programs) is not closed under intersection. In other words, except for particular cases, such intersection cannot be computed in an exact way. However, it could be over-approximated by a CS-program. We are studying this possibility.

References

1. Boichut, Y., Boyer, B., Genet, Th., Legay, A.: Equational abstraction refinement for certified tree regular model checking. In: Aoki, T., Taguchi, K. (eds.) ICFEM 2012. LNCS, vol. 7635, pp. 299–315. Springer, Heidelberg (2012)
2. Boichut, Y., Chabin, J., Réty, P.: Over-approximating descendants by synchronized tree languages. In: RTA, vol. 21 of LIPIcs, pp. 128–142 (2013)
3. Boichut, Y., Chabin, J., Réty, P.: Erratum of over-approximating descendants by synchronized tree languages. Technical report, LIFO, Université d'Orléans (2015). http://www.univ-orleans.fr/lifo/Members/rety/publications.html#erratum
4. Boichut, Y., Courbis, R., Héam, P.-C., Kouchnarenko, O.: Finer is better: abstraction refinement for rewriting approximations. In: Voronkov, A. (ed.) RTA 2008. LNCS, vol. 5117, pp. 48–62. Springer, Heidelberg (2008)
5. Boichut, Y., Héam, P.-C.: A theoretical limit for safety verification techniques with regular fix-point computations. IPL 108(1), 1–2 (2008)
6. Bouajjani, A., Habermehl, P., Rogalewicz, A., Vojnar, T.: Abstract regular (tree) model checking. J. Softw. Tools Technol. Transf. 14(2), 167–191 (2012)
7. Genet, T., Klay, F.: Rewriting for cryptographic protocol verification. In: McAllester, D. (ed.) CADE 2000. LNCS, vol. 1831, pp. 271–290. Springer, Heidelberg (2000)

8. Genet, T., Salmon, Y.: Reachability analysis of innermost rewriting. In: RTA, vol. 36 (2015)
9. Gouranton, V., Réty, P., Seidl, H.: Synchronized tree languages revisited and new applications. In: Honsell, F., Miculan, M. (eds.) FOSSACS 2001. LNCS, vol. 2030, p. 214. Springer, Heidelberg (2001)
10. Kochems, J., Luke Ong, C.-H.: Improved functional flow and reachability analyses using indexed linear tree grammars. In: RTA, vol. 10 of LIPIcs, pp. 187–202 (2011)
11. Limet, S., Réty, P.: E-unification by means of tree tuple synchronized grammars. Discret. Math. Theorit. Comput. Sci. **1**(1), 69–98 (1997)
12. Limet, S., Salzer, G.: Proving properties of term rewrite systems via logic programs. In: van Oostrom, V. (ed.) RTA 2004. LNCS, vol. 3091, pp. 170–184. Springer, Heidelberg (2004)
13. Limet, S., Salzer, G.: Tree tuple languages from the logic programming point of view. J. Autom. Reason. **37**(4), 323–349 (2006)

Formal Specification and Verification of a Selective Defense for TDoS Attacks

Yuri Gil Dantas[1]([✉]), Marcilio O.O. Lemos[2], Iguatemi E. Fonseca[2],
and Vivek Nigam[2]

[1] Computer Science Department, TU Darmstadt, Darmstadt, Germany
dantas@mais.informatik.tu-darmstadt.de
[2] Computer Science Department, UFPB, João Pessoa, Brazil
{marciliolemos,iguatemi,vivek}@ci.ufpb.br

Abstract. Telephony Denial of Service (TDoS) attacks target telephony services, such as Voice over IP, not allowing legitimate users to make calls. There are few defenses that attempt to mitigate TDoS attacks, most of them using IP filtering, with limited applicability. In our recent work, we proposed to use selective strategies for mitigating HTTP Application-Layer DDoS Attacks demonstrating their effectiveness in mitigating different types of attacks. This paper demonstrates that selective strategies can also be successfully used to mitigate TDoS attacks, in particular, two attacks: the Coordinated Call Attack and the Prank Call attack. We formalize a novel selective strategy for mitigating these attacks in the computational tool Maude and verify these defenses using the statistical model checker PVeStA. When compared to our experimental results (reported elsewhere), the results obtained by using formal methods were very similar. This demonstrate that formal methods is a powerful tool for specifying defenses for mitigating Distributed Denial of Service attacks allowing to increase our confidence on the proposed defense before actual implementation.

1 Introduction

Telephony Denial of Service (TDoS) attacks is a type of Denial of Service (DoS) attack that target telephony services, such as Voice over IP (VoIP). With the increase in the popularity of VoIP services, we have witnessed an increase in TDoS attacks being used to target hospital VoIP systems [1,2] and systems for emergency lines (like the American 911 system) [3]. Moreover, according the FBI, 200 TDoS attacks have identified only in 2013 [2].

This paper investigates the use of selective defenses [4] for mitigating two common TDoS attacks: The Coordinated Call [5] and the Dial Call [6] attacks:

The Coordinated Call attack [5] exploits the fact that pairs of attackers, Alice and Bob, can collude to exhaust the resources of the VoIP server. Assume that Alice and Bob are valid registered users.[1] The attack goes by Alice simply calling

---

[1] This can be easily done for many VoIP services.

© Springer International Publishing Switzerland 2016
D. Lucanu (Ed.): WRLA 2016, LNCS 9942, pp. 82–97, 2016.
DOI: 10.1007/978-3-319-44802-2_5

Bob and trying to stay in the call as long as she can. Since the server allocates resources for each call, by using a great number of pairs of attackers, one can exhaust the resources of the server and denying service to honest participants. This is a simple, but ingenious attack, as only a small number of attackers is needed generating a small network traffic (when compared to SIP flooding attack for example). Thus it is hard for the network administrator to detect and counter-measure such attack.

The Dial Call attack [6] is similar to the usual flooding attack [7] denying service by overloading the target resources. It has been carried out to shutdown essential public services, such as the US emergency number (911) and hospital lines. The attack follows by a large number of attackers (or their bots) initiating calls to the target call-center. This causes that many, if not all, telephones in the center to ring. Once the attendant picks up the phone, he can normally notice that this is fake call and puts down the phone. However, since the number of calls is very large, the phone rings again, not allowing legitimate clients to be served.

Formal methods and, in particular, rewriting logic can help developers to design defenses for mitigating DDoS attacks. In our previous work [4] we used selective strategies in the form of the tool SeVen for mitigating HTTP Low-Rate Application-Layer DDoS attacks targetting web-servers. We formalized different attack scenarios in Maude and since our strategies are constructed over some probability functions, we used statistical model checking [8], namely PVeStA [9], to validate our defense. Due to our reasonable preliminary results, we implemented SeVen and carried out experiments over the network obtaining similar results to the ones obtained using formal methods. It took us *only 3 person months* to obtain our results using formal methods, while it took us *24 person months* to obtain our first experimental results. Although we strongly believe that systems should also be validated by means of experiments, the confidence acquired from our formal analysis was invaluable for the success of this project.[2]

This paper continues our general goal of using selective strategies for mitigating DoS attacks, in particular, here for mitigating TDoS attacks. We followed the same methodology as before, first formalizing our defense, the Coordinated Call and the Dial Call attacks in Maude and using PVeStA to validate our defense's effectiveness. While this paper explains the formal model used, in another technical report [10], we detail our initial experimental results on mitigating the Coordinated Call attack using SeVen to defend VoIP servers. The results obtained by using our formal model and our experimental results were very similar.

This paper is organized as follows. Section 2 we review Session Initiation Protocol (SIP) used for initiating a VoIP call and also explain two different TDoS attacks: Coordinated Call and Dial Call attacks. Section 3 explains how SeVen works, while Sect. 4 describes its formalization in Maude. In Sect. 5, we explain our simulation results including our main assumptions, results and discussion of

---

[2] Notice that although our experiments on the network were controlled experiments, they used off-the-shelf tools, such as Apache web-servers, which implement a number of optimizations, and our experiments suffered from interferences that cannot be controlled, such as network latency.

the results obtained. We comment in Sect. 6 related and future work. Finally, the implementation used to carry out our simulations is available for download at [11].

2   VoIP Protocols and DDoS Attacks

We now review the Session Initiation Protocol [12], which is one of the main protocols used to establish Voice over IP (VoIP) connections. Figure 1 shows the message exchanges performed to establish a connection between two registered users, Alice and Bob, where Alice tries to initiate a conversation with Bob. It also contains the messages exchanged to terminate the connection.

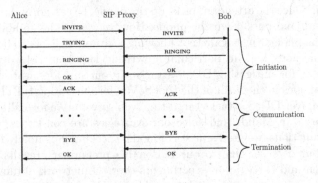

Fig. 1. Exchange of messages between the server and two users (Alice and Bob) during a normal execution of the SIP protocol.

For initiating a call, Alice sends an INVITE message to the SIP server informing that she wants to call Bob. If Bob or Alice is not registered as valid users, the server sends a reject message to Alice. Otherwise, the server sends an INVITE message to Bob.[3] At the same time, the server sends a TRYING message to Alice informing her the server is waiting for Bob's response to Alice's invitation. Bob might reject the request, in which case the server informs Alice (not shown in the Figure), or Bob can accept the call by sending the message RINGING. Finally, the server sends the message RINGING to Alice and the parties exchange OK and ACK messages.

At this point, the communication is established and Alice and Bob should be able to communicate as long as they need/want. (This is represented by the three ellipses in Fig. 1.) The call is then terminated once one of the parties (Alice) sends a BYE message to the server. The server then sends a BYE message to the other party (Bob), which then answers with the message OK, which is forwarded to Alice, and the connection is terminated.

---

[3] In fact, we omit some steps carried out by the server to find Bob in the network. This step can lead to DDoS amplification attacks [13] for which known solutions exists. Such amplification attacks are not, however, the main topic of this paper.

Many attacks have exploited SIP to deny the VoIP service. We detail two different attacks to the SIP protocols. The first one is the Coordinated Call attack and the second one is the Dial Call attack.

Coordinated VoIP Attack. A pair of colluding attackers, A_1 and A_2, that are registered in the VoIP service,[4] call each other and stay in the call for as much time as they can. Once the call is established, the attackers stay in the call for indefinite time. They might be disconnected by some Timeout mechanism establishing some time bounds on the amount of time that two users might call. During the time that A_1 and A_2 are communicating, they are using resources of the server. If many pairs of attackers collude, then the resources of the server can be quickly exhausted. This attack is hard to detect using network analyzers because the traffic generated by attackers is similar to the traffic generated by legitimate clients. The attackers follows correctly the SIP protocol.

Our own experiments [10] replicating this attack show its effectiveness reducing the availability of the VoIP service to less than 15 % of legitimate users.

Dial Call Attack. The Dial Call attack is similar to a flooding attack [7] in that the attackers send a large number of requests targeting essential public resources services, such as the American 911 service. The attacker launches a high volume of calls in order to flood the target VoIP service, reducing the availability to legitimate users. Usually a particular call from the Dial Call attack does not take long, because the callee hangs up the call when he realizes that is a prank call. Dial Call attacks are difficult to track and investigate because the calls are classified as anonymous, hence using traditional traffic analysis tools might not be an efficient approach to mitigate such attacks.

3   SeVen

We proposed recently [4] a new defense mechanism, called SeVen, for mitigating Application-Layer DDoS attacks (ADDoS) using selective strategies. An application using SeVen does not immediately process incoming messages, but waits for a period of time, T_S, called a round. During a round, SeVen accumulates messages received in an internal buffer k. If the number of messages accumulated reaches the maximum capacity of the service being protected and a new incoming request R arrives, SeVen behaves as follows:

1. SeVen decides whether process R or not based on a probability P_1. P_1 is defined using the variable PMod following [14]:

$$\frac{k}{k + \text{PMod}}$$

At the beginning of the round, we set the variable PMod $= 0$. PMod is incremented whenever the application's capacity is exhausted and a new incoming

---

[4] Or alternatively two honest users that have been infected to be zombies by some attacker.

request arrives reducing thus the probability of new incoming request being selected by SeVen during a round.

2. If SeVen decides to process R, then as the application is overloaded, it should decide which request currently being processed should be dropped. This decision is governed by P_2, a distribution probability *which might depend on the state of the existing request.*

3. Otherwise, SeVen simply drops the request R without affecting the requests currently being processed and sends a message to the requesting user informing that the service is temporally unavailable;

At the end of the round, SeVen processes the requests that are in its internal buffer (surviving the selective strategy) sending them to the application.

The intuition of why such a defense works is because whenever a system is overloaded, it is very likely that it is suffering a DoS attack, which means that it is very likely that an attacker request is occupying the resources of the service. Therefore, the probability of dropping an attacker's request is higher than the probability of dropping an honest request. Thus, even under severe attack of multiple attackers, an application running SeVen can maintain fair levels of availability.

There is, however, much space for specifying these probability distributions governing SeVen. In [4], we showed that by using simple *uniform distributions* for dropping existing requests, SeVen can be used to mitigate a number of ADDoS attacks using the HTTP protocol, such as the Slowloris and HTTP POST attacks even in the presence of a large number of attackers.

For mitigating both Dial Call and Coordinated Call attacks described in Sect. 2, we set the probability P_2 to depend on (1) the status of the call and (2) on the duration of a call. We consider two types of call status:

- WAITING: A call is WAITING if it has already sent an INVITE message, but it is still waiting for the responder to join the call, that is, it has not completed the initiation part of the SIP protocol;
- INCALL: A call is INCALL if the messages of initiation part of SIP have been completed and initiator and the responder are already communicating (or simply in a call).

Thus, any incoming INVITE requests assume the status of WAITING, and these can change its status to INCALL once the initiation part of SIP is completed.

We assume here that it is preferable to a VoIP server, when overloaded, to drop WAITING requests than INCALL requests that are communicating not for a *very long duration.* In many cases, it is true that interrupting an existing call is considered to be more damaging to server's reputation than not allowing a user to start a new call. This could also be modeled by configuring the probability distributions of SeVen accordingly. To determine whether a call is taking too long, we assume that the server knows what is the average duration, t_M, of calls.[5]

---

[5] The value of t_M can be obtained by the history of a VoIP provider's usage.

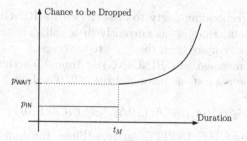

Fig. 2. Graph (not in scale) illustrating the behavior of SeVen according to the status of a call and its duration. p_{WAIT} is the probability of dropping a WAITING call, while p_{IN} the probability of dropping a INCALL call.

The probability of an INCALL request increase using a Poisson distribution[6] once this has a duration of more than t_M. Figure 2 depicts roughly the probability distribution used to drop requests. The actual function d (for drop factor) is of the form, where t is the call duration:

$$d(t) = \begin{cases} p_{WAIT} & \text{if } t = 0 \\ p_{IN} & \text{if } 0 \le t \le t_M \\ p_{WAIT} + e^{\alpha t/t_M} & \text{if } t > t_M \end{cases} \tag{1}$$

We use this probability distribution as an illustration of how SeVen can be used for mitigating VoIP DDoS attacks. Of course, there are many decision options for these probabilities which will depend on the intended application. For instance, one could consider that the Poisson distribution should begin only a period after t_M, or that it should be another distribution, etc. It will depend on the specific requirements of the defense. As our results in Sect. 5 demonstrate, the values chosen are good enough for the VoIP attacks we consider.

We also have developed SeVen as a proxy in C++ which implements the strategy explained above, *e.g.*, using the drop function 1, Poisson distribution and so on. The measures and results (which can be found in another submission [10]) were very similar to the ones detailed in Sect. 5. Such results confirm the success of our formal model proposed here.

3.1 Sample Execution

Consider the following buffer, $\mathcal{B}_i$, at the beginning of a round and assume that $k = 3$, PMod $= 0$, the initial time is 9 and the average call duration is $t_M = 5$ time units:

$$\mathcal{B}_1 = [\langle id_1, \text{WAITING}, \text{undef}\rangle, \langle id_2, \text{INCALL}, 0.5\rangle]$$

$\langle id, st, tm\rangle$ specifies that the call id has status st and the call started at time tm where tm is undef whenever $st = $ WAITING. This buffer specifies that the

---

[6] We used a Poisson distribution because such distributions are normally used for modeling telephone calls arrival.

id_1 is waiting the responding party to answer (with a RINGING message) his invitation request and that id_2 is currently in a call. This means that id_2 is calling already for way more than the expected average.

Assume that a message $\langle id_1, \mathsf{RINGING} \rangle$ at time 9.5 arrives specifying that the responder of the request id_1 answered the call. The buffer is updated to the following:

$$\mathcal{B}_2 = [\langle id_1, \mathsf{INCALL}, 9.5 \rangle, \langle id_2, \mathsf{INCALL}, 0.5 \rangle]$$

Then the message $\langle id_3, \mathsf{INVITE} \rangle$ arrives. Since the buffer is not yet full, a new request is inserted in the buffer and the message TRYING is sent to the requesting user. Notice that the RINGING message is not yet sent to the responding user. The buffer changes to:

$$\mathcal{B}_3 = [\langle id_1, \mathsf{INCALL}, 9.5 \rangle, \langle id_2, \mathsf{INCALL}, 0.5 \rangle, \langle id_3, \mathsf{WAITING}, \mathsf{undef} \rangle]$$

Suppose now that another message $m_1 = \langle id_4, \mathsf{INVITE} \rangle$ arrives at time 10.5. As the buffer is now full, it sets PMod to 1 and the application has to decide whether it will keep m_1. SeVen generates a random number in the interval [0,1] using uniform distribution. Say that this number is less than $(3/3 + 1)$, which means that it will select to process m_1. However, it has to drop some existing request. The probabilities of dropping one the request in the buffer are as follows (see Fig. 2):

- id_1 has probability p_{IN} to be dropped because it is calling for a duration less than t_M: $10.5 - 9.5 < 5$;
- id_2 has a much higher probability to be dropped because it is calling for twice t_M: $10.5 - 0.5 = 2 \times 5$;
- id_3 has probability p_{WAIT} to be dropped because it has WAITING status.

Suppose that the application decides to drop id_2, which means that the call is interrupted by the application. The resulting buffer is:

$$\mathcal{B}_4 = [\langle id_1, \mathsf{INCALL}, 9.5 \rangle, \langle id_4, \mathsf{WAITING}, \mathsf{undef} \rangle, \langle id_3, \mathsf{WAITING}, \mathsf{undef} \rangle]$$

Assume that now the round time is elapsed. The application sends a RINGING message to the responder of the requests id_3 and id_4.

4   Formal Specification

Our specification follows [4,15,16] specifying the attack scenarios using the Actor Model where attackers, clients, and server send and receive messages. These messages are stored in a scheduler that maintains a queue of messages. The attackers do not take control over the channel. Instead they share a channel with clients.

We formalize all actors in the computational system Maude and carry out simulations by using the statistical model checker PVeStA. For sake of simplicity, we considered the server and SeVen as one actor, which means that SeVen is also able to operate as a normal SIP Server, *e.g.*, processing and establishing call connections. Such decision does not affect the analysis of our results, which are similar to the ones of our experiments over the network [10]. In the following, we describe our Maude specification.[7]

```
eq initState =
<name: server | req-cnt: 0.0 , b-set: [0 | none], none >
<name: client-generate | server: server, cnt: 0 , none >
<name: attacker-generate | server: server, cnt: 0 , none >
        {initActor, (attacker-generate <- spawn )}
        {initActor, (client-generate <- spawn )}
        {Ts, server <- ROUND} .
```

The equation for *initState* specifies the initial state of our model, which contains three actors, an attacker generator, a client generation and SeVen. Each actor has an ID and a set of attributes. For example, SeVen is called `server` with attributes `req-cnt` storing the value of PMod and `b-set` the internal buffer with the current call connections. The attributes `cnt` in the other two actors stores how many clients and attackers have been created.

Finally, we also formalize the message configuration between actors that are going to be added in our scheduler. Each message configuration has the parameters delivery time and the message itself. For instance, we use the same `initActor` delivery time to initialize both actors clients and attackers with a message *spawn*. Besides that, we also create a periodically `ROUND` message to control the SeVen's round explained in Sect. 3, which is scheduled to be sent after `Ts` time units.

The equations for generating both clients and attackers are omitted here. Instead, we show their main rewrite rules. The clients have an attribute `status` specifying their call state. Its status is `none` before sending an `INVITE` message to the server which happens when it receives a message `pool` from the equation generating clients[8] as specified by the following rewrite rule:

```
rl [CLIENT-RECEIVE-POOL] :
        <name: c(i) | server: Ser, status: none, AS >
        {c(i) <- poll}
    =>
        <name: c(i) | server: Ser , status: invite, AS >
        { gt + delay, (Ser <- INVITE(c(i)))} .
```

The following rewrite rule specifies the behavior of a client upon receiving a RINGING message from the server. It changes the client's state from *invite* to *connected* and generates a message BYE, scheduled to be sent after some time

---

[7] For the sake of presentation, we simplified here some aspects such as the use of the scheduler appearing in the complete model which can be found in [11].

[8] Note that there is a value `delay` inserted when a message is sent in order to have a more realistic model.

in the interval $]0, \texttt{tMedio}]$. This means that all legitimate clients do not overpass the average time of the duration of calls. We omit the rule specifying when client receives a drop message.

```
rl [CLIENT-RECEIVE-RINGING] :
        <name: c(i) | server: Ser, status: invite, AS >
        {c(i) <- RINGING}
    =>
        <name: c(i) | server: Ser , status: connected, AS >
        { gt + randomNumber(0,tMedio), (Ser <- BYE(c(i)))} .
```

The rewrite rules for the attackers are similar to the client rules. The only difference is that no BYE message is generated, thus, specifying the Coordinated Call attack where attackers attempt to stay in the call for indefinite time. We elide these rules.

```
crl [SeVen-RECEIVE-INVITE] :
        <name: Ser | req-cnt: pmod , b-set: [lenB | B], AS >
        {Ser <- INVITE(Actor)}
    => if (float(lenB) >= floor(lenBufSeVen)) then
            if p1 then ConfAcc {gt, Actor <- TRYING} {gt, ActorDr <- poll}
                else ConfRej {gt + delay , Actor <- poll}
            fi
        else ConfAcc2 {gt + delay, Actor <- TRYING}
        fi
if p1 := sampleBerWithP(accept-prob(pmod))
    /\ { ActorDr, bufDr } := remUser(altPBuf(B, gt), sampleUniWithInt(altPBufLen(B, gt)))
    /\ nBuf := add([lenB + (- 1) | bufDr], < Actor gt INVITE >)
    /\ ConfAcc := <name: Ser | req-cnt: (pmod + 1.0), b-set: nBuf , AS >
    /\ ConfRej := <name: Ser | req-cnt: (pmod + 1.0), b-set: [lenB | B], AS >
    /\ b-setNu := add( [lenB | B], < Actor gt INVITE > )
    /\ ConfAcc2 := <name: Ser | req-cnt: pmod , b-set: b-setNu, AS > .

rl [SeVen-APP-ROUND] :
        <name: Ser | req-cnt: pmod , b-set: [lenB | B], AS >
        {Ser <- ROUND}
    =>
        <name: Ser | req-cnt: 0.0, b-set: [lenB | B], AS >
        {gt, reply(Ser, B, gt)} {gt + Ts, Ser <- ROUND} .
```

Fig. 3. Rewrite rules specifying SeVen's selective strategy.

Figure 3 depicts the rules implementing SeVen's strategy. For each INVITE message received by some actor `Actor`, the rule `SeVen-RECEIVE-INVITE` checks whether the buffer of the server reached its maximum. If not, then the incoming request is added to the server's buffer (`ConfAcc2`) and a message TRYING to the corresponding actor is created. Otherwise, SeVen throws a coin (`p1`) to decide whether the incoming request will be processed using `pmod`. If SeVen decides to process the incoming request, then some request being processed (the one sent by `ActorDr`) is swapped with the new incoming request resulting in the buffer `nBuf` and `pmod` gets incremented, resulting in the configuration `ConfAcc`. Moreover, a `poll` message to `ActorDr` and a TRYING to `Actor` are created. Otherwise, the incoming request is rejected and `pmod` is incremented without affecting the server's buffer resulting in the configuration `ConfRej`. A poll message to `Actor` is also created.

The rule `SeVen-APP-ROUND` specifies that when the round finishes, all surviving requests in the server's buffer are answered, where a new round starts and `pmod` is re-set.

5 Simulation Results

We detail our simulation results obtained from our formal specification using the statistical model checker PVeStA [9]. Our simulations are parametric in the following values:

- Average time of a call – t_M: This is the assumed average time of the of calls of honest users. We assume $t_M = 5$ time units;
- Probability distribution parameters (Func 1) – p_{IN}, p_{WAIT} and α: These are the constants used to configure the distribution probability for dropping requests as shown in Fig. 2;
- SeVen Round Time – t_S: This is the time that SeVen waits accumulating requests, as described in Sect. 3. In our simulations, we use 0.4 time units.
- Size of Buffer – k: This is the upper-bound on the size of $\mathcal{B}$, denoting the processing capacity of the application. $k = 24$;
- Number of calls among honest participants (*countHonest*) and among colluding attackers (*countAttacker*). In all our simulations, we fixed the number of clients to *countHonest* = 24 requests. Whenever we create an honest request, we specify how long the users want to talk, *i.e.*, have the INCALL status;
- Total time of the simulation - *total*: This is the total time of the simulation using PVeStA. We used in our simulations *total* equal to 40 time units, similar to the time used in [15];
- Delay of the Network: We also assumed a delay of 0.1 time units of message in the network;
- Degree of confidence for the simulation: Our simulations were carried out with a degree of confidence of 99 % (see [8,17] for more details on probabilistic model checking).

Quality Measures. In our simulation, we use novel quality measures specific for VoIP services. These are specified by expressions of the QuaTEx quantitative, probabilistic temporal logic defined in [17]. We perform statistical model checking of our defense in the sense of [8]: once a QuaTEx formula and desired degree of confidence are specified, a sufficiently large number of Monte Carlo simulations are carried out allowing for the verification of the QuaTEx formula. The Monte Carlo simulations are carried out by the computational tool Maude [18] and the statistical model checking is carried out by PVeStA.

The QuaTEx formulas, *i.e.*, the quality measures, that we use in our simulations are defined below. The operator $\bigcirc$ is a temporal modality that specifies the advancement of the global time to the time of the next event (see [17] for more details).

– Complete: How many honest calls were able to stay in the INCALL status for the expected duration.

$$complete(total) = \text{if } time > total \text{ then } \frac{countComplete}{countHonest}$$

$$\text{else } \bigcirc complete(total)$$

where *countComplete* is a counter that is incremented whenever an honest call is completed.

– Incomplete: How many honest calls were able to have the INCALL status but were dropped before completing the call, *i.e.* not staying in INCALL status for the expected duration;

$$incomplete(total) = \text{if } time > total \text{ then } \frac{countIncomplete}{countHonest}$$

$$\text{else } \bigcirc incomplete(total)$$

where *countInComplete* = *countIncall* − *countComplete* and *countIncall* is a counter that is incremented whenever an honest calls changes from status WAITING to INCALL.

– Unsuccessful: How many honest calls were not even able to reach the INCALL status. That is, how many calls were not even able to start talking between each other.

$$unsuccessful(total) = \text{if } time > total \text{ then } \frac{countUnsuccess}{countHonest}$$

$$\text{else } \bigcirc unsuccessful(total)$$

where *countUnsuccessful* = *countHonest* − *countIncall*.

– The average of clients incomplete calls: We also measure how many percent in average legitimate clients were able to talk in an incomplete call.

$$avgInCall(total) = \text{if } time > total \text{ then } \frac{totalTimeInCall}{totalIncompleteCall}$$

$$\text{else } \bigcirc avgInCall(total)$$

where *totalTimeInCall* is the sum of how many percent of time clients were able to talk before being interrupted and the *totalIncompleteCall* is the total of clients the were not able to finish their call as explained in Incomplete.

We consider that an honest request that was completed has a better performance than an honest request that was interrupted in the middle of a call which, on the other hand, has a better performance than an honest request that did not even succeed in starting a call, *i.e.*, never reached the INCALL status.

5.1   Coordinated Call Attack

Figure 4 contains our main results for the scenarios where the application is under the Coordinated Call attack discussed in Sect. 2. We considered scenarios where the application is using SeVen (Fig. 4(a)) and not using any defense mechanism (Fig. 4(b)).

Figure 4(a) shows that the application maintains great levels of availability when using SeVen. The Complete calls reduce from 95 % to 81 % of the legitimate calls when the number of attackers increase. The difference is distributed between Incomplete and Unsuccessful calls, where the former is around 13 % and the latter is around 6 % of the legitimate calls. On the other hand, when SeVen is not running, in all simulations, most legitimate users are not able to start a call: When the number of attackers increase, the rate of Unsuccessful call increase from 55 % to 75 % and the rate of Successful call decrease from 45 % to 25 %, which means that when SeVen is running, there is an increase of availability by a factor of 3.

Moreover, the average duration of incomplete calls (Fig. 4(c)) stayed around 70 %, that is, in average, a call that was dropped before completing its duration was able to stay communicating for around 70 % of the intended time.

Comparison with Our Experimental Results. We implemented [10] the Coordinated Call attack and SeVen as described here. Our experimental results were

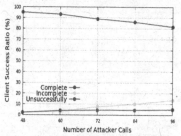

(a) Client Success Ratio when running SeVen.

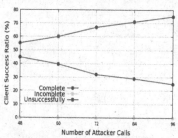

(b) Client Success Ratio when *not* running SeVen.

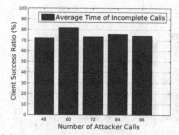

(c) Average Duration of Incomplete Calls when using SeVen

Fig. 4. Simulation results for when the application suffers a Coordinated Call attack.

very similar to the ones we obtained here. In particular, when not running SeVen, we observed very high levels of Unsuccessful calls (85 % of legitimate calls), low levels of Complete calls (15 % of legitimate calls) and no Incomplete calls. These results are very similar to the ones in Fig. 4(b). When running SeVen, our experiments showed a high rate of Successful calls (65 % of legitimate calls), a low rate of Incomplete calls (25 % of legitimate calls) and very low rate of Unsuccessful calls (10 % of legitimate calls). These results are very similar to the ones in Fig. 4(a). Finally, we also measured the average duration of Incomplete calls with an average of 60 % of total call duration being very close to the results in Fig. 4(c).

These results support our claim that Formal Methods can be used for proposing novel selective defenses for mitigating DDoS attacks. We leave to future work the comparison of formal methods results with experimental results for other attacks such as the Dial Call attack.

5.2 Dial Call Attack

Figure 5 shows the results obtained when the application is under a Dial Call attack. We observe that when SeVen is running, the application maintains fair levels of availability. Whereas without SeVen the number of calls that have been completed drops to around 28 % of legitimate calls, it drops to 53 % when SeVen

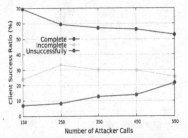

(a) Client Success Ratio when running SeVen.

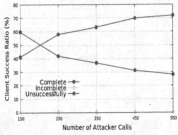

(b) Client Success Ratio when *not* running SeVen.

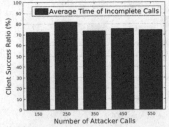

(c) Average Duration of Incomplete Calls

Fig. 5. Simulation results for when the application suffers Dial Call attack.

is running, which means an improve of availability by a factor of almost 2. Moreover, the number of calls that is not even able to reach an INCALL status, the Unsuccessful calls, only increases more sharply to 21 % in the presence of 550 attackers when using SeVen, while it increases considerably when not using SeVen to around 71 %. Finally, the average duration of Incomplete calls (Fig. 5(c)) remains at around 70 % of their intended duration.

These results provide us with strong evidence that SeVen can be used to mitigate the Dial Call attack. We are currently implementing the machinery to carry out experiments on the network.

6   Related and Future Work

This paper formalized a new selective defense to mitigating Coordinated Call and Dial Call attacks. We have shown that using state-dependent probability distributions for selecting which calls are to be processed results in high levels of availability even in the presence of a great number of attackers. The results obtained by our formal model using statistical model checking tools were very similar to the results we obtained running experiments at least for the Coordinated Call attack scenarios.

For VoIP protocols, there have been some defense proposals. For example [19] proposes a filtering mechanism for SIP flooding attacks. It is not clear whether such mechanisms will be enough for mitigating the Coordinated VoIP attack, as the number of messages needed to carry out such attack is much less, a feature of ADDoS. Wu *et al.* [20] have proposed mechanism to identify intruders using SIP by analyzing the traffic data. Although we do not tackle the identification of intruders problem, we find it an interesting future direction.

The formalization of DDoS attacks and their defenses has been subject of other papers. For example, Meadows proposed a cost based model in [21], while others use branching temporal logics [22]. This paper takes the approach used in [15,16,23], where one formalizes the system in Maude and uses the Statistical Model Checker PVeStA to carry out analyses. While [15,16,23] modeled traditional DDoS attacks exploiting stateless protocols on the transport/network layers, we are modeling stateful Application Layer DDoS attacks. Moreover, the quality measures used for VoIP services under TDoS attacks, described in Sect. 3, are different to the quality measures considered in the previous work.

More recently [4], we proposed SeVen showing that it can be used to mitigate ADDoS attacks that exploit the HTTP protocol. This paper shows that SeVen can also be used to mitigate DDoS attacks in VoIP protocols, but in order to do so one needs state-dependent probabilistic distributions. This is because of the quality requirements that we need in VoIP communications. We would like to give a priority to the types of call that should be given more chances to keep using resources of the server. In particular, we give preference to calls that do not take more than the average duration time. Such quality measures are not present in HTTP protocols that we analyzed in [4].

For future work, we are currently implementing controlled experiments with the Dial Call attack carried out on the network. We expect that these experiments also validate our simulation results for this attack. We are also thinking on intrusion detection mechanisms. We are also interested in building defenses for mitigating amplification attacks [13]. We have also been using SeVen for mitigating High-Rate ADDoS attacks using Software Defined Networks [24].

Acknowledgments. This work was supported by the Hessian excellence initiative LOEWE at the Center for Advanced Security Research Darmstadt (CASED), by RNP, by Capes and CNPq.

References

1. Cyber threat bulletin: boston hospital TDoS attack. http://voipsecurityblog. typepad.com/files/cyber-threat-bulletin-13-06-boston-hospital-telephony-denial-of-service-attack.pdf. Accessed 27 Sep 2015
2. TDoS- extortionists jam phone lines of public services including hospitals. https://nakedsecurity.sophos.com/pt/2014/01/22/tdos-extortionists-jam-phone-lines-of-public-services-including-hospitals/. Accessed 27 Sep 2015
3. Situational advisory: recent telephony denial of services (TDoS) attacks. http:// voipsecurityblog.typepad.com/files/ky-fusion_tdos_3-29-13-2.pdf/. Accessed 27 Sep 2015
4. Dantas, Y.G., Nigam, V., Fonseca, I.E.: A selective defense for application layer DDoS attacks. In: JISIC 2014, pp. 75–82 (2014)
5. The Surging Threat of Telephony Denial of Service Attacks. http:// voipsecurityblog.typepad.com/files/tdos_paper_4-11-13.pdf. Accessed 28 Sep 2015
6. TDoS extortionists jam phone lines of public services, including hospitals. https://nakedsecurity.sophos.com/2014/01/22/tdos-extortionists-jam-phone-lines-of-public-services-including-hospitals/. Accessed 28 Nov 2015
7. Zargar, S.T., Joshi, J., Tipper, D.: A survey of defense mechanisms against distributed denial of service (DDoS) flooding attacks. IEEE Commun. Surv. Tutorials **15**(4), 2046–2069 (2013)
8. Sen, K., Viswanathan, M., Agha, G.: On statistical model checking of stochastic systems. In: Etessami, K., Rajamani, S.K. (eds.) CAV 2005. LNCS, vol. 3576, pp. 266–280. Springer, Heidelberg (2005)
9. AlTurki, M., Meseguer, J.: PVESTA: a parallel statistical model checking and quantitative analysis tool. In: Corradini, A., Klin, B., Cîrstea, C. (eds.) CALCO 2011. LNCS, vol. 6859, pp. 386–392. Springer, Heidelberg (2011)
10. Lemos, M.O.O., Dantas, Y.G., Fonseca, I.E., Nigam, V.: A selective defense for mitigating coordinated call attacks (submitted)
11. ygdantas. Seven: repository (2013). https://github.com/ygdantas/SeVen.git
12. SIP: Session initiation protocol. http://www.ietf.org/rfc/rfc3261.txt
13. Shankesi, R., AlTurki, M., Sasse, R., Gunter, C.A., Meseguer, J.: Model-checking DoS amplification for VoIP session initiation. In: Backes, M., Ning, P. (eds.) ESORICS 2009. LNCS, vol. 5789, pp. 390–405. Springer, Heidelberg (2009)
14. Khanna, S., Venkatesh, S.S., Fatemieh, O., Khan, F., Gunter, C.A.: Adaptive selective verification. In: INFOCOM, pp. 529–537 (2008)

15. Eckhardt, J., Mühlbauer, T., AlTurki, M., Meseguer, J., Wirsing, M.: Stable availability under denial of service attacks through formal patterns. In: de Lara, J., Zisman, A. (eds.) FASE 2012. LNCS, vol. 7212, pp. 78–93. Springer, Heidelberg (2012)

16. Eckhardt, J., Mühlbauer, T., Meseguer, J., Wirsing, M.: Statistical model checking for composite actor systems. In: Martí-Oliet, N., Palomino, M. (eds.) WADT 2012. LNCS, vol. 7841, pp. 143–160. Springer, Heidelberg (2013)

17. Agha, G., Meseguer, J., Sen, K.: PMaude: rewrite-based specification language for probabilistic object systems. Electron. Notes Theor. Comput. Sci. **153**(2), 213–239 (2006)

18. Clavel, M., Durán, F., Eker, S., Lincoln, P., Martí-Oliet, N., Meseguer, J., Talcott, C. (eds.): All About Maude. LNCS, vol. 4350. Springer, Heidelberg (2007)

19. Huici, F., Niccolini, S., D'Heureuse, N.: Protecting SIP against very large flooding DoS attacks. In: GLOBECOM 2009, pp. 1369–1374. IEEE Press, Piscataway (2009)

20. Yu-Sung, W., Bagchi, S., Garg, S., Singh, N., Tsai, T.: SCIDIVE: a stateful and cross protocol intrusion detection architecture for voice-over-IP environments. In: DSN 2004, p. 433. IEEE Computer Society, Washington, DC (2004)

21. Meadows, C.: A formal framework and evaluation method for network denial of service. In: CSFW, pp. 4–13 (1999)

22. Mahimkar, A., Shmatikov, V.: Game-based analysis of denial-of-service prevention protocols. In: CSFW, pp. 287–301 (2005)

23. AlTurki, M., Meseguer, J., Gunter, C.A.: Probabilistic modeling and analysis of DoS protection for the ASV protocol. Electr. Notes Theor. Comput. Sci. **234**, 3–18 (2009)

24. Henrique, J., Fonseca, I.E., Nigam, V.: Mitigating high-rate application layer DDoS attacks in software defined networks (submitted)

Egalitarian State-Transition Systems

Óscar Martín[✉], Alberto Verdejo, and Narciso Martí-Oliet

Facultad de Informática, Universidad Complutense de Madrid, Madrid, Spain
{omartins,jalberto,narciso}@ucm.es

Abstract. We argue that considering transitions at the same level as states, as first-class citizens, is advantageous in many cases. Namely, the use of atomic propositions on transitions, as well as on states, allows temporal formulas and strategy expressions to be more powerful, general, and meaningful. We define *egalitarian* structures and logics, and show how they generalize well-known state-based, event-based, and mixed ones. We present translations from egalitarian to non-egalitarian settings that, in particular, allow the model checking of LTLR formulas using Maude's LTL model checker. We have implemented these translations as a prototype in Maude itself.

Keywords: Modular specification · State/transition structure · Rewriting logic · Model checking · Kripke structure · LTS · Temporal logic · Strategy

1 Introduction

There is a case of discrimination in computer science that favors states against transitions (call them events or actions, if you prefer). It is not unlike the discrimination by gender in some human societies. Considering transitions just as a means to go from a state to another is as unfair as considering women just as a means for passing genes from father to son. We want to show that this discrimination (against transitions) hinders specification and programming tasks.

There exist, certainly, transition-oriented formalisms as well as state-oriented ones. State-oriented structures (like Kripke structures) give names to states and assert that some atomic propositions are true on each state. State-oriented temporal logics (like LTL and CTL) use these propositions as basic formulas. On the other hand, transition-oriented structures (like labeled transition systems, LTSs) also give names to states; transitions are associated to a non-unique action name. The only way to identify a transition is by looking at the adjacent states. Action names are used in formulas in transition-oriented temporal logics, like HML (Hennessy-Milner logic) [10] and ACTL* [6], but they are not formulas by themselves. In both types of logics, formulas are evaluated on states or on

Partially supported by MINECO Spanish project StrongSoft (TIN2012–39391–C04–04), Comunidad de Madrid program N-GREENS Software (S2013/ICE-2731), and UCM-Santander grant GR3/14.

D. Lucanu (Ed.): WRLA 2016, LNCS 9942, pp. 98–117, 2016.
DOI: 10.1007/978-3-319-44802-2_6

computations starting at an initial state. Even the idea of evaluating a formula on a transition sounds odd.

The origin of this discriminating view is a model of information systems in which indivisible and instantaneous events occur that change the system's state. We argue that, as successful as this model has been, it is not the whole story.

An imperative program is a sequence of instructions and it is natural to see a state in the gap between two consecutive instructions. The evolution of (part of) one such program can be represented like this:

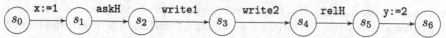

We used `askH` as an abbreviation for "ask for handle to file" and `relH` for "release handle". The s_i are names for states. Suppose now that this is not the only program or process running in the system, and the two `write` instructions involve a shared resource and need to be executed in mutual exclusion. There is a critical section, and it is natural to consider it as an unrefined composed state. This would be a bird's-eye view of the program:

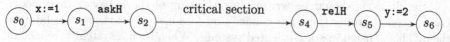

Now, we can define the proposition `in-crit`$_1$ to be true in the critical section; and `in-crit`$_2$ for the other program. We can assert mutual exclusion by the LTL formula

$$\text{MUTEX} := \Box(\neg\texttt{in-crit}_1 \lor \neg\texttt{in-crit}_2)$$

and perform verification as needed.

There is a better way. There is no reason why states s_2 and s_4 should be considered to be in the critical section. Indeed, the very question of whether a state belongs to the critical section is dubious: mutual exclusion is required when *doing* something, not while standing still. The alternative is to consider the critical section as an unrefined composed instruction:

However, mutual exclusion algorithms specified in this way are rare. In rewriting logic, specifications in the spirit of the one on the left are way more usual than the one on the right:

```
rl [enter] : rem  => crit .        rl [crit] : entering => exiting .
rl [exit]  : crit => rem  .        rl [rem]  : exiting  => entering .
```

The reason, or one of them, is that the formula MUTEX involves atomic propositions, and these are usually only available on states. If propositions on transitions were available, we could define `in-crit` to hold true on both writing instructions and then use the same formula MUTEX.

Another desirable property of such a program is that the shared file is not used unless access to it has been granted previously. In a state-based setting this could be expressed by the formula

$$\Box(\texttt{in-crit} \rightarrow \Diamond\texttt{gotFileH})$$

with $\diamond$ meaning "at some past time". We would declare `in-crit` to hold on s_3, and `gotFileH` to hold on s_2. However, an unexpected way to go from s_1 to s_2 is discovered: through the action `hackH`, that gets a handle in a non-standard way, without asking or letting the system know. So, the question is not whether the program got access to the file, but how it did so. We need to refer to transitions in our formula. If we had action names available as basic formulas, we could use

$$\text{ASKB4USE} := \Box(\text{write1} \rightarrow \diamond\text{askH})$$

as a more fitting formula. But note the difference between MUTEX and ASKB4USE as written above: while the former reflects mutual exclusion by itself, and is valid for any programs in which `in-crit` can be defined, the latter is only meaningful for file-sharing programs whose actions are named exactly as they appear in the formula. The way to go is by defining propositions on transitions `using-res` and `asking-for-res`, making them hold, for our example system, on the transitions labeled `write1` and `askH`, respectively, and then using the formula

$$\Box(\text{using-res} \rightarrow \diamond\text{asking-for-res}).$$

This is a meaningful and general formula.

Consider now strategy languages. If, instead of verifying, we want to control the programs so as to ensure mutual exclusion, we can impose the following regular-expression strategy:

$$((\text{askH}_1; \text{ other*} ; \text{relH}_1) \mid (\text{askH}_2 ; \text{ other*} ; \text{relH}_2))*$$

We have added process indices to instructions, and `other` is a shorthand for the disjunction of all instructions different from `askH` and `relH`. This expression ensures that after `askH`$_1$ no other instruction related to file handling is possible until `relH`$_1$ is performed; in particular, `askH`$_2$ is forbidden in between. And vice versa. Again, this expression can only be applied to systems that use these same labels, and often this is not possible or reasonable.

Specifications should be written just thinking of the behavior they model. Later, atomic propositions are defined and formulas or strategies are built on them. This is usual in state-oriented systems. When such a system is refined or otherwise modified, propositions are redefined if needed, but their names do not need to change, let alone the formulas.

The approach we propose to improve the strategy is to define `enter` and `exit` as propositions on transitions, common to both programs, representing the entrance to and exit from the critical section, respectively. These are true, for our example system, of `askH` and `relH`, respectively, and false otherwise. In Maude-like syntax, we would define, for both programs:

```
var enter exit : Prop .
eq askH |= enter = true .
eq relH |= exit = true .
eq I:Instruction |= P:Prop = false [owise] .
```

We can thus build the strategy:

$$(\text{enter} ; (\neg\text{enter})* ; \text{exit})*$$

Then, if there is the need to specify a system with exclusive access to a communication channel, using instructions, say, `get-channel` and `release-channel`, the same proposition names and the same strategy expression can be used.

In a word, the advantage of propositions on transitions (and on states) is *decoupling*: writing the system specification and writing the temporal property are independent tasks. The definition of propositions provides an interface. Changes in the identifiers used in the system need not be accompanied by changes in temporal formulas, but just in the definition of propositions. Temporal formulas and strategy expressions gain in generality.

Our proposal of giving transitions first-class citizenship is visually represented by making a box appear in the middle of every arrow representing a transition, with states in rounded shapes and transitions in rectangles—Petri-net style:

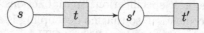

In this way, every element—state or transition—is explicit and can be treated the same. The same as only states were treated before. There remains an only source of discrimination: while a state can have several arrows going in and out, a transition only has one of each. Monogamy for her, polygamy for him. (But see section on future work.)

1.1 Related Work

Several temporal logics have been proposed that make joint use of actions and propositions on states: ACTL* [6], RLTL [18], SE-LTL [4], TLR* [16], ESTL [11]. There are also definitions of structures with mixed ingredients: LKS [4], L^2TS [5], Petri nets [17].

The best moves towards fairness we know of are the *temporal logic of rewriting*, TLR*, and the *event-and-state-based temporal logic*, ESTL, the former designed for rewriting logic and the latter for Petri nets. The explanations and examples in [16] and [11] are good arguments for an egalitarian view. In both cases, the point is that some properties of systems can only be directly specified if we can talk about states and transitions within the same logic. Our formula ASKB4USE above was inspired by an example in [11]. In another example, this time from [16], fairness for a rule ℓ is expressed by the formula:

$$\Box \Diamond \text{ enabled-}\ell \rightarrow \Box \Diamond \text{ taken-}\ell$$

The proposition enabled-ℓ is on states: it means that the current state of the system has the form needed to apply rule ℓ to it. But taken-ℓ is on transitions: it tells that the transition being executed is according to rule ℓ. Propositions on transitions are unavoidable. Or, rather, they are avoidable at the price of *cooking* the system (in Meseguer's terminology), making it artificially complex, so that some information about transitions is kept in states.

In ESTL, formulas are evaluated on *cuts* that are composed of places and transitions mixed together. A basic ESTL formula is a name of a place or of a transition. This is indeed an egalitarian view. What ESTL does not achieve is decoupling, as it uses literally names from the Petri net. We are not discussing

Petri nets, and egalitarian structures are not directly related to them, although at least part of our work can probably be adapted to them through the implementation on rewriting logic proposed in [15].

Rewriting logic is an appropriate formalism to be egalitarian, because, as pointed out in [15], transitions are represented by proof terms, in the same way as states are represented by state terms. We expand on this below. But TLR* stays a step away from our aim, because, while it uses atomic propositions on states, it uses proof-term patterns (called *spatial actions*) to express properties of transitions. These patterns are less powerful than general propositions (for an example, a pattern cannot represent the set of proof terms in which a given variable has been instantiated with an even integer). But the real drawback is that a TLR* formula is only meaningful for algebraically specified systems, and for a particular algebraic specification. Spatial actions use literally elements from the text of the specification, so that no decoupling is achieved. In contrast, formulas using propositions—on states, like in CTL*, or on transitions, as we advocate—are meaningful for any system where the atomic propositions can be defined, irrespective of the formalism used to specify it. Notably, we know of three implementations of model checkers for (the linear-time subset of) TLR*, and all of them propose some kind of propositions on transitions [1,2,13].

1.2   Our Contributions in This Paper

In Sect. 2, we propose *egalitarian structures*, and show how they encompass typical state-based and event-based structures. In Sect. 3, we show how systems (especially rewrite ones) can be given egalitarian semantics. In Sect. 4, we describe translations from egalitarian structures to state-based ones. Correspondingly, we describe a way to split each rule of a rewrite system into two *halves*, so that new states arise that represent the transitions of the original system. In Sect. 5, we show how also temporal logics can be translated, and how all this allows performing verification on the resulting state-based systems to draw conclusions about the original, egalitarian systems. In Sect. 6, we describe our implementation, that allows the specification and model checking of egalitarian structures in Maude. Sections on future work and conclusions complete the paper.

There is an extended version of this paper available at http://maude.sip. ucm.es/syncprod. The Maude code for our implementation and some examples can also be found there.

2   Egalitarian Structures

Let us recall the usual definitions of labeled transition system (LTS) and Kripke structure. An LTS is given by a tuple (S, Λ, δ), where S is the set of states, Λ the alphabet of actions, and $\delta : S \times \Lambda \to 2^S$ the non-deterministic transition function. A Kripke structure is given by a tuple (S, R, AP, L), where S is again the set of states, $R \subseteq S^2$ the transition relation, AP the set of atomic propositions, and $L : S \to 2^{\mathrm{AP}}$ the labeling function, that assigns to each state the set of propositions that hold true on it. Graphically:

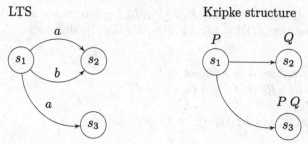

In some cases, both action names and atomic propositions on states are used in a mixed structure. We propose egalitarian structures as a generalization of all these cases. An *egalitarian structure* is given by a tuple $(S, T, R, \mathrm{AP}, L)$, where:

- S is the set of states;
- T is the set of transitions;
- $R \subseteq (S \times T) \cup (T \times S)$ is the bipartite accessibility relation that is functional on T, that is, for each $t \in T$ there are exactly one $s \in S$ and exactly one $s' \in S$ such that $(s, t) \in R$ and $(t, s') \in R$;
- AP is the set of atomic propositions on both states and transitions;
- $L : S \cup T \to 2^{\mathrm{AP}}$ is the labeling function for both states and transitions.

The same atomic proposition can be defined on states and on transitions in the same structure. Indeed, it is plausible that a proposition that is satisfied on several consecutive states also holds on the transitions between them. As pointed out in the introduction, the functionality of R on T is the only discriminatory requirement we allow.

Egalitarian structures generalize LTSs and Kripke structures. An LTS $\mathcal{L} = (S_{\mathcal{L}}, \Lambda_{\mathcal{L}}, \delta_{\mathcal{L}})$ can readily be made into an equivalent egalitarian structure $\mathcal{E}(\mathcal{L}) = (S_{\mathcal{E}}, T_{\mathcal{E}}, R_{\mathcal{E}}, \mathrm{AP}_{\mathcal{E}}, L_{\mathcal{E}})$ by defining:

- $S_{\mathcal{E}} := S_{\mathcal{L}}$;
- $T_{\mathcal{E}} := \{(s, \lambda, s') \in S_{\mathcal{L}} \times \Lambda_{\mathcal{L}} \times S_{\mathcal{L}} : s' \in \delta_{\mathcal{L}}(s, \lambda)\}$;
- $R_{\mathcal{E}}$ is given by $s\, R_{\mathcal{E}}\, (s, \lambda, s')$ and $(s, \lambda, s')\, R_{\mathcal{E}}\, s'$;
- $\mathrm{AP}_{\mathcal{E}} := \Lambda_{\mathcal{L}}$;
- $L_{\mathcal{E}}((s, \lambda, s')) := \{\lambda\}$, and $L_{\mathcal{E}}(s) := \emptyset$.

Graphically:

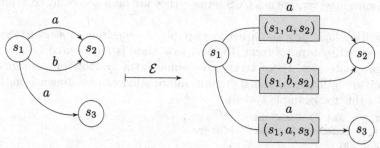

Atomic propositions in $\mathcal{E}(\mathcal{L})$ represent actions in $\mathcal{L}$, so it seems fitting that states are assigned no label. The equivalence between these two structures is left at the intuitive level and we do not care to make it formal in this paper.

A Kripke structure $\mathcal{K} = (S_\mathcal{K}, R_\mathcal{K}, \text{AP}_\mathcal{K}, L_\mathcal{K})$ can be made into an equivalent egalitarian structure $\mathcal{E}(\mathcal{K}) = (S_\mathcal{E}, T_\mathcal{E}, R_\mathcal{E}, \text{AP}_\mathcal{E}, L_\mathcal{E})$ by defining:

- $S_\mathcal{E} := S_\mathcal{K}$;
- $T_\mathcal{E} := R_\mathcal{K}$ (considered as a subset of ${S_\mathcal{K}}^2$);
- $R_\mathcal{E}$ is given by $s \, R_\mathcal{E} \, (s, s')$ and $(s, s') \, R_\mathcal{E} \, s'$;
- $\text{AP}_\mathcal{E} := \text{AP}_\mathcal{K}$;
- $L_\mathcal{E}(s) := L_\mathcal{K}(s)$, and $L_\mathcal{E}((s, s')) := L_\mathcal{K}(s) \cap L_\mathcal{K}(s')$.

Graphically:

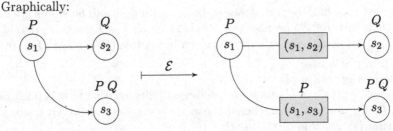

The choice $L_\mathcal{E}((s, s')) := L_\mathcal{K}(s) \cap L_\mathcal{K}(s')$ allows the continuity of satisfaction, that is, that a proposition true on two consecutive states is also true while traveling between them. Whether this is appropriate depends on the precise concept of equivalence between $\mathcal{K}$ and $\mathcal{E}(\mathcal{K})$, but, again, we do not care to make it formal. We will have something more to say on this below when dealing with rewriting logic.

3   Egalitarian Semantics for Rewrite Systems

The embedding of Kripke structures in egalitarian ones given above implies that any specification that is interpretable on the former can use the latter instead. The definition of transitions as pairs of states can be improved in some cases, because we can produce *objects* (read *terms*, if you prefer) that properly identify transitions without explicitly relying on the states around. In [3], for instance, it is shown how transitions in CCS can be represented by *proof terms* derived from the system of rules that implement the semantics of the language. These proof terms, however, are not CCS terms—they are built according to a different syntax.

Rewriting logic provides a better example. A transition in a rewrite system is represented by a proof term [15], just as a state is represented by a term of the appropriate sort. Proof terms need some extra symbols in the signature, but they are still terms, and structural information can be drawn from them. Consider this toy example system:

```
ops f g : Nat -> SomeSort .
op _+_ : SomeSort SomeSort -> State .
var N : Nat .
rl [a] : N => N + 1 .
rl [b] : f(N) => f(3) .
```

From the initial state `g(1) + f(2)` the three possible transitions are shown here, with their respective proof terms:

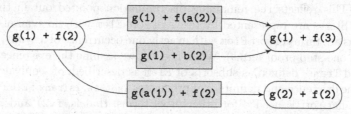

Each proof term includes the rule label in the context in which it is being applied, and with the values that instantiate the variables in the rule. Seen in this way, rewrite systems are naturally egalitarian, and are easily interpretable on egalitarian structures. (Indeed, as rewriting logic is well suited for implementing language syntax and semantics, proof terms become available for any language, if only in this indirect way.)

We propose a definition of rewrite system slightly different from the usual one, in order to make its egalitarian nature clearer, and also so that our ensuing exposition gets easier. Namely, we include in its signature the declaration of rule labels. It is not the definition of a more egalitarian kind of rewrite system, but a more egalitarian definition of the same concept.

In the setting of rewriting logic, the standard definition of a rewrite system (or rewrite theory) is given by a tuple $(S, O, E \cup Ax, R)$, where S is a set of declarations of sorts (sometimes with a subsort relation among them), O is a set of declarations of function symbols (operators), E is a set of equations, Ax is a set of equational attributes, and R is a set of rewrite rules. Sometimes, S and O are denoted together by Σ and called the *signature*.

The egalitarian definition of a rewrite system is a tuple $(S, O, L, E \cup Ax, R)$, where L, the only novelty, is a set of declarations of rule labels. As rule labels are used to identify transitions (by building proof terms), it is fair that they are declared, as operators are. Each rule-label declaration has the same form as an operator declaration, that is, it contains argument sorts and a result sort. For the example above, the rule label declarations would be:

```
lb a : Nat -> Nat .
lb b : Nat -> SomeSort .
```

The argument sorts are the ones of the variables that appear in the rule with that label (in their textual order if there are several variables, or the empty list of sorts if there are none). It is a requirement for any valid rewrite rule that both sides are terms of the same kind. We add to this that the result sort of the rule label has to be of the same kind as well. In a simple but typical case, both sides of the rule would be terms of the same sort `State`, and so will be the result sort of its label.

For verification and other purposes, one often assumes, in the standard setting, that S includes declarations for sorts `State` and `Prop`, and that O includes the infix symbol $\models$: `State` $\times$ `Prop` $\rightarrow$ `Bool`. For the egalitarian setting we assume the sort `Elem` to represent both states and proof terms. We also still need `Prop`.

Thus, the operator $\models$ is declared as $\models\,:\,$Elem $\times$ Prop $\to$ Bool. Any sort can include terms built using symbols from O and from L, but with either one or no symbol from L. (This reflects the remaining discrimination pointed out in the introduction.) States are represented by terms of sort Elem with no symbol from L; transitions are terms of sort Elem with exactly one occurrence of a symbol from L (so-called one-step proof terms). When needed, we assume the existence of sorts State and Trans, defined as subsorts of Elem as described; or, equivalently, we assume the existence and definition of predicates isState, isTrans : Elem $\to$ Bool. No particular sort is needed for other proof terms, that is, f(2) and b(2) are both of sort SomeSort. (More precise, though slightly different, algebraic definitions are given in [13].)

The semantic function, that we denote as $\mathcal{E}'$, is now easy. For a rewrite system $\mathcal{R} = (S_\mathcal{R}, O_\mathcal{R}, L_\mathcal{R}, E_\mathcal{R} \cup Ax_\mathcal{R}, R_\mathcal{R})$, its semantics are given by $\mathcal{E}'(\mathcal{R}) = (S_\mathcal{E}, T_\mathcal{E}, R_\mathcal{E}, \mathrm{AP}_\mathcal{E}, L'_\mathcal{E})$, where:

- $S_\mathcal{E} := T_{S_\mathcal{R} \cup O_\mathcal{R} / E_\mathcal{R} \cup Ax_\mathcal{R}, \text{State}}$ (terms of sort State modulo equations);
- $T_\mathcal{E} := T_{S_\mathcal{R} \cup O_\mathcal{R} \cup L_\mathcal{R} / E_\mathcal{R} \cup Ax_\mathcal{R}, \text{Trans}}$ (terms of sort Trans modulo equations);
- $R_\mathcal{E}$ is given by $s\,R_\mathcal{E}\,t$ and $t\,R_\mathcal{E}\,s'$ for each t that is a proof term for a one-step derivation from s to s';
- $\mathrm{AP}_\mathcal{E} := T_{S_\mathcal{R} \cup O_\mathcal{R} / E_\mathcal{R} \cup Ax_\mathcal{R}, \text{Prop}}$ (terms of sort Prop modulo equations);
- $L'_\mathcal{E}(s) := \{p \in \mathrm{AP}_\mathcal{E} : s \models p = \mathbf{true}$ modulo $E_\mathcal{R} \cup Ax_\mathcal{R}\}$, for $s \in S_\mathcal{E}$;
- $L'_\mathcal{E}(t) := L'_\mathcal{E}(s) \cap L'_\mathcal{E}(s')$ for $t \in T_\mathcal{E}$, and s, s' such that $s\,R_\mathcal{E}\,t$ and $t\,R_\mathcal{E}\,s'$.

The definition of the labeling, in particular, reflects the one for the embedding of Kripke structures in egalitarian ones given in the previous section to guarantee continuity of satisfaction. Thus, we have that this diagram commutes:

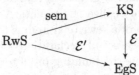

In it, we denote as RwS the class of rewrite systems, as KS the class of Kripke structures, and as EgS the class of egalitarian structures. Also, "sem" is the semantics based on term algebras described in [7], $\mathcal{E}$ is the embedding of Kripke structures in egalitarian ones from Sect. 2, and $\mathcal{E}'$ is the semantics just defined.

The labeling deserves a deeper thought. In a rewrite system, seen in an egalitarian way, atomic propositions and the equations defining them apply equally to states and to transitions. Often, a state and a neighboring transition have similar algebraic shapes, and that eases a continuous definition of satisfaction for them. In the simple example above, consider this proposition has-g1:

```
op has-g1 : Prop .
var E : Elem .
eq g(1) + E |= has-g1 = true .
eq E |= has-g1 = false [owise] .
```

This equational definition makes at once the proposition $\mathbf{true}$ for the transition g(1) + b(2) and for the state g(1) + f(2), and $\mathbf{false}$ for the transition g(a(1)) + f(2) and for the state g(2) + f(2).

Considering this, a better, more egalitarian, and more flexible definition of the labeling for any `Elem` e is:

- $L_{\mathcal{E}}(e) := \{p \in \mathrm{AP}_{\mathcal{E}} : e \models p = \text{true} \text{ modulo } E_{\mathcal{R}} \cup Ax_{\mathcal{R}}\}$.

The semantics of rewrite systems as egalitarian structures according to this labeling is denoted as $\mathcal{E}$ (instead of the previous $\mathcal{E}'$) from now on.

4   Translation to Familiar Grounds

We define now functions $\mathcal{K}$ and "split" so that the following diagram commutes:

$$
\begin{array}{ccc}
\text{EgRwS} & \xrightarrow{\;\;\mathcal{E}\;\;} & \text{EgS} \\
{\scriptstyle \text{split}}\Big\downarrow & & \Big\downarrow{\scriptstyle \mathcal{K}} \\
\text{RwS} & \xrightarrow[\text{sem}]{} & \text{KS}
\end{array}
$$

EgRwS is the class of rewrite systems defined in the egalitarian way. (More precisely, the diagram commutes only when monogamy of transitions is guaranteed; more on this below.)

Our aim is to benefit from tools and concepts available for the lower half of the diagram, and use them in the egalitarian systems and structures on the upper half. For instance, in Sect. 5 we define the satisfaction of a temporal formula on an egalitarian structure based on the standard satisfaction on a Kripke structure, and in Sect. 6 we use existing model checkers with a new mission.

Also note that, although rewriting logic is egalitarian in nature, as discussed above, because states and transitions are represented as like terms, Maude is not so, as proof terms are not Maude objects. The function "split", as we describe below, makes transitions appear as new states, allowing thus to be egalitarian in an indirect way. Our implementation, described in Sect. 6, is based on this idea.

Sometimes we call *split* systems or structures the ones that result from applying $\mathcal{K}$ or "split". Also, the states of a split system or structure that were originally a transition are called *t-states*; the others are *s-states*.

Transforming an egalitarian structure into a Kripke one is accomplished in this simple way:

$$
(S, T, R, \mathrm{AP}, L) \quad \xrightarrow{\;\;\mathcal{K}\;\;} \quad (S \cup T, R, \mathrm{AP}, L).
$$

That is, we make old states and transitions into new states. Visually, this is reflected by changing square shapes into rounded ones:

(Note that this is not the inverse of the embedding $\mathcal{E} : \mathrm{KS} \to \mathrm{RwS}$ given above.)

The transformation "split" on rewrite systems, designed to reflect $\mathcal{K}$, is more involved. The idea is removing each rule

| crl [ℓ] : $l(\overline{x}) \to r(\overline{x})$ if $C(\overline{y})$

and adding in its place

| crl [ℓ_1] : $l(\overline{x}) \to \ell(\overline{x}, \overline{y})$ if $C(\overline{y})$ and   rl [ℓ_2] : $\ell(\overline{x}, \overline{y}) \to r(\overline{x})$

with the straightforward simplification for non-conditional rules. The condition applies to the firing of the rule, not to its continuation. The variables in the tuple $\overline{y}$ are the new ones, not in $\overline{x}$, that appear in matching and rewriting conditions in C.

This splitting of a rule into two produces new states in the split rewrite system that correspond to the new states produced by $\mathcal{K}$. With rules a and b (from the beginning of Sect. 3) split in the way described, we get a rewrite system

```
rl [a1] : N => a(N) .
rl [a2] : a(N) => N + 1 .
rl [b1] : f(N) => b(N) .
rl [b2] : b(N) => f(3) .
```

whose standard Kripke semantics includes this:

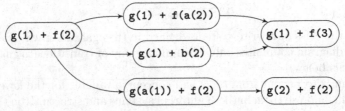

This is exactly $\mathcal{K}$ applied to the egalitarian structure for the original system, as drawn in Sect. 3.

More formally now, given $\mathcal{R} = (S_1, O_1, L_1, E_1 \cup Ax_1, R_1)$, we build split($\mathcal{R}$) = $(S_2, O_2, E_2 \cup Ax_2, R_2)$ by this series of steps:

1. S_2 is produced by renaming sorts State to SState, Trans to TState and Elem to State in S_1 (so SState and TState are subsorts of State); this renaming must be propagated all through the specification;
2. letting $O_2 := O_1 \cup L_1$ (that is, rule labels are transformed into operators);
3. letting $E_2 := E_1$, and $Ax_2 := Ax_1$;
4. splitting rules in R_1 to produce the ones in R_2, as explained above.

There is still a difficulty with the resulting system. For it to be equivalent to the original one, we need to ensure that half-rule ℓ_1 is always immediately followed by ℓ_2, for each original rule ℓ. Otherwise, another half-rule ℓ_1' could take place in between, a behavior not possible in the original system. Again, this reflects the discrimination of monogamy for transitions, polygamy for states.

A solution is restricting our attention to *topmost* rewrite systems. Many interesting rewrite systems are topmost or can be easily transformed into an equivalent one that is topmost and formally similar [9]. A topmost rewrite system is one in which all rewrites happen on the whole state term—not on its subterms. Formally, this is guaranteed by requiring that all rule labels have result sort Elem (or its subsort Trans), and that the sort Elem does not appear as argument in any constructor or rule label, so that no term of sort Elem can be subterm of another term of the same sort. In particular, this prevents that the left-hand side of a rule is a variable (of sort State). If this happened, the resulting proof term would have shape $\ell(S)$, for S of sort State, so the split system would not be topmost even though the original one was.

In a topmost system, the term $\ell(t_1, \ldots, t_n)$, resulting from applying the half-rule ℓ_1, can only be rewritten using half-rule ℓ_2, as we need. Or, this is so if there are no two rules with the same label and the same argument sorts. We assume that our systems fulfill this mild requirement. This is the same reasonable requirement made to overloaded function symbols.

We assume from now on that transition monogamy is guaranteed in split systems in some way. Thus, the diagram at the beginning of this section is commutative. The definitions have been chosen so that the proof of that result is straightforward.

5   Temporal Logics on Egalitarian Structures

As LTSs and Kripke structures can be seen as particular cases of egalitarian structures, any temporal logic designed for the former ones can also be interpreted on the latter. This includes HML [10] and the μ-calculus [12], and all the CTL* family [8]. More interestingly, mixed logics like ACTL* [6] that use at the same time action identifiers and atomic propositions on states, are interpretable on egalitarian structures.

As introduced above, we would like to define and verify the satisfaction of temporal formulas on egalitarian structures by translating the problem to well-known non-egalitarian settings. That is, we want temporal logics TL_1 and TL_2 and a translation σ to complete the previous diagram to this one:

$$
\begin{array}{ccccc}
\text{EgRwS} & \xrightarrow{\ \mathcal{E}\ } & \text{EgS} & & TL_1 \\
\text{split} \downarrow & & \downarrow \mathcal{K} & & \downarrow \sigma \\
\text{RwS} & \xrightarrow[\text{sem}]{} & \text{KS} & & TL_2
\end{array}
$$

TL_2 is any state-based logic, like LTL. In Meseguer's terminology [16], the maps

$$(\mathcal{K}, \sigma) : \text{EgS} \times TL_1 \to \text{KS} \times TL_2$$
$$(\text{split}, \sigma) : \text{EgRwS} \times TL_1 \to \text{RwS} \times TL_2$$

must be *faithful maps of tandems*, that is, the satisfaction relation must be preserved. Indeed, instead of giving a new, independent definition for semantics, we consider they are given by σ and define satisfaction on the upper half of the diagram as satisfaction of translations on the lower half:

$$\mathcal{R}, e \models_{\text{eg}} \varphi \quad \text{iff} \quad \text{split}(\mathcal{R}), e \models \sigma(\varphi).$$

Here, $\models_{\text{eg}}$ is the egalitarian satisfaction relation, $\mathcal{R}$ is an egalitarian rewrite system, e a state or transition, and φ a temporal formula. Remember that, for this definition of $\models_{\text{eg}}$ to work as expected, we need monogamous transitions in split$(\mathcal{R})$.

Raw LTL. The perfect temporal logic to play the role of TL_1 would also be egalitarian, to exploit the full potential of egalitarian structures. By that we mean a logic able to use propositions both on states and on transitions as its basic formulas, and to evaluate formulas on transitions. In a different way: we want σ to be onto. To the best of our knowledge, no such logic has been proposed, although TLR* [16] and SE-LTL [4] come close.

The obvious onto transformation is the identity: $TL_1 = TL_2 = LTL$ and $\sigma = $ id. Thus, for example, the *next* operator $\bigcirc$ has to be interpreted on an egalitarian structure as "in all outgoing transitions" when on a state, and "in the destination state" when on a transition. That gives the specifier full power. This is equally valid for state-based temporal logics other than LTL. The moral is: instead of (or in addition to) looking for new state-and-transition-based temporal logics, use well-known state-based logics on split systems.

From LTL$_{eg}$ to LTL. Consider a Kripke structure $\mathcal{K}$ and an LTL formula φ interpreted on $\mathcal{K}$. We can interpret φ on $\mathcal{E}(\mathcal{K})$, the embedding of $\mathcal{K}$ as egalitarian structure, by pretending that transitions are not present and jumping from state to state. Let us refer to LTL with these semantics on egalitarian structures as LTL$_{eg}$. We want to find the σ that makes faithful the map of tandems $(\mathcal{K}, \sigma)$: EgS $\times$ LTL$_{eg}$ $\rightarrow$ KS $\times$ LTL. From a practical point of view this is pointless, as it amounts to translating a problem $(\mathcal{K}, \varphi)$ on KS $\times$ LTL to the more complex one $(\mathcal{K}(\mathcal{E}(\mathcal{K})), \sigma(\varphi))$ on the same setting; but it is an interesting exercise.

The *next* operator $\bigcirc$ is originally only interested in states, so it must skip t-states. The translation σ must duplicate this operator: $\sigma(\bigcirc\varphi) := \bigcirc\bigcirc\sigma(\varphi)$. The *at all future times* operator $\square$, being an LTL operator, must rather be understood as *on all future states*. The translation σ must make it skip every second state, which is known to be non-doable in LTL [19]. We have to use the atomic proposition isTrans, true for t-states and false otherwise, and define $\sigma(\square\,\varphi) := \square(\text{isTrans} \vee \sigma(\varphi))$.

However, intuitively, something is wrong in the specification of a system if a property that is supposed to hold at all future times does not hold while transitions are being executed. If I am feeling sleepy until lunch and also after lunch, so would I be while having lunch. Remember the discussion at the end of Sect. 3 about the proposition has-g1. For another example, think of a system whose states are given as *soups* of objects, that is, independent objects tied by a commutative and associative operator (often represented by empty syntax). This could be such a state:

```
<client1, waiting, info1> <client2, running, info2> <server, client2>
```

We are interested in knowing whether some client is waiting. The proposition some-waiting can be defined like this:

```
eq <C, waiting, I> Rest |= some-waiting = true .
eq Conf |= some-waiting = false [owise] .
```

When client2 finishes its communication with the server, the system executes the rule

```
rl [finish] : <C, running, I> <server, C>
           => <C, finished, I> <server, noclient> .
```

and goes to state

| `<client1, waiting, info1> <client2, finished, info2> <server, noclient>`

by means of the transition

| `<client1, waiting, info1> finish(client2, info2)`

The point to note is that **some-waiting** is true, as defined, in both states and in the transition.

From TLR* to CTL*. The approach to propositions on transitions in TLR* is through the use of so-called *spatial actions*, that is, patterns for proof terms. A single rule label ℓ, for instance, is a valid spatial action. Variable instantiations and contexts for rewriting can also be specified. For each of these patterns, an equivalent atomic proposition on t-states can be defined. Equivalent in the sense that a t-state satisfies the proposition iff it matches the pattern. This was implemented in [1] and in [13]. We assume this equivalence, so that any spatial action appearing in a TLR* formula can appear as a proposition in a CTL* formula. (Defining a proposition equivalent to a single rule-label pattern involves exploring the proof term to search for the label at any nesting level. However, rules tend to be applied at particular spots in the term. Compare to operators: it is rare that we are interested in whether a particular operator appears at any nesting level on a state term, and then define atomic propositions according to it.)

In TLR*, propositions on states and spatial actions are clearly separate entities: the former are only tested on states, the latter only on transitions. But when interpreted on $\mathcal{K}(\mathcal{R})$ both are propositions on states. In order to be able to define σ, we need that $\mathcal{K}(\mathcal{R})$ includes two subsorts of **Prop**: **SProp** and **TProp**.

From TLR*'s point of view, a transition is tied to its origin state. Thus, if P_t is a **TProp** and P_s is an **SProp**, the formula $\bigcirc(P_t \wedge P_s)$ means "P_s must hold on the next state, and P_t must hold on the transition going out from that next state". Likewise, the formula $\square\, P_t$ means "P_t must hold in all future transitions".

This deserves formalization. Taking as primitive constructs for TLR* negation, disjunction, *next*, *until*, and existential quantification on paths, we define $\sigma : \text{TLR*} \to \text{CTL*}$ by:

- $\sigma(P) = P$, if P has sort **SProp**;
- $\sigma(P) = \bigcirc P$, if P has sort **TProp**;
- $\sigma(\neg\varphi) = \neg\sigma(\varphi)$;
- $\sigma(\varphi_1 \vee \varphi_2) = \sigma(\varphi_1) \vee \sigma(\varphi_2)$;
- $\sigma(\bigcirc\varphi) = \bigcirc\bigcirc\sigma(\varphi)$;
- $\sigma(\varphi_1 \, \mathbf{U} \, \varphi_2) = (\text{isState} \to \sigma(\varphi_1)) \, \mathbf{U} \, (\text{isState} \wedge \sigma(\varphi_2))$;
- $\sigma(\mathbf{E}\,\varphi) = \mathbf{E}\,\sigma(\varphi)$.

The proposition **isState**, as explained in Sect. 3, needs to be defined in $\mathcal{K}(\mathcal{E})$ as **true** on s-states and **false** on t-states.

The previous two examples defined new semantics for raw LTL and LTL$_{\text{eg}}$ through the translations σ. This case is different, because TLR* already has semantics [16]. It can be shown that these semantics agree. The proof is in the extended version of this paper.

6   Our Implementation

We have implemented in Maude the translation just defined, but restricted to the linear-time subset of TLR*, called LTLR, and to topmost systems. That is:

$$(\text{split}, \sigma) : \text{EgRwS} \times \text{LTLR} \rightarrow \text{RwS} \times \text{LTL}.$$

The implementation and some examples are available for download from our website: http://maude.sip.ucm.es/syncprod. The extended version of this paper, also available from our website, contains an appendix with detailed instructions for using the implementation.

The function "split" is implemented by a module operator SPLIT[ModName]. It produces a module with each original rule split into two, and with the original rule labels added as operators to the signature. Users, after coding a system module, say Orig, can import the split module by using protecting SPLIT[Orig]. Then, they have available sorts StateOrig (a renaming of the original State) and TransOrig, and also a new sort State, which is a supersort of the other two.

In the exposition in Sect. 3 we proposed the name Elem to include states and transitions. However, we want to be ready for our future developments in which we anticipate that nested module operators will be used. That is why we always assume that the input system has a sort named State, and we guarantee that the same is true for the produced system. Module operators observing this convention can be combined. For instance, SPLIT[SPLIT[Orig]] is a valid module expression.

If model checking is the aim, atomic propositions on s-states and t-states can be declared and their satisfaction defined by the usual means. The model-checking function, modelCheck, expects an LTL formula, that it interprets in the split module (without any consideration to the fact that it is a split module). We have implemented the syntax of LTLR and the translation σ described at the end of the previous section (except that we do not need quantification on paths, as we restrict to linear time). The function that performs the translation is called LTLR. We have not included in this implementation spatial actions, so our flavor of LTLR uses propositions on transitions and no spatial actions. The syntax for LTLR formulas has been defined with a symbol "@" attached to each logical symbol, to avoid clashes with LTL syntax: @True, @->, and so on. Not a beautiful choice, but acceptable for a prototype. The formula LTLR(@- P @-> Q), for example, can be used in the model checker, assuming propositions P and Q have been properly declared and defined, each one either of sort SProp or TProp.

To test the performance of our tool, we have found useful an example system about a communication channel described in [16]. The system contains a parameter, maxFaults, that limits the number of duplications and losses of messages the communication can suffer. This single number allows tuning the size of the state space and drawing some conclusions on the performance of the model checker.

We have chosen a pure LTL formula and have model checked it in the standard way. Then, we have split the system specification and translated the formula (considering it is in LTLR) and have model checked it again. In short, we are performing an equivalent model checking in a more involved and costly way. The aim is to get an idea of how much is lost in performance to pay for being egalitarian, for being interested in transitions. Part of the data is in this table:

	Standard LTL		Split	
maxFaults	States	Secs	States	Secs
7	26,077	1	202,686	2
9	61,676	1	518,097	4
11	129,695	3	1,157,874	10
13	249,981	8	2,344,098	30
15	450,261	33	4,396,666	105

(It must be noted that this system has an infinite number of reachable states. It is a surprise that Maude's model checker behaves gracefully on it. The reason must be that the system is finitely branching and that the property we try to verify is indeed satisfied in finite time in every computation.)

According to the table, the transitions in the original system seem to outnumber the states, and this results in large split systems. Each state on the split system needs less mean time to be processed than each state on the original, presumably because t-states have unique in and out arrows.

Note that this extra complexity is not introduced by our splitting translation, but by our egalitarian view. Transitions have to be explored, either as such transitions or as new states after the translation.

6.1   An Alternative Translation

Already in [16], Meseguer proposed a different translation from TLR* to CTL*, with a corresponding translation of rewrite systems. It was later implemented in Maude by Bae for LTLR in [2], with the explicit aim of using Maude's LTL model checker. Both their translation and their implementation differ from ours.

They include in each state the information about the transition that took to it. If a given state has several transitions leading to it, the resulting system has a copy of the state for each such transition. The number of states added is usually much larger in our translation, but each state is more complex in theirs. This is a different way to pay for being interested in transitions.

The translation of temporal formulas is based on the replacement of each occurrence of a proposition on transitions P by $\bigcirc P$: what was a property of a transition associated to the current state, becomes a property of the *transition part* of the next state.

Their implementation does not require the system to be topmost. Our own translation, on the other hand, seems more intuitive, because it just adds new states in each arrow, without really changing the structure. Consider this simple system (on the left), our translation (in the middle), and theirs (on the right):

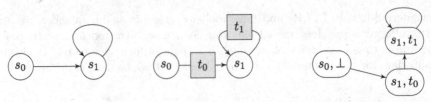

The implementation in [2] works at the metalevel, as does the theoretical description in [16]. Basically, they emulate the original rewrite system with a single rule $\mathtt{rl}\ t \rightarrow \mathtt{next}(t)$, with the function $\mathtt{next}$ doing all the work and the term t including all the information about the original module, the current state, and some bookkeeping needed for the emulation. In contrast, we use the metalevel to produce a new object-level module, which we then model check. Obtaining modules at the object level is important for us because, as noted above, we foresee we will be using nested module operators in the future.

Our method's performance is better on the systems we have tested. This is most probably due to the fact that we work at the object level, with simpler terms being rewritten. The following data comes from model checking the same communication-channel system cited above, this time with a formula containing a proposition on transitions (resp., a spatial action):

maxFaults	Our method		[2]'s method	
	States	Secs	States	Secs
2	3,886	0	2,406	2
3	35,459	1	20,281	25
4	77,804	2	42,937	57
5	332,256	12	172,510	278
6	568,066	30	not run	

It has to be noted that Bae and Meseguer took one more step and modified Maude's model checker at the C++ level to allow for model checking LTLR directly.

7 Future Work

We want to point out three directions in which our proposals could be profitable. We intend to pursue some of them in the near future.

Concurrent Proof Terms. The persistence of a discrimination in the definition of egalitarian systems is a hint that we are midway to somewhere. Remember the discrimination: transitions have unique in and out arrows. Bipartite alternating automata—or any bipartite structures—can be seen as extensions of egalitarian structures where the discrimination has been dropped in a particular way.

In a different spirit, Petri nets also represent a generalization of our egalitarian structures, allowing several arrows in and out of a transition.

Removing the *topmost* requirement seems more interesting, thus allowing several rules to be *executing* simultaneously. For instance, the toy system we used above, with the rule `rl [a] : N => N + 1`, allows the derivation

$$f(1) + g(1) \quad \longrightarrow \quad f(a(1)) + g(1) \quad \longrightarrow \quad f(a(1)) + g(a(1))$$

This last term represents two concurrent executions of rule `a`. Suppose `f` and `g` represent two components of a software system, and the argument is their version number. Rule `a` is version updating for each component. It happens, however, that version 2 of each component is only compatible with version 2 of the other. Any sequential, interleaved execution (like the ones performed by Maude's engine) necessarily visits a state with incompatibility. This same engine will find the right way on a split system.

Synchronization and Strategies. In [14], we study the possibility of synchronized execution of several Maude systems. In principle, the synchronization happens on states by agreement on their propositions, but on transitions only by identity of rule labels. This is often not enough, and having propositions on transitions opens interesting possibilities.

A use of such synchronized execution will be the implementation of strategic control. Strategy languages for rewrite systems usually include rule labels to denote actions, but more general tests (or propositions) on states. The use of propositions on transitions, as already pointed, would allow decoupling the tasks of system specification and strategy design. If, for example, the system is refined, or modified in some way, the definition of the propositions can also be modified correspondingly, with no change in the name or meaning of the propositions, let alone in the formulas to be verified.

Shrinking the Size of Systems. Several methods for shrinking the size of systems, especially with model checking in mind, are in common use: invisible-transition collapse, partial order reduction, equational abstraction, folding abstractions, well-structured transition systems. Some of them focus only on states and others only on transitions. An egalitarian view could result in new insights.

8 ˙ Conclusion

We have tried to convince the reader that granting to transitions all the privileges enjoyed by states can help in specification and verification tasks. In particular, we advocate for the free use of atomic propositions on transitions, as well as on states. Mixing both kinds of propositions helps make specifications, both of systems and of their temporal properties, more powerful and intuitive. Indeed, it allows to definitely decouple specification tasks from verification ones: entities from the system specification are not used literally in formulas, because propositions provide an interface. For strategy languages, propositions on transitions make it possible to give general meaning to strategies, independent from the particular formalization of the system to be controlled.

Structures that allow general propositions on transitions are not common. Egalitarian structures are designed to play this role, and labeled transition systems and Kripke structures can be embedded in them. Rewriting logic is particularly well suited for an egalitarian view, that is, there are natural semantics from rewrite systems as egalitarian structures.

There are ways to apply existing tools and concepts to egalitarian structures. Faithful maps of tandems can be given from egalitarian structures and logics to better-known settings. This paper presents a prototype implementation in Maude, allowing the specification of egalitarian systems and their verification using the available LTL model checker.

Acknowledgements. It is comforting to realize how much a paper can improve with the help of capable referees. We are most grateful to ours.

References

1. Bae, K., Meseguer, J.: The linear temporal logic of rewriting Maude model checker. In: Ölveczky, P.C. (ed.) WRLA 2010. LNCS, vol. 6381, pp. 208–225. Springer, Heidelberg (2010)
2. Bae, K., Meseguer, J.: A rewriting-based model checker for the linear temporal logic of rewriting. In: Kniesel, G., Pinto, J.S. (eds.) Rule 2008. ENTCS, vol. 290, pp. 19–36. Elsevier (2012)
3. Boudol, G., Castellani, I.: A non-interleaving semantics for CCS based on proved transitions. Fundamenta Informaticae **11**, 433–452 (1988)
4. Chaki, S., Clarke, E.M., Ouaknine, J., Sharygina, N., Sinha, N.: State/event-based software model checking. In: Boiten, E.A., Derrick, J., Smith, G.P. (eds.) IFM 2004. LNCS, vol. 2999, pp. 128–147. Springer, Heidelberg (2004)
5. De Nicola, R., Vaandrager, F.: Three logics for branching bisimulation. J. ACM **42**(2), 458–487 (1995)
6. De Nicola, R., Vaandrager, F.W.: Action versus state based logics for transition systems. In: Guessarian, I. (ed.) Semantics of Systems of Concurrent Processes. LNCS, vol. 469, pp. 407–419. Springer, Heidelberg (1990)
7. Eker, S., Meseguer, J., Sridharanarayanan, A.: The Maude LTL model checker. In: Gadducci, F., Montanari, U. (eds.) WRLA 2002. ENTCS, vol. 71, pp. 162–187. Elsevier (2004)
8. Emerson, E.A., Halpern, J.Y.: "Sometimes" and "not never" revisited: on branching versus linear time temporal logic. J. ACM **33**(1), 151–178 (1986)
9. Escobar, S., Meseguer, J.: Symbolic model checking of infinite-state systems using narrowing. In: Baader, F. (ed.) RTA 2007. LNCS, vol. 4533, pp. 153–168. Springer, Heidelberg (2007)
10. Hennessy, M., Milner, R.: Algebraic laws for nondeterminism and concurrency. J. ACM **32**(1), 137–161 (1985)
11. Kindler, E., Vesper, T.: ESTL: a temporal logic for events and states. In: Desel, J., Silva, M. (eds.) ICATPN 1998. LNCS, vol. 1420, pp. 365–384. Springer, Heidelberg (1998)

12. Kozen, D.: Results on the propositional μ-calculus. TCS **27**(3), 333–354 (1983)
13. Martín, Ó., Verdejo, A., Martí-Oliet, N.: Model checking TLR* guarantee formulas on infinite systems. In: Iida, S., Meseguer, J., Ogata, K. (eds.) Specification, Algebra, and Software. LNCS, vol. 8373, pp. 129–150. Springer, Heidelberg (2014)
14. Martín, Ó., Verdejo, A., Martí-Oliet, N.: Synchronous products of rewrite systems. Technical report, Facultad de Informática, Universidad Complutense de Madrid (2016). http://maude.sip.ucm.es/syncprod
15. Meseguer, J.: Conditional rewriting logic as a unified model of concurrency. TCS **96**(1), 73–155 (1992)
16. Meseguer, J.: The temporal logic of rewriting: a gentle introduction. In: Degano, P., De Nicola, R., Meseguer, J. (eds.) Concurrency, Graphs and Models. LNCS, vol. 5065, pp. 354–382. Springer, Heidelberg (2008)
17. Reisig, W.: Petri Nets: An Introduction. EATCS Monographs on TCS, vol. 4. Springer, Heidelberg (1985)
18. Sánchez, C., Samborski-Forlese, J.: Efficient regular linear temporal logic using dualization and stratification. In: Reynolds, M., Terenziani, P., Moszkowski, B. (eds.) Proceedings of TIME 2012, pp. 13–20. IEEE (2012)
19. Wolper, P.: Temporal logic can be more expressive. Inf. Control **56**(1–2), 72–99 (1983)

Towards Generic Monitors for Object-Oriented Real-Time Maude Specifications

Antonio Moreno-Delgado[1]($\boxtimes$), Francisco Durán[1], and José Meseguer[2]

[1] University of Málaga, Málaga, Spain
{amoreno,duran}@lcc.uma.es
[2] University of Illinois at Urbana-Champaign, Champaign, USA
meseguer@illinois.edu

Abstract. Non-Functional Properties (NFPs) are crucial in the design of software. Specification of systems is used in the very first phases of the software development process for the stakeholders to make decisions on which architecture or platform to use. These specifications may be analyzed using different formalisms and techniques, simulation being one of them. During a simulation, the relevant data involved in the analysis of the NFPs of interest can be measured using monitors. In this work, we show how monitors can be parametrically specified so that the instrumentation of specifications to be monitored can be automatically performed. We prove that the original specification and the automatically obtained specification with monitors are bisimilar by construction. This means that the changes made on the original system by adding monitors do not affect its behavior. This approach allows us to have a library of possible monitors that can be safely added to analyze different properties, possibly on different objects of our systems, at will.

1   Introduction

As system complexity grows, specification of systems becomes an even more important task during the first phases of the software life cycle. With the proliferation of distributed systems due to Cloud-computing systems, Internet of Things, etc., with software being present in all activities of our lives, Non-Functional Properties (NFPs) are gaining relevance in design decisions.

Specification of software and its simulation can be used to get insights about how the system is going to behave. Furthermore, by adding monitors or observers to system specifications, software engineers can analyze those NFPs of interest [9]. System specifications have to be instrumented in order to get probes of executions. One may think of different NFPs, such as response time, throughput, mean cycle time or rate of failures. However, different NFPs have to be monitored by different observers, and such observers are typically hard-coded in the specifications.

To cope with this lack of modularity, many alternatives have been proposed. For example, in Aspect-Oriented Programming, code is instrumented by monitors as a cross-cutting concern. Other works, as the one presented in [16], propose

© Springer International Publishing Switzerland 2016
D. Lucanu (Ed.): WRLA 2016, LNCS 9942, pp. 118–133, 2016.
DOI: 10.1007/978-3-319-44802-2_7

adding observers as new elements (objects) of the language. See [17] for a discussion of how to monitor non-functional properties in component-based systems.

In most cases, and even with more emphasis in the case of distributed or concurrent systems, these specifications are written with, among others, the purpose of verification. Different kinds of verification can be achieved depending on the desired level of evidence and precision in the proofs. Furthermore, some formalisms are more amenable to perform some proofs or checks than others. For example, a specification in Promela/Spin [8] is more amenable to perform model-checking that a specification in UML. Likewise, a specification in Coq [1] is well-suited to perform theorem-proving. This means that a tight dependence between formalisms and the verification one can perform exists. Among all kind of formalisms, we find very attractive those which can be executed, since the software engineers involved in the software development can get insights on where they are failing or on which parts they have to stress.

Execution of a system specification means that the system at hand can be simulated in the very first phases of software design, and, at very low additional cost, software engineers can test different designs and approaches, thus getting insight about how the system is going to fulfill the required NFPs. However, to analyze the behavior of a system under simulation, we have to measure the properties we want to study.

Rewriting logic [10] provides a formal framework where concurrent and distributed systems can be naturally defined. Since the specification remains within a formal environment, different kinds of verification can be performed: confluence, model-checking, reachability analysis or invariant analysis. Additionally, rewriting logic specifications are executable, providing prototypes that can be simulated and tested.

In this work we propose the definition of monitors in a very general way. If monitors are defined following certain guidelines, their addition to any real-time object-oriented specification is automatic, and what more important, the original behavior of the system after being instrumented is not changed.

We focus on object-oriented modules that must be defined using Real-Time Maude [14], since the main applications we envision are real-time and stochastic systems. On these specifications, we are interested in measuring system properties, i.e., properties that affect the whole system as throughput, and individual properties, i.e., properties related to concrete objects as traffic or utilization.

Monitors can be defined just by querying data. Thus, we give a skeleton Maude module which can be used to define any kind of monitor query by specifying the data structure to use and the query to perform.

Besides the theoretical results, a tool in the rewriting logic language Maude is presented to include generically defined monitors to system specifications. Using the reflective capabilities of Maude, we have defined module operations that take the specifications to be analized and the generic monitors to be used on them, and generate new modules with the instrumented specifications. We have used the extensibility capabilities of Full Maude [4,6] to provide a new module expression giving access to such module operation. Thus, we can not only automatically instrument our specifications with reusable monitors, but also use them in our specifications and commands as any other module.

The rest of the paper is structured as follows. Section 2 presents the rewriting logic language Maude and its Real-Time Maude extension, which allows us to define systems with time annotations. Section 3 presents the structure of monitors we use and basic principles of the approach. Section 4 presents the automatic transformation and the module operation implementing it. Section 5 provides the proof for bisimilarity between the original specification and the instrumented one. Section 6 provides one additional example. Section 7 wraps up the paper with some conclusions and ideas for further extensions and improvements.

2   Maude and Real-Time Maude

Maude [2,3] is an executable formal specification language based on rewriting logic [10], a logic of change that can naturally deal with states and non-deterministic concurrent computations. A rewrite logic theory is a tuple (Σ, E, R), where (Σ, E) is an *equational theory* that specifies the system states as elements of the initial algebra $T_{(\Sigma, E)}$, and R is a set of rewrite rules that describe the one-step possible concurrent transitions in the system.

Rewriting operates on congruence classes of terms modulo E. This of course does not mean that an implementation of rewriting logic must have an E-matching algorithm for each equational theory E that a user might specify. The equations E are divided into a set A of structural axioms for which matching algorithms are available and a set E of equations. Then, for having a complete agreement between the specification's initial algebra and its operational semantics by rewriting, a rewrite theory $(\Sigma, E \cup A, R)$ is assumed to be such that the set E of equations is (ground) Church-Rosser and terminating modulo A, and the rules R are (ground) coherent with the equations E modulo A (see [5,7]).

Maude provides support for rewriting modulo associativity, commutativity and identity, which perfectly captures the evolution of systems made up of objects linked by references. Maude has a rich set of verification and validation tools, and its use is widespread in many fields of research. Furthermore, Maude has demonstrated to be a good environment for rapid prototyping, and also for application development (see [3]).

Among the tools and extensions of Maude, one interesting tool for specifying distributed and concurrent systems is Real-Time Maude [14], a rewriting-logic-based specification language and formal analysis tool that supports the formal specification and analysis of *real-time systems*. Real-Time Maude provides a sort Time to model the time domain, which can be either discrete or dense. Then, passage of time is modelled with *tick rules* of the form

$$\texttt{crl}\,[l] : \{t, T\} => \{t', T + \tau\}\,\texttt{if}\,C.$$

where t and t' are system states, T is the global time, and τ is a term of sort Time that denotes the *duration* of the rewrite, and that advances by τ the *global time elapse*. Since tick rules advance the global time, in Real-Time Maude time elapse is usually modeled by one single tick rule, and the system dynamic behavior by instantaneous transitions [14]. Although there are other sampling strategies, in the most convenient one this single tick rule models time elapse by using two functions: the `delta` function, that defines the effect of time elapse over every model element, and the `mte` (maximal time elapse) function, that defines the maximum amount of time that can elapse before any action can be performed. Then, time can advance non-deterministically by any time amount τ, which must be less than or equal to the maximum time elapse of the system.

$$\text{crl [tick]} : \{t, T\} => \{\text{delta}(t, \tau), T + \tau\} \text{ if } 0 < \tau \leq \text{mte}(t) \wedge C.$$

3   General Monitors

In this section we present our proposal for the specification of system-independent monitors. Given a Real-Time Maude object-oriented system specification we provide operations to automatically add objects to measure different properties. We distinguish two types of properties, namely, those on individual objects, e.g., the number of messages received by each node in a network, or the number of defective pieces produced by each machine in a production line, and those on global systems, e.g., the average time taken by messages in reaching their destination or the average failure rate of the machines in a system. We handle both cases uniformly by assuming that there are classes in our specification whose objects "represent" the subsystems being monitored. For instance, we might assume that our network of nodes has a *net* object with references to all the nodes in it. This would allow us to use an individual monitor associated to the net object instead of a system monitor associated to all the node objects. This might be the case if we wanted to consider, for instance, multiple nets in the same system and separately monitor information on them.

We assume a Real-Time Maude object-oriented specification, with a flat configuration of objects and messages (i.e., no nested configurations) and with all rewrite rules of the system defined on terms of sort `System`, that is, on terms of the form {*Conf, T*}, with *Conf* a flat configuration and *T* a term of sort `Time`.

To present and illustrate our monitors, we use a very simple specification of a messaging system, shown in Fig. 1, where we have interconnected nodes, some of which belong to a subclass a message creator nodes, which create messages to be delivered through the net via specific neighbors. The `Node` class is defined with an attribute `neighbors` of type `List{Oid}`. Its `MsgCreator` subclass has, in addition, attributes `targets`, with the identifiers of the nodes it may be addressing messages to, and a `counter` to limit the number of generated messages. The `Net` class represents the entire net of nodes. It has an attribute `elems` with the identifiers of the nodes in the net. Messages are of the form `to T via N`, without sender identifier nor any contents to simplify the specification, where `T` is the identifier of the target node and `N` is the neighbor node the message is being sent through. The auxiliary operation `pickOne` is used to select an element in a list, which will be used in the `create-msg` and `resend-msg` rules to randomly select

```
omod SMP is
 pr NAT-TIME-DOMAIN-WITH-INF .
 inc RANDOM + COUNTER .
 pr LIST{Oid} .

 var   Msg : Msg .                      vars O O1 ON : Oid .
 var   VCreator : MsgCreator .          var   VNode : Node .
 var   VNet : Net .                     vars T T' : TimeInf .
 vars L L' EL EL' : List{Oid} .         var   N : Nat .
 var   Atts : AttributeSet .            var   Conf : Configuration .

 sort System .
 op {_,_} : Configuration TimeInf -> System [ctor] .

 class Net | elems : List{Oid} .
 class Node | neighbors : List{Oid} .
 class MsgCreator | targets : List{Oid}, counter : Nat .
 subclass MsgCreator < Node .
 msg to_via_ : Oid Oid -> Msg .

 op delay : Msg Time -> Msg .
 eq delay(Msg, 0) = Msg .

 rl [create-msg] :
   { < ON : VNet | elems : (EL O EL') >
     < O : VCreator | targets : L, neighbors : L',
       counter : s(N), Atts > Conf, T }
   =>
   { < ON : VNet | elems : (EL O EL') >
     < O : VCreator | targets : L, neighbors : L', counter : N, Atts >
     delay(to pickOne(L, random(counter) rem size(L))
            via pickOne(L', random(counter) rem size(L')),
          random(counter) rem 500)
     Conf, T } .
 rl [get-msg] : { < ON : VNet | elems : (EL O EL') >
                  < O : VNode | Atts > (to O via O1) Conf, T }
   => { < ON : VNet | elems : (EL O EL') >
        < O : VNode | Atts > Conf, T } .
 crl [resend-msg] : { < ON : VNet | elems : (EL O EL') >
                      < O : ,VNode | neighbors : L, Atts >
                      (to O1 via O) Conf, T }
   => { < ON : VNet | elems : (EL O EL') >
        < O : VNode | neighbors : L, Atts >
        delay(to O1 via pickOne(L, random(counter) rem size(L)),
              random(counter) rem 5) Conf, T }
   if O =/= O1 .

 op pickOne : List{Oid} Nat ~> Oid .
 eq pickOne(O L, 0) = O .
 eq pickOne(O L, s(N)) = pickOne(L, N) .

 op mte : Configuration -> TimeInf .
 eq mte(delay(Msg, T) Conf) = min(T, mte(Conf)) .
 eq mte((to O via O1) Conf) = 0 .
 eq mte(Conf) = INF [owise] .

 op delta : Configuration Time -> Configuration .
 eq delta(delay(Msg, T) Conf, T')
   = delay(Msg, T monus T') delta(Conf, T') .
 eq delta(Conf, T) = Conf [owise] .

 crl [tick] : { Conf, T } => { delta(Conf, T'), T + T' }
   if T' := mte(Conf) /\ 0 < T' /\ T' < INF .
endom
```

Fig. 1. Specification of a simple messaging system

```
omod MONITOR is
 pr CONFIGURATION .
 pr NAT-TIME-DOMAIN-WITH-INF .
 sort Data .
 class @Monitor | o : Object, data : Data .
 op eval : Data Time Object Configuration Configuration Configuration
      -> Data .
 op mon : Oid -> Oid [ctor] .
endom
```

Fig. 2. Core of monitors

elements in the list of targets and neighbors. The `create-msg` rule creates a new message addressed to a random target via a random neighbor, the `get-msg` specifies the reception of a message by its addressee, and the `resend-msg` rule specifies the action in which a node receives a message that is not addressed for it and resends it via one of its neighbors. Note that such rule will resend the message via one of its randomly chosen neighbors. Delays in message delivery is specified with the usual `delay` operator (see [14]). Real-Time Maude's `tick` rule and `mte` and `delta` functions are defined as usual.

Inspired by the works on wrapper objects, and specifically on the Onion-Skin pattern [11, 13], we add monitors to our specification by means of wrappers. We will show a generic monitor structure that, by specifying the definition of the *data structure* and the query for the monitor to use, can be instantiated to a concrete monitor to be added to our system.

Each object to be monitored is wrapped inside a monitor object that will observe its behavior and will collect the required information on it. This generic monitor structure is defined by the `MONITOR` module in Fig. 2. There is a class `@Monitor` whose instances will wrap objects in their o attributes. The data of the monitor is stored in the attribute `data`, of sort `Data`, to be later instantiated depending on the specific kind of monitor defined. There is an operation `eval`, that will be used to recalculate the monitored information, depending on the

```
omod TRAFFIC-MONITOR is
 inc MONITOR .
 pr NAT .
 subsort Nat < Data .

 var  N : Nat .
 var  T : Time .
 var  Obj : Object .
 vars LConf RConf GConf : Configuration .

 eq eval(N, T, Obj, LConf, RConf, GConf)
   = N + #msgs(LConf) .

 op #msgs : Configuration -> Nat .
 eq #msgs(Msg Conf) = s(#msgs(Conf)) .
 eq #msgs(Conf) = 0 [owise] .
endom
```

Fig. 3. Traffic monitors

actions specified in individual rules, with parameters: (i) the current monitor's data, (ii) the time at which the expression is evaluated, (iii) the monitored object in the LHS of the rule, (iv) the objects and messages explicitly stated in the rule's LHS, (v) the objects and messages in the rule's RHS, and (vi) the rest of the LHS' configuration. The individual monitor of an object with identifier O will have identifier $\mathrm{mon}(O)$.

Specific monitors can be defined by specifying of the function *eval*, which could be defined over any data structure, just by appropriately subsorting the sort *Data*. For example, given the simple messaging system specified in the module in Fig. 1, we may count the number of messages received by each of the nodes

```
var   Msg : Msg .                 vars O O1 ON : Oid :
var   VCreator : MsgCreator .     var   VNode : Node .
vars L L' EL EL' : List{Oid} .    var   N : Nat .
vars Atts @Atts : AttributeSet .  var   Conf : Configuration .
vars T T' : TimeInf .             var   VNet : Net .
var   @D : Data .

rl [create-msg] :
  { < ON : VNet | elems : (EL O EL') >
    < mon(O) : @Monitor |
      o : < O : VCreator |
             targets : L, neighbors : L', counter : s(N) > >
    Conf , T }
  =>
  { < ON : VNet | elems : (EL O EL') >
    < mon(O) : @Monitor |
      o : < O : VCreator |
             targets : L, neighbors : L', counter : N > >
    delay(to pickOne(L, random(counter) rem size(L))
            via pickOne(L', random(counter) rem size(L')),
          random(counter) rem 500)
    Conf , T } .
rl [get-msg] : { < ON : VNet | elems : (EL O EL') >
                   < mon(O) : @Monitor | o : < O : VNode | Atts > >
                   (to O via O1) Conf, T }
  => { < ON : VNet | elems : (EL O EL') >
         < mon(O) : @Monitor | o : < O : VNode | Atts > > Conf, T } .
crl [resend-msg] : { < ON : VNet | elems : (EL O EL') >
                       < mon(O) : @Monitor |
                         o : < O : VNode | neighbors : L >,
                         data : @D >
                       (to O1 via O) Conf, T }
  => { < ON : VNet | elems : (EL O EL') >
         < mon(O) : @Monitor |
           o : < O : VNode | neighbors : L >,
           data : eval(@D, T,
                   < O : VNode | neighbors : L >,
                   (< ON : VNet | elems : (EL O EL') >
                   < O : VNode | neighbors : L > (to O1 via O)),
                   (< ON : VNet | elems : (EL O EL') >
                   < O : VNode | neighbors : L >
                   delay(to O1
                           via pickOne(L, random(counter) rem size(L)),
                           random(counter) rem 5)),
                   Conf) >
         delay(to O1 via pickOne(L, random(counter) rem size(L)),
               random(counter) rem 5) Conf, T }
  if O =/= O1 .
```

Fig. 4. Rules of the simple messaging system with individual monitors

in the system by wrapping each of them inside monitor objects as in Fig. 4, and by defining the `eval` function in a module `TRAFFIC-MONITOR` extending the `MONITOR` module, given an auxiliary `#msgs` function which counts the number of messages in a configuration, as shown in Fig. 3. Note that the `data` attribute remains unchanged in the `create-msg` rule, but it is recalculated in rules `get-msg` and `resend-msg`, those rules in which node objects receive messages.

The `subsort` relation states the data type of the monitor data. This monitor is going to store only a natural number, used to count the number of messages the node at hand has processed. Note that the operation `eval` is total and it will increment the natural number stored in the monitor with the number of messages in the rule's LHS.

By rewriting our initial configuration with our nodes wrapped inside monitor objects using the rules in Fig. 4, we get a final configuration in which the `data` attributes of each of the monitor objects contains the number of messages received by that node.

4   Construction of the Instrumented Specification

The construction of instrumented specifications has been automated by providing a module expression `MONITOR` that takes as arguments the specification to be monitored, the class whose objects are to be wrapped, the set of rules on which the measures are to be evaluated, and a concrete monitor to apply to it, in which the `Data` sort and the `eval` functions are defined, and that produces the corresponding new module. The module expression is integrated in Full Maude and is handled as any other module expression [6].

Given an object-oriented system specification S, a class C, a set of rule labels LS, and a concrete monitor M, the rewrite theory $M[S, C, LS, E]$ denotes the system S but now instrumented with the monitor E as follows:

- $M[S, C, LS, E]$ includes both S and M, plus transformed copies of the rules of S so that each rule of the form

```
crl [L] : { < O : C' | Atts > Conf , T }
    => { < O : C' | Atts' > Conf' , T }
  if Cond .
```

with C' a subclass of C or C itself, and L in LS, generates a new rule

```
crl [L] :
    { < mon(O) : Monitor | o : < O : C | Atts >, data : D > Conf , T }
    =>
    { < mon(O) : Monitor |
        o : < O : C | Atts' >,
        data : eval(D , T ,
                    < O : C | Atts >,
                    Conf ,
                    < O : C | Atts' > Conf') >
      Conf' ,
      T }
  if Cond .
```

- All other occurrences of objects

$< O : C \mid Atts >$

of subclasses of C in rules, equations and memberships will be rewritten as

`< mon(O) : Monitor | o : < O : C | Atts >, data : D >`.

- All other objects in rules are left as they were.
- In case multiple objects appear in the same rule/equation/membership, different D variables will be consistently used. E.g., if L is not in LS, for a rule with two objects of class C in its left-hand side, the following rule will be generated:

```
crl [L] :
  { < mon(O1) : Monitor | o : < O1 : C | Atts1 >, data : D1 >
    < mon(O2) : Monitor | o : < O2 : C | Atts2 >, data : D2 >
  Conf, T }
  =>
  { < mon(O1) : Monitor | o : < O1 : C | Atts1' >, data : D1 >
    < mon(O2) : Monitor | o : < O2 : C | Atts2' >, data : D2 >
  Conf', T }
```

Note that:

- Those rules with no objects in subclasses of C remain as in the original module, and
- There might be more than one object in subclasses of C in the lefthand side of a rule, in which case the above transformation has to be applied to each of them, that is, we must consider all possible matches of the above pattern. E.g., given a rule

```
crl [L] :
  { < O1 : C1 | Atts1 >
    < O2 : C2 | Atts2 >
  Conf, T }
  =>
  { < O1 : C1 | Atts1' >
    < O2 : C2 | Atts2' >
  Conf', T }
  if Cond .
```

with $C1$ and $C2$ subclasses of C and L in LS, we get the rule

```
crl [L] :
  { < mon(O1) : Monitor | o : < O1 : C1 | Atts1 >, data : D1 >
    < mon(O2) : Monitor | o : < O2 : C2 | Atts2 >, data : D2 >
  Conf, T }
  =>
  { < mon(O1) : Monitor |
        o : < O1 : C1 | Atts1' >,
        data : eval(D1, T,
                      < O1 : C1 | Atts1 >,
                      < O2 : C2 | Atts2 > Conf,
                      < O1 : C1 | Atts1' > < O2 : C2 | Atts2' > Conf') >
    < mon(O2) : Monitor |
        o : < O2 : C2 | Atts2' >,
        data : eval(D2, T,
                      < O2 : C2 | Atts2 >,
                      < O1 : C1 | Atts1 > Conf,
                      < O1 : C1 | Atts1' > < O2 : C2 | Atts2' > Conf') >
  Conf', T }
  if Cond .
```

Given the SMP module shown in Fig. 1 and the module TRAFFIC-MONITOR in Fig. 3 defining the counter of received messages, the module expression

```
MONITOR[SMP, Node, get-msg resend-msg, TRAFFIC]
```

produces the instrumented version of the SMP module as previously explained. This module operation is indeed integrated in Full Maude and can be used, for example, to execute the following rewrite command:

```
rew in MONITOR[SMP, Node, get-msg resend-msg, TRAFFIC-MONITOR] :
{ < n   : Net | elems : (n1 n2 n3 n4 n5 n6 n7) >
  < mon(n1) : @Monitor |
       o : < n1 : MsgCreator | targets : (n2 n3 n4 n5 n6 n7),
                               neighbors : (n2 n3 n4 n5 n6),
                               counter : 500 >,
       data : 0 >
  < mon(n2) : @Monitor | o : < n2 : Node | neighbors : (n1 n3 n7) >,
                              data : 0 >
  < mon(n3) : @Monitor | o : < n3 : Node | neighbors : (n1 n2 n4) >,
                              data : 0 >
  < mon(n4) : @Monitor | o : < n4 : Node | neighbors : (n1 n3 n5) >,
                              data : 0 >
  < mon(n5) : @Monitor | o : < n5 : Node | neighbors : (n1 n4 n6) >,
                              data : 0 >
  < mon(n6) : @Monitor | o : < n6 : Node | neighbors : (n1 n5 n7) >,
                              data : 0 >
  < mon(n7) : @Monitor | o : < n7 : Node | neighbors : (n1 n6 n2) >,
                              data : 0 >, 0 } .
result GoodSystem :
{ < n : Net | elems : (n1 n2 n3 n4 n5 n6 n7) >
  < mon(n1) :. @Monitor |
       o : < n1 : MsgCreator | neighbors : (n2 n3 n4 n5 n6),
                               targets : (n2 n3 n4 n5 n6 n7),
                               counter : 0 >,
       data : 923 >
  < mon(n2) : @Monitor | o : < n2 : Node | neighbors : (n1 n3 n7) >,
                              data : 459 >
  < mon(n3) : @Monitor | o : < n3 : Node | neighbors : (n1 n2 n4) >,
                              data : 545 >
  < mon(n4) : @Monitor | o : < n4 : Node | neighbors : (n1 n3 n5) >,
                              data : 537 >
  < mon(n5) : @Monitor | o : < n5 : Node | neighbors : (n1 n4 n6) >,
                              data : 530 >
  < mon(n6) : @Monitor | o : < n6 : Node | neighbors : (n1 n5 n7) >,
                              data : 470 >
  < mon(n7) : @Monitor | o : < n7 : Node | neighbors : (n1 n6 n2) >,
                              data : 219 >,
  1238 }
```

5 Addition of Individual Monitors Preserves Behavior

Adding individual monitors to our specification should not modify the behavior of the system specification, in the sense that there must be a one-to-one correspondence between the rewrites in the original specification and the instrumented one. This idea is captured by the notion of bisimulation, defined as a simulation relation whose inverse relation is also a simulation [12]. In this section we provide bisimulation proofs for the addition of monitors.

We will name S a generic system defined as an object-oriented system with time annotations. We assume a Real-Time Maude specification as above described. We will denote by E a particular monitor to be added to S. The result of the composition of E in S, with a distinguish class C of S and a set of labels of rules LS of S, will be denoted as $M[S, C, LS, E]$. In this section we prove that adding this general individual monitors does not modify the behavior of our system by showing that a bisimulation between $M[S, C, LS, E]$ and S exists.

First, notice that the transformation injecting the monitors depends on the class whose objects are to be monitored, and that in order to define a total function we need to restrict the kind of systems we may consider. We introduce sorts $GoodSystem_S$ and $GoodSystem_{M[S,C,LS,E]}$ respectively as subsorts of $System_S$ and $System_{M[S,C,LS,E]}$. The kind of object configurations permitted in these sorts satisfy all the usual requirements of object configurations (no repeated object identifiers, no repeated attributes in objects, objects have attributes defined in their classes or superclasses, etc.). Moreover, all objects in configurations of terms of sort $GoodSystem_{M[S,C,LS,E]}$ wrapped in monitor objects are instances of class C or subclasses of it. We define these good-system sorts using conditional memberships.

By using techniques related to ground invariance [15], and assuming that the term algebra $\mathcal{T}_{\Sigma_S/E_S, GoodSystem_S}$ is closed under the relation $\to_{\mathcal{R}_S}$, we prove that $\mathcal{T}_{\Sigma_{M[S,C,LS,E]}/E_{M[S,C,LS,E]}, GoodSystem_{M[S,C,LS,E]}}$ is closed under $\to_{\mathcal{R}_{M[S,C,LS,E]}}$. If not total, a transition relation $\to$ can be extended to $\to^\bullet$ by adding pairs of the form $a \to^\bullet a$ when a cannot be rewritten (see [3,12] for an automatic transformation). Assuming a set of propositions AP and labeling functions $L_S : GoodConfig_S \to P(AP)$ and $L_{M[S,C,LS,E]} : GoodConfig_{M[S,C,LS,E]} \to P(AP)$, which associates to each state with the set of atomic propositions that hold in it, we extend S and $M[S, C, LS, E]$ to Kripke structures $\mathsf{A}_S = (\mathcal{T}_{\Sigma_S/E_S, GoodSystem_S}, \to_S, L_S)$ and $\mathsf{A}_{M[S,C,LS,E]} = (\mathcal{T}_{\Sigma_{M[S,C,LS,E]}/E_{M[S,C,LS,E]}, GoodSystem_{M[S,C,LS,E]}}, \to_{M[S,C,LS,E]}, L_S \circ H)$, respectively, where H is the function defined below.

Let us consider the following map H and let us prove it is a (strict) simulation:

$$H : GoodSystem_{M[S,C,LS,E]} \to GoodSystem_S$$

First of all, note that, since we have labeling functions L and $H \circ L$, H preserves labeling functions in a *strict* sense. Given variables O, C, *Atts*, D and *Conf* of sorts $\texttt{Oid}$, C, $\texttt{AttributeSet}$, $\texttt{Data}$ and $\texttt{Configuration}$, respectively, we define the H function using a recursively-defined auxiliary function H' as follows:

$$H(\{Conf, T\}) = \{ H'(Conf), T\}$$
$$H'(< \texttt{mon}(O) : \texttt{@Monitor} \mid \texttt{o} : < O : C \mid Atts >, \texttt{data} : D > Conf)$$
$$= < O : C \mid Atts > H'(Conf)$$
$$H'(Conf) = Conf \quad otherwise$$

H is a function that removes all monitor objects, leaving the monitored objects as they were (without wrappers). Other objects and all messages are just left as such.

Following the methods introduced in [12], we split the rules $R_{M[S,C,LS,E]}$ into the following three disjoint sets of rules:

- Let $R^1_{M[S,C,LS,E]}$ be the set of rules without modifications, i.e., rules in R_S (rules with no objects of subclasses of C are not changed in the transformation, either if in LS or not).
- Let $R^2_{M[S,C,LS,E]}$ be the set of rules whose labels are not in LS but include objects of subclasses of C.
- Let $R^3_{M[S,C,LS,E]}$ be the set of rules whose labels are in LS and include objects of subclasses C.

Theorem 1. *H defines a (strict) simulation map from an instrumented system specification $M[S, C, LS, E]$ to a system specification S.*

Proof. Let $\rightarrow_{k,M[S,C,LS,E]}$, with $k \in \{1, 2, 3\}$, be the transition relation defined by $R^k_{M[S,C,LS,E]}$. We differentiate two cases:

- $a \in GoodSystem_{M[S,C,LS,E]}$ is rewritten to $a' \in GoodSystem_{M[S,C,LS,E]}$ using a rule in $R^1_{M[S,C,LS,E]}$, i.e., $a \rightarrow^1_{1,M[S,C,LS,E]} a'$. Since rules in $R^1_{M[S,C,LS,E]}$ do not have monitored objects, $H(a) = b \in GoodSystem_S$ can be rewritten to $H(a') = b' \in GoodSystem_S$ using a transition in $\rightarrow_S$.
- $a \in GoodSystem_{M[S,C,LS,E]}$ is rewritten to $a' \in GoodSystem_{M[S,C,LS,E]}$ using a rule L in $R^2_{M[S,C,LS,E]}$ or $R^3_{M[S,C,LS,E]}$, i.e. $a \rightarrow^1_{k,M[S,C,LS,E]} a'$, with $k = 2\ or\ 3$. Then the rewritten subterm contains monitored objects that are removed by H. The rule in R_S from which the rule with label L was generated may then be used to rewrite $H(a) = b \in GoodSystem_S$ into $H(a') = b' \in GoodSystem_S$. □

Theorem 2. *The relation*

$$H^{-1} : GoodSystem_S \rightarrow GoodSystem_{M[S,C,LS,E]}$$

defines a (strict) simulation map from the system specification S to the instrumented system $M[S, C, LS, E]$.

Proof. H^{-1} is a relation from *valid* states in S to states in $M[S, C, LS, E]$ with monitor objects. Given a state $a \in GoodSystem_S$ which by $\rightarrow_S$ may be rewritten to another state $a' \in GoodSystem_S$. Using H^{-1}, a may be lifted to a possibly infinite number of states in $GoodSystem_{M[S,C,LS,E]}$. Basically, $H^{-1}(a)$ will yield states where objects of subclasses of C have been wrapped into monitor objects. All other objects and messages in the configurations will be left as such. The structure of the monitor objects introduced, including their identifier is fixed, but their **data** attribute may take any value in the **Data** sort. We prove that for all states b in $GoodSystem_{M[S,C,LS,E]}$ such that $H(a) = b$, a transition to a state $H(a') = b'$ in $GoodSystem_{M[S,C,LS,E]}$ exists in $\rightarrow_{M[S,C,LS,E]}$.

We reason by cases:

- if the state a is rewritten into a' using a rule with no objects of subclasses of C, then $H^{-1}(a) = b \in System_{M[S,C,LS,E]}$ and b is rewritten to some $H^{-1}(a') = b'$ using a rule in $R^1_{M[S,C,LS,E]}$.

– if the state a is rewritten by a rule whose label is not in LS but that involves objects of subclasses of C, these objects will be wrapped by monitor objects by $H^{-1}(a)$. This is the case in which a state $H^{-1} = b \in GoodSystem_{M[S,C,LS,E]}$ will be rewritten using a rule in $R^2_{M[S,C,LS,E]}$. In this case, there is an infinite number of possible wrappers since the variable D is free. However, since the rule label is not in LS, the value of D remains unchanged, and therefore, the state b transitions to b' so that $H(b') = a'$ in $GoodSystem_S$.

– if the state a is rewritten using a rule in $R^3_{M[S,C,LS,E]}$, then a can be lifted to an infinite number of possible monitor wrappers $b \in H^{-1}(a)$. Moreover, since b will transition using a monitored rule, the value of the attribute **data** matters. However, since **eval** is assumed to be a well-defined total function, for every value of D of sort $Data$, the state b can transition to a state b' such that $H(b') = a'$. □

Then, since H is a bisimulation of Kripke structures $A_{M[S,C,LS,E]}$ and A_S, since strict simulations always reflect satisfaction of CTL^* formulas [12, Theorem 2], we have that given any CTL^* formula ϕ, and a configuration $a \in GoodSystem_{M[S,C,LS,E]}$,

$$H(a) \models_{A_S} \phi \iff a \models_{A_{M[S,C,LS,E]}} \phi$$

6   The Throughput Monitor

As an example of a *global* monitor, suppose we want to calculate the number of messages passing through nodes per time unit. By using the definition of **Data** and the **eval** function in a module extending the **MONITOR** module as shown in Fig. 5, we may count the number of messages forwarded by rules per time unit.

In the module **THROUGHPUT-MONITOR**, sort **Data** is declared a supersort of 2-tuples in which the first component keeps the number of messages and the second one the current throughput. We assume that if the number of messages in the left- and right-hand sides is the same it is because the message is being forwarded, in which case the number of messages in the **data** attribute is increased and the current number of messages is divided by the actual time.

We may rewrite the system using the **MONITOR** module expression as follows:

```
rew in MONITOR[SMP, Net, resend—msg, THROUGHPUT—MONITOR] :
  { < mon(n) : @Monitor |
        o : < n  : Net | elems : (n1 n2 n3 n4 n5 n6 n7) >,
        data : {0, 0.0} >
    < n1 : MsgCreator | targets : (n2 n3 n4 n5 n6 n7),
                        neighbors : (n2 n3 n4 n5 n6),
                        counter : 500 >
    < n2 : Node | neighbors : (n1 n3 n7) >
    < n3 : Node | neighbors : (n1 n2 n4) >
    < n4 : Node | neighbors : (n1 n3 n5) >
    < n5 : Node | neighbors : (n1 n4 n6) >
    < n6 : Node | neighbors : (n1 n5 n7) >
    < n7 : Node | neighbors : (n1 n6 n2) >, 0 } .
  result GoodSystem:
  { < n1 : MsgCreator | neighbors : (n2 n3 n4 n5 n6),
                        targets : (n2 n3 n4 n5 n6 n7),
```

```
                     counter : 0 >
< n2 : Node | neighbors : (n1 n3 n7) >
< n3 : Node | neighbors : (n1 n2 n4) >
< n4 : Node | neighbors : (n1 n3 n5) >
< n5 : Node | neighbors : (n1 n4 n6) >
< n6 : Node | neighbors : (n1 n5 n7) >
< n7 : Node | neighbors : (n1 n6 n2) >
< mon(n) : @Monitor |
   o : < n : Net | elems : (n1 n2 n3 n4 n5 n6 n7) >,
   data : { 3683, 2.9797734627831716 } >,
1238}
```

```
omod THROUGHPUT-MONITOR is
 inc MONITOR .
 pr CONVERSION .

 sort 2Tuple .
 op '{_',_'} : Nat Float -> 2Tuple [ctor] .
 subsort 2Tuple < Data .

 var   N : Nat .                     var  T : Time .
 var   Obj : Object .                var  Thp : Float .
 vars LConf RConf Conf : Configuration .   var  Msg : Msg .

 eq eval({ N, Thp}, T, Obj, LConf, RConf)
   = if (#msgs(LConf) == #msgs(RConf))
     then { N + #msgs(LConf)),
            float(N + #msgs(LConf)) / float(T)  }
     else { N, Thp}
     fi .

 op #msgs : Configuration -> Nat .
 eq #msgs(Msg Conf) = s(#msgs(Conf)) .
 eq #msgs(Conf) = 0 [owise] .
endom
```

Fig. 5. Throughput system monitor

The result shows, that for this execution, messages have been re-sent 3683 times, with around 2.98 messages re-sent per time unit.

7   Conclusions and Future Work

We have presented a methodology to define monitors that can be added to any real-time object-oriented system specification.

We have proven that the addition of these generic monitors to a system specification does *not* change its behavior. Furthermore, due to properties of simulations, safety formulas are preserved after instrumenting the specifications. This assures bisimulation by construction for any monitor and system.

Besides the theoretical results, we have presented a Maude tool which performs the *weaving* of monitors and specifications, as well as two case studies. The instrumentation has been implemented as part of Full Maude following its reflective and extensible design. We have provided a module expression that allows us to instantiate predefined generic monitors in a very simple way, perfectly integrated with Full Maude. The extended version of Full Maude, and several examples are available at http://maude.lcc.uma.es/monitors.

There is much work ahead. We believe that the need for indicating the rules to be monitored may be avoided when the `eval` functions have all the required information to decide when the information needs to be computed. Views from parameter monitors to specific systems may be provided, thus reducing the coupling with monitors and increasing flexibility: we may want to specify monitors depending on multiple classes or on other parameters. Multiple monitors should be used on the same systems to monitor different properties on different objects. First steps towards this kind of composition have already been taken, but the constructions will be presented elsewhere.

Acknowledgements. This work has been partially supported by Spanish MINECO/FEDER project TIN2014-52034-R, and Universidad de Málaga, Campus de Excelencia Internacional Andalucía Tech. Partially supported by NSF Grant CNS 13-19109.

References

1. Bertot, Y., Castéran, P.: Interactive Theorem Proving and Program Development. Coq'Art: The Calculus of Inductive Constructions. Springer, Heidelberg (2004). http://www.labri.fr/perso/casteran/CoqArt/index.html
2. Clavel, M., Durán, F., Eker, S., Lincoln, P., Martí-Oliet, N., Meseguer, J., Quesada, J.: Maude: specification and programming in rewriting logic. Theoret. Comput. Sci. **285**, 187–243 (2002)
3. Clavel, M., Durán, F., Eker, S., Lincoln, P., Martí-Oliet, N., Meseguer, J., Talcott, C.: All About Maude - A High-Performance Logical Framework: How to Specify, Program, and Verify Systems in Rewriting Logic. LNCS, vol. 4350. Springer, Heidelberg (2007)
4. Durán, F.: The extensibility of Maude's module algebra. In: Rus, T. (ed.) AMAST 2000. LNCS, vol. 1816, p. 422. Springer, Heidelberg (2000)
5. Durán, F., Lucas, S., Marché, C., Meseguer, J., Urbain, X.: Proving operational termination of membership equational programs. High.-Order Symbolic Comput. **21**(1–2), 59–88 (2008)
6. Durán, F., Meseguer, J.: Maude's module algebra. Sci. Comput. Program. **66**(2), 125–153 (2007)
7. Durán, F., Meseguer, J.: On the Church-Rosser and coherence properties of conditional order-sorted rewrite theories. J. Log. Algebr. Program. **81**(7–8), 816–850 (2012)
8. Holzmann, G.J.: The SPIN Model Checker. Addison-Wesley, Boston (2003)
9. Lee, I., Kannan, S., Kim, M., Sokolsky, O., Viswanathan, M.: Runtime assurance based on formal specifications. In: Arabnia, H.R. (ed.) Proceedings of the International Conference on Parallel and Distributed Processing Techniques and Applications, PDPTA 1999, 28 June–1 July 1999, Las Vegas, Nevada, USA, pp. 279–287. CSREA Press (1999)
10. Meseguer, J.: Conditional rewriting logic as a unified model of concurrency. Theoret. Comput. Sci. **96**(1), 73–155 (1992)

11. Meseguer, J.: Taming distributed system complexity through formal patterns. Sci. Comput. Program. **83**, 3–34 (2014)
12. Meseguer, J., Palomino, M., Martí-Oliet, N.: Algebraic simulations. J. Log. Algebr. Program. **79**(2), 103–143 (2010)
13. Meseguer, J., Talcott, C.: Semantic models for distributed object reflection. In: Magnusson, B. (ed.) ECOOP 2002. LNCS, vol. 2374, p. 1. Springer, Heidelberg (2002)
14. Ölveczky, P.C., Meseguer, J.: Semantics and pragmatics of Real-Time Maude. High.-Order Symbolic Comput. **20**(1–2), 161–196 (2007)
15. Rocha, C., Meseguer, J.: Proving safety properties of rewrite theories. In: Corradini, A., Klin, B., Cîrstea, C. (eds.) CALCO 2011. LNCS, vol. 6859, pp. 314–328. Springer, Heidelberg (2011)
16. Troya, J., Vallecillo, A., Durán, F., Zschaler, S.: Model-driven performance analysis of rule-based domain specific visual models. Inf. Softw. Technol. **55**(1), 88–110 (2013)
17. Zschaler, S.: Formal specification of non-functional properties of component-based software systems. Softw. Syst. Model. **9**(2), 161–201 (2010)

Proving Reachability-Logic Formulas Incrementally

Vlad Rusu[1]([✉]) and Andrei Arusoaie[1,2]

[1] Inria, Lille, France
Vlad.Rusu@inria.fr, Andrei.Arusoaie@inria.fr
[2] "Al. I. Cuza" University of Iaşi, Iaşi, Romania

Abstract. Reachability Logic (RL) is a formalism for defining the operational semantics of programming languages and for specifying program properties. As a program logic it can be seen as a language-independent alternative to Hoare Logics. Several verification techniques have been proposed for RL, all of which have a circular nature: the RL formula under proof can circularly be used as a hypothesis in the proof of another RL formula, or even in its own proof. This feature is essential for dealing with possibly unbounded repetitive behaviour (e.g., program loops). The downside of such approaches is that the verification of a set of RL formulas is monolithic, i.e., either all formulas in the set are proved valid, or nothing can be inferred about any of the formula's validity or invalidity. In this paper we propose a new, incremental method for proving a large class of RL formulas. The proposed method takes as input a given RL formula under proof (corresponding to a given program fragment), together with a (possibly empty) set of other valid RL formulas (e.g., already proved using our method), which specify sub-programs of the program fragment under verification. It then checks certain conditions are shown to be equivalent to the validity of the RL formula under proof. A newly proved formula can then be incrementally used in the proof of other RL formulas, corresponding to larger program fragments. The process is repeated until the whole program is proved. We illustrate our approach by verifying the nontrivial Knuth-Morris-Pratt string-matching program.

1 Introduction

Reachability Logic (RL) [1–4] is a language-independent logic for defining the operational semantics of programming languages and for specifying properties of programs. For instance, on the sum program in Fig. 1, the RL formula

$$\langle \text{sum}, \text{n} \mapsto a \rangle \wedge a \geq 0 \Rightarrow (\exists i, s)\langle \text{skip}, \text{n} \mapsto a \ \text{i} \mapsto i \ \text{s} \mapsto s \rangle\rangle \wedge s = sum(a) \qquad (1)$$

specifies that after the complete execution of the sum program from a configuration where the program variable n is bound to a non-negative value a, a configuration where s is bound to a value $s = sum(a)$ is reached. Here, $sum(a)$ is a mathematical definition of the sum of natural numbers up to a.

© Springer International Publishing Switzerland 2016
D. Lucanu (Ed.): WRLA 2016, LNCS 9942, pp. 134–151, 2016.
DOI: 10.1007/978-3-319-44802-2_8

```
i := 1;
s := 0;
while (i <= n) do
    s := s + i;
    i := i + 1
end
```

Fig. 1. Program sum.

Existing RL verification tools [1,2,4–6] would typically verify formula (1) as follows. First, they would consider (1) together with, e.g., the following formula (2), where while denotes the program fragment consisting of the while-loop in Fig. 1. The formula (2) is intended to specify the while loop, just like (1) specifies the whole program, and can be seen as encoding a loop invariant.

$$\langle \text{while}, \text{n} \mapsto a \; \text{i} \mapsto i \; \text{s} \mapsto s \rangle \land 0 < i \le a + 1 \land s = sum(i - 1) \qquad (2)$$
$$\Rightarrow (\exists i', s') \langle \text{skip}, \text{n} \mapsto a \; \text{i} \mapsto i' \; \text{s} \mapsto s' \rangle \land s' = sum(a)$$

Then, the tool would symbolically execute at least one instruction in the programs in the left-hand side of both (1) and (2) using the semantics of the instructions of the language (assumed to be also expressed as RL formulas[1]), and then execute the remaining programs in the left-hand sides of the resulting formulas *as if both* (1) *and* (2) *became new semantical rules of the language.* For example, when the program executed in (1) reaches the while loop, the rule (2) can be applied instead of the rule defining the semantics of the while instruction - that is, when proving (1), (2) is assumed to hold. Similarly, when the program in (2) completes one loop iteration, the left-hand side of (2) contains again the same while loop as initially, with other values mapped to the variables. Then, (2) is applied instead of the rule defining the semantics of the while instruction. Thus, it is assumed that (2) holds after having completed one loop iteration.

The *circular* reasoning illustrated in the above example is sound, in the sense that if such a proof succeeds, all the formulas under proof are (semantically) valid. However, if the proof does not succeed, nothing can be said about the validity of the formulas. In our example, (1) or (2) (or both) could be invalid.

Contribution. In this paper we propose a new method for proving a significant subset of RL formulas, which, unlike existing verification methods, is *incremental*. In our example, the proposed method would first prove (2), and then would prove (1) knowing for a fact (i.e., not assuming) that (2) is valid. Thus, if the proof of (1) fails for some reason, the user still knows that (2) holds, and can take action for fixing the proof based on this knowledge. Of course, for a simple program such as the above example the advantage of incremental RL verification is not obvious, but it turns out to make quite a difference when verifying more challenging programs, such as the KMP program illustrated later in the paper.

---

[1] For the language of interest in this paper the rules are shown in Sect. 2.

We first establish an equivalence between the validity of RL formulas and two technical conditions (one condition is an invariance property, and the other one regards the so-called capturing of terminal configurations). Then we propose a graph-construction approach that takes a given RL formula under proof (corresponding to a given program fragment), together with a (possibly empty) set of other valid RL formulas (e.g., proved using a previous iteration of our approach, or by any other sound RL formula verification method). The latter formulas specify sub-programs of the program fragment currently under verification. The invariance and terminal-configuration capturing conditions are then checked on the graph, thus establishing the validity of the RL formula under proof. The newly proved formula can then be incrementally used in the proof of other RL formulas, corresponding to larger program fragments. The same process is then repeated until, eventually, the whole program is proved.

Of course, the proposed method has limitations, since verification of RL formulas is in general undecidable. The graph construction may not terminate, or the conditions to be checked on it may not hold. One situation that a purely incremental method cannot handle is mutually recursive function calls, in which none of the functions can be verified individually unless (coinductively) assuming that the other function's specifications hold. A natural solution here is to use an incremental method as much as possible, and to locally apply a circular approach only for subsets of formulas that the incremental method cannot handle.

In order to demonstrate the feasibility of our approach we illustrate it on the nontrivial Knuth-Morris-Pratt KMP string-matching program. The program is written in a simple imperative language, whose syntax and semantics is defined in Maude [7]. We chose Maude in order to benefit from its reflective capabilities, which turned out to be very useful for implementation purposes. We are using a specific version of Maude that has been interfaced with the Z3 solver [8], which is here used for simplifying conditions required for proving RL formula validity.

Paper Organisation. After this introduction we present in Sect. 2 the Maude-based definition of a simple imperative programming language IMP+ that includes assignments, conditions, loops, and simple procedures operating on global variables. In Sect. 3 we present background notions: Reachability Logic, and how the language definition from the previous section fits in this framework (Sect. 3.1); and language-parametric symbolic execution, together with its implementation by rewriting based on transforming the semantical rules of a language (Sect. 3.2). In Sect. 4 we present the incremental RL-formula verification method. In Sect. 5 we illustrated our method on the KMP string-matching algorithm, and in Sect. 6 we conclude and present related and future work. An extended version containing detailed proofs of technical results is available at https://hal.inria.fr/hal-01282379.

2   Defining a Simple Programming Language

In this section we define the language IMP+ in Maude. IMP+ is simple enough so that its Maude code is reasonably small (less than two hundred lines of code), yet expressive enough for programming algorithms on arrays such as the KMP. We assume Maude is familiar to readers; for details the standard reference is [7].

Datatypes. IMP+ computes over Booleans, integers, and integer arrays. We use the builtin Booleans and integers of Maude, and provide a standard algebraic definition of arrays. The constructor `array : Nat -> IntArray` creates an array of a given length. The operation `store : IntArray Nat Int -> IntArray` stores a given integer (third argument) at a given natural-number index. An operation `select : IntArray Nat -> Int` returns the element at the position given by the second argument. These functions are defined equationally. They return error values in case of attempts to access indices out of an array's bounds.

Syntax. The syntax on IMP+ consists of expressions (arithmetic and Boolean) and statements. Each of these syntactical categories is defined by a sort, i.e., `AExp`, `BExp`, and `Stmt`. Allowed arithmetical operations are addition, substraction, and array selector, denoted by `_++_`, `_--_`, and `_[_]` respectively, in order to avoid confusion with the corresponding Maude operations on the datatypes. In the same spirit, Boolean operations are less-or-equal-than (`_<==_`) and equality (`_===_`); negation `!`; and conjunction `_&&_`. Such expressions are built from identifiers (i.e., program variables) and constants (Maude integers and Booleans).

The statements of IMP+ are: assignments to integer variables and array elements (`_:=_`); conditional (`if_then_else_endif`); while loops (`while_do_end`); parameterless function declaration (`function_(){_}`) and call (`_()`); a `print` instruction; and finally, a sequencing `_;_` instruction that, for convenience, is declared associative with the "do-nothing" `skip` instruction as a neutral element.

Semantics. Semantical rules operate on *configurations*, which consist of a program to be executed, a mapping of integer variables to values and of function names to statements, and a list of integers denoting the output of the program. In Maude we write a constructor `<_,_,_,_> : Stmt Map Funs Ints -> Cfg`. Getters and setters for the `Map` and `Funs` maps are also equationally defined.

The semantics of IMP+ then consists in evaluating expressions (in a given map, assigning values to variables) and statements (in a given configuration, describing all the infrastructure required for statements to execute). Expressions are evaluated using equations, and statements are evaluated using rewrite rules.

Evaluating Expressions. This amounts to writing a function `eval` and equations:

```
op eval : AExp Map -> Int .
eq eval(I, M) = I .
eq eval(X, (M (X -> J))) = J .
eq eval(X[E], (M (X -> A))) = select(A,eval(E,(M (X -> A)))) .
...
op eval : BExp Map -> Bool .
eq eval(B,M) = B .
eq eval(Cnd1 && Cnd2, M) = eval(Cnd1,M) and eval(Cnd2,M) .
...
```

That is, `eval` goes through the structure of an expression and evaluates it in a given mapping of values to variables. Here, e.g., M (X -> J) denotes an associative-commutative map, constructed as the anonymous juxtaposition operation __ of a map variable M with a map of the identifier X to the integer J.

Evaluating Statements. This is performed by rewrite rules, some of which are:

```
rl [assign]: <((X := E) ; S), M, F, O > => < S, set(X, eval(E, M), M), F, O > .

crl [if-true]: <(if Cnd then S1 else S2 endif) ; S, M, F, O > => < S1 ; S, M, F, O >
          if  eval(Cnd,M) .

crl [if-false]: <(if Cnd then S1 else S2 endif) ; S, M, F, O > => < S2 ; S, M, F, O >
          if  not eval(Cnd,M) .

rl [while]: <(while Cnd do S1 end) ; S, M, F, O > =>
          <(if Cnd then S1 ; while Cnd do S1 end else skip endif) ; S, M, F, O > .

rl [print]: < (print E) ; S, M, F, O >   => < S, M, F, (O ; eval(E,M)) > .
```

The first rule deals with assigment to a program-variable X of an arithmetic expression E. It uses the `set` function on maps in order to update the map so that X is mapped to the value of E. Another rule, not shown here, deals with assignments to array elements. The following two rules describe the two possible outcomes of a conditional instruction, depending on the value of the condition. The rule for the while loop consists essentially in loop unrolling. The rule for the printing instruction appends the value of the instruction's argument to the list of integers (last argument of configurations) denoting the program's output.

3 Reachability Logic and Symbolic Execution

In this section we present background material used in the rest of the paper. We illustrate the concepts with examples from the IMP+ language.

3.1 Reachability Logic

Several versions of RL have been proposed in the last few years [1–4]. Moreover, RL is built on top of *Matching Logic* (ML), which also exists in several versions [9–11]. (The situation is somewhat similar to the relationship between rewriting logic and the equational logics underneath it.) We adopt the recent *all-paths* interpretation of RL [4], built upon a minimal ML that is enough to express typical practically-relevant properties about program configurations and is amenable to *symbolic execution* by rewriting, a key ingredient of our method.

The formulas of ML that we consider are called *patterns* and are defined as follows. Assume an algebraic signature Σ with a set S of sorts, including two distinguished sorts $Bool, Cfg \in S$. We write $T_{\Sigma,s}(Var)$ for the set of terms of sort s over a set Var of S-indexed variables and $T_{\Sigma,s}$ for the set of ground terms of sort s. We identify the $Bool$-sorted operations in Σ with a set Π of predicates.

Example 1. Consider the Maude definition of the IMP+ language. Then, Σ is the algebraic signature containing all the sorts and operations described in the previous section, including the Bool and Cfg sorts. The operation eval : BExp Map -> Bool has sort Bool and is thus identified with a predicate in the set Π. The sort Cfg has the constructor <_,_,_,_> : Stmt Map Funs Ints -> Cfg.

Definition 1 (Pattern). *A pattern is an expression of the form $(\exists X)\pi \wedge \phi$, where $X \subset Var$, $\pi \in T_{\Sigma,Cfg}(X)$ and ϕ is a FOL formula over the FOL signature (Σ, Π) with free variables in X.*

We often denote patterns by φ and write $\varphi \triangleq (\exists X)\pi \wedge \phi$ to emphasise its components: the quantified variables X, the *basic pattern* π, and ϕ, the *condition*. We let *FreeVars*(φ) denote the set of variables freely occurring in a pattern φ, defined as usual (i.e., not under the incidence of a quantifier). We often identify basic patterns π with $(\exists\emptyset)\pi \wedge true$, and *elementary patterns* $\pi \wedge \phi$ with $(\exists\emptyset)\pi \wedge \phi$.

Example 2. The left and right-hand sides of the rules defining the semantics of IMP+ are basic patterns, < S, M, F, O > /\ eval(true,M) is an elementary pattern, and $(\exists O)$ < S, M, F, O > /\ eval(true,M) is a pattern.

We now describe the semantics of patterns. We assume a model M of the algebraic signature Σ. In the case of the Maude specification of IMP+ the model M, M is the initial model induced by the specification's equations and axioms. For sorts $s \in S$ we write M_s for the interpretation (a.k.a. carrier set) of the sort s.

We call *valuations* the functions $\rho : Var \rightarrow M$ that assign to variables in Var a value in M of a corresponding sort, and *configurations* the elements in M_{Cfg}.

Definition 2 (Pattern Semantics). *Given a pattern $\varphi \triangleq (\exists X)\pi \wedge \phi$, $\gamma \in M_{Cfg}$ a configuration, and $\rho : Var \rightarrow M$ a valuation, the satisfaction relation $(\gamma, \rho) \models \varphi$ holds iff there exists a valuation ρ' with $\rho'|_{Var \setminus X} = \rho|_{Var \setminus X}$ such that $\gamma = \rho'(\pi)$ and $\rho' \models \phi$ (where the latter $\models$ denotes satisfaction in FOL, and $\rho|_{Var \setminus X}$ denotes the restriction of the valuation ρ to the set $Var \setminus X$).*

We let $[\![\varphi]\!]$ denote the set $\{\gamma \in M_{Cfg} \mid (\exists \rho : Var \rightarrow M)(\gamma, \rho) \models \varphi\}$. A formula φ is *valid in M*, denoted by $M \models \varphi$, if it is satisfied by all pairs (γ, ρ).

We now recall Reachability-Logic (RL) formulas, the transition systems that they induce, and their all-paths semantics [4] that we will be using in this paper.

Definition 3 (RL Formulas). *An RL formula is a pair of patterns $\varphi \Rightarrow \varphi'$.*

Examples of RL formulas were given in the introduction. The rules defining the semantics of IMP+ are also RL formulas (for the conditional rules, just assume that the expression following if is the condition of the rule's left-hand side).

Let S denote a fixed set of RL formulas, e.g., the semantics of a given language. We define the transition system defined by S together with some notions related to this transition system, and then the notion of validity for RL formulas.

Definition 4 (Transition System Defined by $\mathcal{S}$). *The transition system defined by $\mathcal{S}$ is $(M_{Cfg}, \Rightarrow_{\mathcal{S}})$, where $\Rightarrow_{\mathcal{S}} = \{(\gamma, \gamma') \mid (\exists \varphi \Rightarrow \varphi' \in \mathcal{S})(\exists \rho)(\gamma, \rho) \models \varphi \wedge (\gamma', \rho) \models \varphi'\}$. We write $\gamma \Rightarrow_{\mathcal{S}} \gamma'$ for $(\gamma, \gamma') \in \Rightarrow_{\mathcal{S}}$. A state γ is terminal if there is no γ' such that $\gamma \Rightarrow_{\mathcal{S}} \gamma'$. A path is a sequence $\gamma_0 \cdots \gamma_n$ such that $\gamma_i \Rightarrow_{\mathcal{S}} \gamma_{i+1}$ for all $0 \leq i \leq n - 1$. Such a path is complete if γ_n is terminal.*

An RL *formula $\varphi \Rightarrow \varphi'$ is valid, written $\mathcal{S} \models \varphi \Rightarrow \varphi'$, if for all pairs (γ_0, ρ) such that $(\gamma_0, \rho) \models \varphi$, and all complete paths $\gamma_0 \Rightarrow_{\mathcal{S}} \cdots \Rightarrow_{\mathcal{S}} \gamma_n$, there exists $0 \leq i \leq n$ such that $(\gamma_i, \rho) \models \varphi'$.*

Note that the validity of RL formulas is only determined by finite, complete paths. Infinite paths, induced by nonterminating programs, are not considered. Thus, termination is assumed: as a program logic, RL is a logic of partial correctness. We restrict our attention to RL formulas satisfying the following assumption:

Assumption 1. *RL formulas have the form $\pi_l \wedge \phi_l \Rightarrow (\exists Y) \pi_r \wedge \phi_r$ and satisfy $FreeVars(\pi_r) \subseteq FreeVars(\pi_l) \cup Y$, $FreeVars(\phi_r) \subseteq FreeVars(\pi_l) \cup FreeVars(\pi_r)$, and $FreeVars(\phi_l) \subseteq FreeVars(\pi_l)$.*

That is, the left-hand side is an elementary pattern, and the right hand side is a pattern, possibly with quantifiers. Such formulas are typically expressive enough for expressing language semantics (for this purpose, quantifiers are not even required)[2] and program properties. For program properties, existentially quantified variables in the right-hand side are useful to denote values computed by a given program, which are not known before the program computes them, such as s - the sum of natural numbers up to a given bound - in the formula (1).

3.2 Language-Parametric Symbolic Execution

We now briefly present symbolic execution, a well-known program analysis technique that consists in executing programs with symbolic input (e.g. a symbolic value x) instead of concrete input (e.g. 0). We reformulate the language-independent symbolic execution approach we already presented elsewhere [6], with some simplifications (e.g., unlike [6] we do not use coinduction). The approach consists in transforming the signature Σ and semantics $\mathcal{S}$ of a programming language so that, under reasonable restrictions, executing a program with the modified semantics amounts to executing the program symbolically.

Consider the signature Σ corresponding to a language definition. Let *Fol* be a new sort whose terms are all FOL formulas, including existential and universal quantifiers. Let *Id* and *IdSet* be new sorts denoting identifiers and sets of identifiers, with a union operation $\_, \_$. Let Cfg^s be a new sort, with constructor $(\exists \_) \_ \wedge \_ : IdSet \times Cfg \times Fol \to Cfg^s$. Thus, patterns $(\exists X) \pi \wedge \phi$ correspond to terms $(\exists X) \pi \wedge \phi$ of sort Cfg^s in the enriched signature and reciprocally. Consider also the following set of RL formulas, called the *symbolic version of $\mathcal{S}$*:

$$\mathcal{S}^s \triangleq \{(\exists \mathcal{X}) \pi_l \wedge \psi \Rightarrow (\exists \mathcal{X}, Y) \pi_r \wedge (\psi \wedge \phi_l \wedge \phi_r) \mid \pi_l \wedge \phi_l \Rightarrow (\exists Y) \pi_r \wedge \phi_r \in \mathcal{S}\}$$

with ψ a new variable of sort *Fol*, and $\mathcal{X}$ a new variable of sort *IdSet*.

---

[2] See, e.g., the languages defined in the $\mathbb{K}$ framework: http://k-framework.org.

Example 3. The following conditional rule is part of the semantics $\mathcal{S}$ of IMP+:
`< if C then S1 else S2 endif ; S, M, F, 0 > => < S1 ; S, M, F, 0 > if eval(C,M)`   Written as an RL formula (with patterns in left and right-hand sides) it becomes[3]
`<if C then S1 else S2 endif ; S, M, F, 0 >` $\wedge$ `eval(C,M)=> < S1 ; S, M, F, 0 >`
The corresponding rule in $\mathcal{S}^s$ becomes an unconditional rule: $(\exists \mathcal{X})$
`<if C then S1 else S2 endif ; S, M, F, 0 >` $\wedge\psi$ => $(\exists \mathcal{X})$ `<S1 ; S, M, F, 0 >`
$\wedge\,(\psi \wedge$ `eval(C,M)`$)$.

The interest of the above nontrivial construction is that, under reasonable assumptions, stated below, rewriting with the rules in $\mathcal{S}^s$ achieves a *simulation* of rewriting with the rules in $\mathcal{S}$, which is a result that we need for our approach.

Assumption 2. *There exists a* builtin subsignature $\Sigma^b \subsetneq \Sigma$. *The sorts and operations in Σ^b are builtin, while all others are non-builtin. The sort Cfg is not builtin. Non-builtin operation symbols may only be subject to a (possibly empty) set of* linear, regular, *and* non-collapsing *axioms.*

We recall that an axiom $u = v$ is linear if both u, v are linear (a term is linear if any variable occurs in it at most once); it is regular if both u, v have the same set of variables; and it is non-collapsing if both u, v have non-builtin sorts.

Example 4. For the IMP+ language specification we assume that the non-builtin sorts are Cfg, Stmt (for statements), and Funs (which map function identifiers to statements). Statements were declared to be associative with unity, whereas maps of identifiers to statements were taken to be associative and commutative with unity. All these axioms have the properties requested by Assumption 2.

In order to formulate the simulation result we now define the transition relation generated by the set of symbolic RL rules $\mathcal{S}^s$. It is essentially rewriting modulo the congruence $\cong$ on $T_\Sigma(Var)$ induced by the axioms in Assumption 2. Let $Var^b \subset Var$ be the set of variables of builtin sorts. We first need the following technical assumption, which does not restrict the generality of our approach:

Assumption 3. *For every* $\pi_l\wedge\phi_l \Rightarrow (\exists Y)\pi_r\wedge\phi_r \in \mathcal{S}$, $\pi_l \in T_{\Sigma\setminus\Sigma^b}(Var)$, π_l *is linear, and* $Y \subseteq Var^b$.

The assumption can always be made to hold by replacing in π_l all non-variable terms in Σ^b and all duplicated variables by fresh variables, and by equating in the condition ϕ_l the new variables to the terms that they replaced.

For the sake of complying with the definition of rewriting we need to extend the congruence $\cong$ to terms of sort Cfg^s by $(\exists X)\pi_1\wedge\phi \cong (\exists X)\pi_2\wedge\phi$ iff $\pi_1 \cong \pi_2$.

Definition 5 (Relation $\Rightarrow_{\alpha^s}$). *For* $\alpha^s \triangleq (\exists \mathcal{X})\pi_l\wedge\psi \Rightarrow (\exists \mathcal{X}, Y)\pi_r\wedge(\psi \wedge \phi_l \wedge \phi_r)$
$\in \mathcal{S}^s$ *we write* $(\exists X)\pi\wedge\phi \Rightarrow_{\alpha^s} (\exists X, Y)\pi'\wedge\phi'$ *whenever* $(\exists X)\pi\wedge\phi\ \alpha^s$ *is rewritten by* α^s *to* $(\exists X, Y)\pi'\wedge\phi'$, *i.e., there exists a substitution* σ' *on* $Var \cup \{\mathcal{X}, \psi\}$ *such that* $\sigma'((\exists \mathcal{X})\pi_l\wedge\psi) \cong (\exists X)\pi\wedge\phi$ *and* $\sigma'((\exists \mathcal{X}, Y)\pi_r\wedge(\psi \wedge \phi_l \wedge \phi_r)) = (\exists X, Y)\pi'\wedge\phi'$.

---

[3] We liberally use a mixture of Maude and math notation for the sake of the example.

Lemma 1 ($\Rightarrow_{\alpha^s}$ **Simulates** $\Rightarrow_\alpha$). *For all* $\gamma, \gamma' \in M_{Cfg}$, *all patterns* φ *with* $FreeVars(\varphi) \subseteq Var^b$, *and all valuations* ρ, *if* $(\gamma, \rho) \models \varphi$ *and* $\gamma \Rightarrow_\alpha \gamma'$ *then there exists* φ' *with* $FreeVars(\varphi') \subseteq Var^b$ *such that* $\varphi \Rightarrow_{\alpha^s} \varphi'$ *and* $(\gamma', \rho) \models \varphi'$.

As a consequence, any concrete execution (following $\Rightarrow_S$) such that the initial configuration satisfies a given initial pattern φ is simulated by a symbolic execution (following $\Rightarrow_{S^s}$) starting in φ. We shall also use the following notion of *derivative*, which collects all the symbolic successors of a pattern by a rule:

Definition 6 (Derivatives). $\Delta_\alpha(\varphi) = \{\varphi' \mid \varphi \Rightarrow_{\alpha^s} \varphi'\}$ *for any* $\alpha \in \mathcal{S}$.

Since the symbolic successors are computed by rewriting, the derivative operation is computable and always returns a finite set of patterns.

4   Proving RL Formulas Incrementally

In this section we present an incremental method for proving RL formulas. We first state two technical conditions and prove that they are equivalent to RL formula validity. The equivalence works for so-called *terminal* formulas, whose right-hand side specifies a completed program; however, a generalisation to non-terminal formulas, required for incremental verification, is also given. Thus, RL formula verification amounts to checking the two above-mentioned conditions.

For this, we present a graph construction based on symbolic execution that, if it terminates successfully, ensures that the two conditions in question hold for a given RL formula. The graph construction is parameterised by a set of formulas that have already been proved valid (using the same method, or any other sound one). These formulas correspond to subprograms of the given program fragment that the current formula under proof specifies. The current formula, once proved, can then be used in proofs of formulas specifying larger program fragments.

We consider a fixed set $\mathcal{S}$ or RL formulas and their transition relation $\Rightarrow_S$. The first of the two following definitions says that all terminal configurations reachable from a given pattern "end up" as instances of a quantified basic pattern:

Definition 7 (Capturing All Terminal Configurations). *We say that a pattern* $(\exists Y)\pi'$ *captures all terminal configurations for a pattern* φ *if for all* (γ, ρ) *such that* $(\gamma, \rho) \models \varphi$, *and all complete paths* $\gamma \Rightarrow_S \cdots \Rightarrow_S \gamma'$, $(\gamma', \rho) \models (\exists Y)\pi'$.

The second definition characterises FOL formulas that hold in a given quantified pattern, i.e., conditions satisfied by all configurations reachable from a given initial pattern whenever they "reach" the quantified pattern in question:

Definition 8 (Invariant at, Starting from). *We say that a FOL formula* $(\exists Y)\phi'$ *is invariant at a pattern* $(\exists Y)\pi'$ *starting from a pattern* φ *if for all* (γ, ρ) *such that* $(\gamma, \rho) \models \varphi$, *all paths* $\gamma \Rightarrow_S \cdots \Rightarrow_S \gamma'$, *and all valuations* ρ' *with* $\rho'|_{Var\backslash Y} = \rho|_{Var\backslash Y}$, *if* $\gamma' = \rho'(\pi')$, *then* $\rho' \models \phi'$.

Note that the *same* values of the variables Y were used for satisfying π' and ϕ'.

Definition 9. *A basic pattern π' is terminal if for all valuations ρ, $\rho(\pi')$ is a terminal configuration. A rule $\pi \wedge \phi \Rightarrow (\exists Y)\pi' \wedge \phi'$ is terminal if π' is terminal.*

The following proposition characterises the validity of terminal RL formulas:

Proposition 1 (Equivalent Conditions for Terminal Formula Validity). *Consider a terminal formula $\pi \wedge \phi \Rightarrow (\exists Y)\pi' \wedge \phi'$. Then $\mathcal{S} \models \pi \wedge \phi \Rightarrow (\exists Y)\pi' \wedge \phi'$ iff*

1. *$(\exists Y)\phi'$ is invariant at $(\exists Y)\pi'$ starting from $\pi \wedge \phi$, and*
2. *$(\exists Y)\pi'$ captures all terminal configurations for $\pi \wedge \phi$.*

Remark 1. The $(\Leftarrow)$ implication in Proposition 1 is the important one for the soundness of our method. Its proof naturally follows from definitions. For the reverse implication, the following assumption is required: for all right-hand sides $\varphi_r \triangleq (\exists Y)\pi_r \wedge \phi_r$ of rules in $\mathcal{S}$, if $\rho(\pi_r) = \rho'(\pi_r)$ then $\rho|_{FreeVars(\pi_r)} = \rho'|_{FreeVars(\pi_r)}$. The assumption does not restrict generality as it can always be made to hold, by replacing subterms of patterns by fresh variables (and adding equations to the condition) and by noting that the *Cfg* sort is interpreted syntactically in the model M. Then, $\pi_r \triangleq f(x_1, \ldots, x_n)$ where f is the constructor for the *Cfg* sort, and $\rho(f(x_1, \ldots, x_n)) = \rho'(f(x_1, \ldots, x_n))$ iff $\rho(x) = \rho'(x_i)$ for all variables x_i.

Remark 2. Proposition 1 works for terminal RL formulas. We shall need the following observation: assume that an RL formula of the following form $\langle P \ldots \rangle \wedge \phi \Rightarrow (\exists Y)\langle skip \ldots \rangle \wedge \phi'$ has been proved valid, where P is a program, $skip$ denotes the empty program, and suspension dots denote the rest of the configurations (which depend on the programming language). Then, assuming a sequencing operation[4] denoted by semicolon, the following formula $\langle P; Q \ldots \rangle \wedge \phi \Rightarrow (\exists Y)\langle Q \ldots \rangle \wedge \phi'$ is also valid: if each terminal path executing P ended up in the empty program, then each path executing $P; Q$ still has Q to execute after having executed P. As shown later in this section, the validity of such "generalized" formulas enables us to incrementally use a proved-valid formula in the proofs of other formulas.

Proposition 1 is the basis for proving RL formulas, by checking the conditions (1) and (2). We now show how the conditions can be checked mechanically.

Symbolic Graph Construction. The graph-construction procedure in Fig. 2 uses symbolic execution and is used to check the conditions (1) and (2) in Proposition 1. Before we describe the procedure we introduce the components that it uses.

A Partial Order $<$ on $\mathcal{S}$. The procedure assumes a set of RL formulas $\mathcal{S}$, which consist of the semantical rules $\mathcal{S}_0$ of a programming language and a (possibly empty) set of RL formulas $\mathcal{G}$ that were already proved valid in an earlier step of our envisaged incremental verification method. Such formulas, sometimes called *circularities* in RL verification, specify subprograms of the program under verification, and are assumed here to have the form $\langle P; Q, \ldots \rangle \wedge \phi \Rightarrow (\exists Y)\langle Q, \ldots \rangle \wedge \phi'$

---

[4] "Sequencing" and "empty" do not need to be actual statements of the programming language; they can just be artifacts required by the language's operational semantics.

0: $G = (N \triangleq \{\pi \wedge \phi\}, E \triangleq \emptyset)$, *Failure* $\leftarrow$ *false*, *New* $\leftarrow N$
1: **while** not *Failure* and *New* $\neq \emptyset$

    2: **choose** $\varphi \triangleq (\exists X_n)\pi_n \wedge \phi_n \in New$; *New* $\leftarrow New \setminus \{\varphi\}$
    3: **if** $match_{\simeq}(\pi_n, \pi') = \emptyset$ **then**
       4: **if** $\bigvee_{\alpha \in min(<)} inclusion(\varphi, lhs(\alpha)) = true$ **then**
          5: **forall** $\alpha \in min(<)$, **forall** $\varphi' \in \Delta_\alpha(\varphi)$
             6: **if** $inclusion(\varphi', \varphi)$ **then** $E \leftarrow E \cup \{\varphi \xrightarrow{\alpha} (\pi \wedge \phi)\}$
             7: **else** *New* $\leftarrow New \cup \{\varphi'\}$; $E \leftarrow E \cup \{\varphi \xrightarrow{\alpha} \varphi'\}$ **endif**
         8: $N \leftarrow N \cup New$
       9: **else** *Failure* $\leftarrow true$ **endif**
    10: **elseif** not $inclusion(\varphi, (\exists Y)\pi' \wedge \phi')$ **then** *Failure* $\leftarrow true$ **endif**.

Fig. 2. Graph construction. $match_{\simeq}()$ is matching modulo the non-bultin axioms (cf. Sect. 3.2), and $inclusion()$ is the object of Definition 10.

(cf. Remark 2). During symbolic execution, circularities can be symbolically applied "in competition with" rules in the semantics (e.g., when the program to be executed is $P; Q$, the symbolic version of the above rule can be applied, but the symbolic version of the semantical rule for the first instruction of P can be applied as well). We solve the conflict between semantical rules and circularities by giving priority to the latter.

We use the following notations. Let $lhs(\alpha)$ denote the left-hand side of a formula α. Let $\mathcal{G} < \mathcal{S}_0$ denote the fact that for every $g \in \mathcal{G}$ and $\alpha \in \mathcal{S}_0$, $g < \alpha$. Let $\mathcal{S}_0 \models \mathcal{G}$ denote $\mathcal{S}_0 \models g$, for all $g \in \mathcal{G}$, and $min(<)$ denote the minimal elements of $<$.

Assumption 4. *We assume a partial order relation* $<$ *on* $\mathcal{S} \triangleq \mathcal{S}_0 \cup \mathcal{G}$ *satisfying:* $\mathcal{G} < \mathcal{S}_0$, $\mathcal{S}_0 \models \mathcal{G}$, *and for all* $\alpha' \in \mathcal{S}$ *and pairs* (γ, ρ), *if* $(\gamma, \rho) \models lhs(\alpha')$ *then there exists a rule* $\alpha \in min(<)$ *such that* $(\gamma, \rho) \models lhs(\alpha)$.

This assumption is satisfied by taking as minimal elements of $<$ previously proved circularities, which gives them priority over rules in the semantics that can be applied in competition with them. The other rules in the semantics, which are not in competition with circularities, are not related by $<$ with other formulas and are thus minimal by definition (and valid, since $\alpha \in \mathcal{S}$ implies $\mathcal{S} \models \alpha$).

Inclusion Between Patterns. The graph-construction procedure uses a test of inclusion between patterns, which satisfies the following definition.

Definition 10 (Inclusion). *An inclusion test is a function that, given patterns* φ, φ', *returns true if for all pairs* (γ, ρ), *if* $(\gamma, \rho) \models \varphi$ *then* $(\gamma, \rho) \models \varphi'$.

The Graph Construction. We are now ready to present the procedure in Fig. 2. The procedure takes as input an RL formula $\pi \wedge \phi \Rightarrow (\exists Y)\pi' \wedge \phi'$ and a set $\mathcal{S}$ of RL formula with an order $<$ on $\mathcal{S}$ as discussed earlier in this section. It builds a graph (N, E) with N the set of nodes (initially, $\{\pi \wedge \phi\}$) and E the set of edges (initially empty). It uses two variables to control a while loop: a Boolean variable *Failure* (initially *false*) and a set of nodes *New* (initially equal to $N = \{\pi \wedge \phi\}$).

At each iteration of the while loop, a node $\varphi_n \triangleq (\exists X_n)\pi_n \wedge \phi_n$ is taken out from *New* (line 2) and checks whether there is a matcher modulo $\cong$ (cf. Sect. 3.2) of π' onto π_n (line 3). If this is the case, then π_n is an instance of the (terminal) basic pattern π', and the procedure goes to line 10 to check whether φ_n "as a whole" is included in $(\exists Y)\pi' \wedge \phi'$. If this is not the case, then, informally, this indicates a terminal path that does not satisfy the right-hand side of the formula under proof, i.e., of the fact that $(\exists Y)\phi'$ is not invariant at $(\exists Y)\pi'$, in contradiction with the first hypothesis of Proposition 1 that the procedure is checking; *Failure* is reported, which terminates the execution of the procedure. However, if the test at line 3 indicated that π_n is not an instance of the terminal pattern π', then another inclusion test is performed (line 4): whether there exists a minimal rule in $\mathcal{S}$ (i.e., a rule in the language's semantics, or a circularity already proved, as discussed earlier in this section) whose left-hand side includes φ_n. If this is not the case then, informally, this indicates a terminal configuration that is not an instance of $(\exists Y)\pi'$, which contradicts the second hypothesis of Proposition 1, making the procedure terminate again with *Failure* = *true*.

If, however, the inclusion test at line 4 succeeds then all symbolic successors φ'_n of φ_n by minimal rules α w.r.t. $<$ are computed. Each of these patterns is tested for inclusion in the initial node $\pi \wedge \phi$. If inclusion holds then an edge is added from φ_n to the initial node, labelled by the rule that generated the symbolic successor in question. Otherwise, a new node φ'_n is created, and an edge from the current node φ_n to the new node, labelled by the rule that generated it, is created, and the while loop proceeds to the next iteration.

The graph-construction procedure does not terminate in general, since the verification of RL formulas is undecidable. However, if it does terminate with *Failure* = *false* then the two conditions equivalent to the validity of the procedure's input $\pi \wedge \phi \Rightarrow (\exists Y)\pi' \wedge \phi'$ hold, i.e., $\mathcal{S} \models \pi \wedge \phi \Rightarrow (\exists Y)\pi' \wedge \phi'$, which is the desired conclusion. This is established by the results in the rest of this section.

The paths in the constructed graph simulate concrete execution paths whose transitions are given by rules from $\mathcal{S}_0$. This is formalised and used in the proof of the main theorem states that the hypotheses of Proposition 1, equivalent to RL formula validity, are checked by the graph-construction procedure.

Theorem 1. *If the procedure in Fig. 2 terminates with Failure = false on a terminal RL formula $\pi \wedge \phi \Rightarrow (\exists Y)\pi' \wedge \phi'$, then $(\exists Y)\phi'$ is invariant at $(\exists Y)\pi'$ starting from $\pi \wedge \phi$, and $(\exists Y)\pi'$ captures all terminal configurations starting from $\pi \wedge \phi$.*

Theorem 1 uses the following (and last) assumptions on RL formulas:

Assumption 5. *All rules $\varphi_l \Rightarrow \varphi_r \in \mathcal{S}$ have the following properties:*

1. *for all pairs (γ, ρ) such that $(\gamma, \rho) \models \varphi_l$ there exists γ' such that $(\gamma', \rho) \models \varphi_r$[5].*
2. $[\![\varphi_l]\!] \cap [\![\varphi_r]\!] = \emptyset$.

The first of the above assumptions says that if the left-hand side of a rule matches a configuration then there is nothing in the right-hand side preventing the application. This property is called *weak well-definedness* in [4] and is shown there

---

[5] This property is called weak well-definedness in [4].

to be a necessary condition for obtaining a sound proof system for RL. The second condition just says that the left and right-hand sides of rules cannot share instances - such rules could generate self-loops on instances, which are useless. We then obtain as a corollary the soundness of our RL formula proof method:

Corollary 1 (Soundness). *If procedure in Fig. 2 terminates with Failure = false on a terminal RL formula $\pi \wedge \phi \Rightarrow (\exists Y)\pi' \wedge \phi'$ then $\mathcal{S} \models \pi \wedge \phi \Rightarrow (\exists Y)\pi' \wedge \phi'$.*

Incremental Verification. We are now ready to describe our incremental RL formula verification method. The method works in a setting where each formula has an associated *code* that it specifies, and that for a given RL formula f, $code(f)$ returns the given code. Considering the RL formulas (1) and (2) in Sect. 1, $code(1)$ is the sum program in Fig. 1 and $code(2)$ is the while subprogram.

The problem to be solved is: given two sets of formulas: $\mathcal{S}$ (the semantics of a language) and $\mathcal{G}$ (the specification of a given program and of some of its subprograms) prove *for all $g \in \mathcal{G}$, $\mathcal{S} \models g$* (for short, $\mathcal{S} \models \mathcal{G}$).

We use partial orders $<$ on $\mathcal{S}$ (initially empty) and $\sqsubset$ on $\mathcal{G}$, defined by $g_1 \sqsubset g_2$ whenever $code(g_1)$ is a strict subprogram of $code(g_2)$. Without restriction of generality we take the formulas in $\mathcal{G}$ to be terminal (which is natural: a piece of code is specified by stating what the code "does" when it terminates). The verification consists repeatedly applying the following steps while $\mathcal{G} \neq \emptyset$:

- choose $g \in \mathcal{G}$ minimal w.r.t. $\sqsubset$ and prove it, based on Corollary 1;
- remove g from $\mathcal{G}$, transform g into a non-terminal formula (cf. Remark 2) and add the resulting formula g' to $\mathcal{S}$;
- extend $<$ on the newly obtained set $\mathcal{S}$ so that g' is smaller than any formula in $\mathcal{S}$ that can be applied concurrently with g'.

Example 5. Consider the sum program in Fig. 1. $\mathcal{S}$ consists of the semantical rules of IMP+, and $\mathcal{G}$ consists of formulas (1) and (2) in Sect. 1, with (2) $\sqsubset$ (1).

At the first iteration (2) is chosen. It is verified based on Corollary 1 (which builds the graph according to the procedure shown in Fig. 2), then transformed into a nonterminal formula, removed from $\mathcal{G}$ and added to $\mathcal{S}$. The relation $<$ is extended so that the newly added formula is smaller than the semantical rule for the while instruction, since the two rules can be applied concurrently.

At the second (and final) iteration, (1) is verified. The graph-construction procedure exploits the fact that (2) is minimal in $\mathcal{S}$ and thus it will be applied instead of the semantical rule for while, producing a finite graph by avoiding an infinite loop unfolding, and allowing Corollary 1 to establish that (1) is valid.

5   Incrementally Verifying the KMP Algorithm

The KMP (Knuth-Morris-Pratt) algorithm is a linear-time string-matching algorithm. The algorithm optimises the naive search of a pattern P into a text T by using some additional information collected from the pattern.

For instance, let us consider $T = \texttt{ABADABCDA}$ and $P = \texttt{ABAC}$. It can be easily observed that $\texttt{ABAC}$ does not match $\texttt{ABADABCDA}$ starting with the first position because there is a mismatch on the fourth position, namely $\texttt{C} \neq \texttt{D}$. A naive algorithm, after having detected this, would restart the matching process of P at the second position of T (which fails immediately) then at the third one, where it woud first match an $\texttt{A}$ before detecting another mismatch (between $\texttt{B}$ and $\texttt{D}$). The KMP optimises this by comparing directly the $\texttt{B}$ and $\texttt{D}$, as it "already knows" that they are both preceded by $\texttt{A}$, thereby saving one redundant comparison.

The overall effect is that the worst-case complexity of KMP is determined by the sum of the lengths of P and T, whereas that of a naive algorithm is determined by the product of the two lengths.

The KMP algorithm pre-processes the pattern P by computing a so-called *prefix function* π. Let P_j denote the subpattern of P up to a position j. For such position j, $\pi(j)$ equals the *length of the longest proper prefix of P_j, which is also a suffix of P_j*. In the case of a mismatch between the position i in T and the position j in P, the algorithm proceeds with the comparison of the positions i and $\pi[j]$. This is why, in the above example, KMP direcly compared the $\texttt{B}$ and $\texttt{D}$.

We prove that the KMP algorithm is correct, i.e., given a non-empty pattern P and a non-empty string T, the algorithm finds *all* the occurrences of P in T. We use the incremental method presented in Sect. 4 on an encoding of KMP in the IMP+ language formally defined in Maude (cf. Sect. 2).

The program is shown in Fig. 3. Its specification uses the following notions:

Definition 11. – P_j *denotes the prefix of P up to (and including) j. P_0 is the empty string ϵ. If a string P' is a strict suffix of P we write $P' \sqsupset P$.*
- *The prefix function for P is $\pi : \{1, \ldots, m\} \rightarrow \{0, \ldots, m-1\}$ defined by $\pi(i) = max\{j \mid 0 \leq j < i \wedge P_j \sqsupset P_i\}$. We let $\pi^*(q) = \{\pi(q), \pi(\pi(q)), \ldots\}$.*
- *Let T be a string of length n. We define $\theta : \{1, \ldots, n\} \rightarrow \{0, \ldots, m\}$ the function which, for a given $i \in \{1, \ldots, n\}$, returns the longest prefix of P which is a suffix of T_i: $\theta(i) = max\{j \mid 0 \leq j \leq m \wedge P_j \sqsupset T_i\}$.*
- *Let T be a string of length n and Out a list. The function $allOcc(Out, P, T, i)$ returns true iff the list Out contains all the occurrences of P in $T[1..i]$.*

The grey-text annotations, written as pre/post conditions and invariants, are syntactical sugar for RL formulas. The annotations are numbered (C_1 to C_6) according to the order in which the RL formulas are verified by our incremental method. So, for example, the annotation for the inner loop of the `computePrefix` function is the first to be verified, and corresponds to an RL formula for the form
$$\langle \texttt{while C do} \ldots \texttt{endwhile}, \ldots \rangle \wedge C \wedge C_1 \Rightarrow \langle \texttt{skip}, \ldots \rangle \wedge \neg C \wedge C_1$$
where `while C do ... endwhile` denotes the inner loop of `computePrefix`. Similarly, the specification of the KMP program is an RL formula of the form:
$$\langle \texttt{KMP}, \ldots, \texttt{.Ints} \rangle \wedge C_6 \Rightarrow \langle \texttt{skip}, \ldots, \texttt{Out} \rangle \wedge allOcc(Out, \ldots),$$
where KMP denotes the whole program, `.Ints` denotes an empty list of integers (cf. Sect. 2), Out is a list of integers denoting the program's output, and $allOcc(Out, \ldots)$ states that Out contains all positions of the pattern in the text.

The RL formulas corresponding to the annotations ($C_1 \ldots C_6$) were verified in the given order. Once a formula was verified, it was generalised (cf. Remark 2)

```
/*C3: m >= 1 */
function computePrefix(){
  k := 0;
  pi[1] := 0;
  q := 2;
  while (q <== m) do
  /*C2: 0 <= k /\ k < q /\ q <= m+1 /\
  (forall u:1..k)(p[u]=p[q-1-k+u]) /\
  (forall u:1..q-1)(pi[u]=Pi(u)) /\
  (forall j)((j > k /\ j in Pi*(q-1))
            implies p[j+1] != p[q]) /\
  k in Pi*(q-1) /\ Pi(q)<=k+1  */
    while !(k <== 0) &&
        !(p[k ++ 1] === p[q]) do
    /*C1: 0 <= k /\ k < q /\ q <= m /\
    (forall u:1..k)(p[u]=p[q-1-k+u]) /\
    (forall u:1..q-1)(pi[u]=Pi(u)) /\
    (forall j)((j > k /\ j in Pi*(q-1))
              implies p[j+1] != p[q]) /\
    k in Pi*(q-1) /\ Pi(q)<=k+1  */
      k := pi[k]
    endwhile
    if (p[k ++ 1] === p[q]) then
      k := k ++ 1
    else skip
    endif
    pi[q] := k;
    q := q ++ 1;
  endwhile}
/*(forall u:1..m)(pi[u]=Pi(u)) */
```

```
/*Main program  */
/*C6: m>=1 /\ n>=1 */
q := 0;
i := 1;
computePrefix();
while (i <== n) do
/*C5: *1 <= m /\ 0 <=q <= m /\ 1 <= i<= n+1 /\
  (forall u:1..q)(p[u]=t[i-1-q+u]) /\
  (forall u:1..m)(pi[u]=Pi(u)) /\
  (exists v)((forall u:v+1..i-1) Theta(u)<m /\
                    allOcc(Out,p,t,v))/\

  Theta(i)<=q+1 */
  while !(q <== 0) && !(p[q ++ 1] === t[i]) do
  /*C4: 1<=m /\ 0<=q<m /\ 1 <= i <= n/\
    (forall u:1..q)(p[u]=t[i-1-q+u]) /\
    (forall u:1..m)(pi[u]=Pi(u)) /\
    (exists v)((forall u:v+1..i-1)
            Theta(u)<m /\ allOcc(Out,p,t,v))/\
    Theta(i)<=q+1 */
    q := pi[q]
  endwhile
  if (p[q ++ 1] === t[i]) then q := q ++ 1
  else skip endif;
  if (q === m) then print (i -- m) ; q := p[q]
  else skip endif;
  i := i ++ 1
endwhile
/*allOcc(Out, p, t, n) */
```

Fig. 3. The KMP algorithm in IMP+: prefix function (left) and the main program (right). Grey-text annotations are syntactic sugar for RL formulas. Pi, Theta, allOcc, and Pi* denote the functions π, θ, and $allOcc$, and the set π^* respectively (cf. Definition 11).

and added to the rules denoting the semantics of IMP+ as new, prioritary rules. Each rule verification follows the construction of a graph (cf. procedure in Fig. 2), performed by symbolic execution, implemented by rewriting as described in Sect. 3. For this purpose we have intensively use Maude's metalevel mechanisms in order to control the application of rewrite rules.

The main verification effort (besides coming up with the annotations $C_1 \ldots C_6$) went into the inclusion test between patterns that occurs in our graph-construction procedure. For this purpose we have used certain properties of the π, π^*, and θ mathematical functions from [12], which we include in Maude as equations used for the purpose of simplification. Some elementary simplifications involving properties of integers and Booleans were performed via Maude's interface to the Z3 solver. Collectively, these properties can be seen as axioms that define the class of models in which the correctness of our KMP program holds.

Benefits of Incremental Verification. In earlier work [5] we attempted to verify KMP using a circular approach of the "all-or-nothing" variety. The main difficulty with such approaches is that, if verification fails, one is left with nothing: any of the formulas being (simultaneously) verified could be responsible for the failure.

The consequence was that (as we realised afterwards by revisiting the problem) our earlier verification was incorrect. We found some versions of the annotations $C_1 \dots C_6$, which, as RL formulas, would only hold under unrealistic assumptions about the problem-domain functions π, π^*, and θ.

We decided to redo the KMP verification incrementally, starting with smaller program fragments, and rigorously proving at each step the required facts about the problem domain. Our incremental approach was first a language-*dependent* one [12], as it was based on proving pre/post conditions of functions and loop invariants. Of course, not all languages have the same kinds of functions and loops; some lack such constructions altogether. The method proposed in this paper is (with some restrictions) both incremental and language-independent, is formally proved correct, and was instrumental in successfully proving the KMP program, this time, under valid assertions regarding the problem domain.

6   Conclusion, Related Work and Future Work

In this paper we propose an incremental method for proving a class of RL formulas useful in practical situations. Mainly, RL formula verification is reduced to checking two technical conditions: the first is an invariance property, while the second is related to the so-called capturing of terminal configurations. Formally, the conjunction of these conditions is shown to be equivalent to RL formula validity. We also present a graph construction procedure based on symbolic execution which, if it terminates successfully, ensures that these conditions hold for a given RL formula. The method is successfully applied on the nontrivial Knuth-Morris-Pratt algorithm for string matching, encoded in a simple imperative language. The syntax and the semantics of this language have been defined in Maude, whose reflective features were intensively used for implementation purposes.

Using the proposed approach RL formulas are proved in a systematic manner. One first proves formulas that specify sub-programs of the program under verification, and then exploits the newly proved formulas to (incrementally) prove other formulas that specify larger subprograms. By contrast, monolithic/circular approaches [1–4,6,13] attempt to prove all formulas at once, in no particular order. In case of failure, in a monolithic approach, *any* circularly dependent subset of formulas under proof might be responsible for the failure; whereas in an incremental approach, there is only one subset of formulas to consider (and to modify in order to progress in the proof): the formula currently under proof, together with some already proved valid formulas. Thus, an incremental method saves the user some effort in the trial-and-error process of program verification.

Related Work. Besides the already mentioned work on RL we cite some approaches in program verification; an exhaustive list is outside the scope of this paper.

Some approaches are based on exploring the state-space of a program, e.g., [14], in which software model checking is combined with symbolic execution and abstraction techniques to overcome state-space explosion. Our approach has some similarities with the above: we also use symbolic execution to construct a graph, which is an abstraction of the reachable state space of a program.

Some verification tools (e.g., Why3 [15]) are based on deductive methods. These tools use the program specifications (i.e., pre/post-conditions, invariants) to generate proof obligations, which are then discharged to external provers (e.g., COQ, Z3, ...). Similarly, our implementation uses a version of Maude which includes a connection to the Z3 SMT solver (used for simplifying conditions).

In the same spirit, compositional methods for the formal verification (e.g., [16]) shift the focus of verification from global to local level in order to reduce the complexity of the verification process.

Future Work. One issue that needs to be addressed is the handling of domain-specific properties. Each program makes computations over a certain domain (e.g., arrays), and in order to prove a program, certain properties of the underlying domain are required (e.g., relations between selecting and storing elements in an array). Currently, these properties are stated as axioms in Maude, and we are planning to connect Maude to an inductive prover in order to interactively prove the axioms in questions as properties satisfied by more basic definitions.

References

1. Roşu, G., Ştefănescu, A.: Towards a unified theory of operational and axiomatic semantics. In: Czumaj, A., Mehlhorn, K., Pitts, A., Wattenhofer, R. (eds.) ICALP 2012, Part II. LNCS, vol. 7392, pp. 351–363. Springer, Heidelberg (2012)
2. Roşu, G., Ştefănescu, A.: Checking reachability using matching logic. In: Proceedings of the 27th Conference on Object-Oriented Programming, Systems, Languages, and Applications (OOPSLA 2012), pp. 555–574. ACM (2012)
3. Roşu, G., Ştefănescu, A., Ciobâcă, Ş., Moore, B.M.: One-path reachability logic. In: Proceedings of the 28th Symposium on Logic in Computer Science (LICS 2013), pp. 358–367. IEEE, June 2013
4. Ştefănescu, A., Ciobâcă, Ş., Mereuţă, R., Moore, B.M., Şerbănuţă, T.F., Roşu, G.: All-path reachability logic. In: Dowek, G. (ed.) RTA-TLCA 2014. LNCS, vol. 8560, pp. 425–440. Springer, Heidelberg (2014)
5. Arusoaie, A., Lucanu, D., Rusu, V.: A generic framework for symbolic execution: theory and applications. Research report RR-8189. Inria, September 2015
6. Arusoaie, A., Lucanu, D., Rusu, V.: A generic framework for symbolic execution. Research report RR-8189. Inria, September 2015. https://hal.inria.fr/hal-00766220
7. Clavel, M., Durán, F., Eker, S., Lincoln, P., Martí-Oliet, N., Meseguer, J., Talcott, C. (eds.): All About Maude. LNCS, vol. 4350. Springer, Heidelberg (2007)
8. de Moura, L., Bjørner, N.S.: Z3: an efficient SMT solver. In: Ramakrishnan, C.R., Rehof, J. (eds.) TACAS 2008. LNCS, vol. 4963, pp. 337–340. Springer, Heidelberg (2008)
9. Roşu, G., Ellison, C., Schulte, W.: Matching logic: an alternative to Hoare/Floyd logic. In: Johnson, M., Pavlovic, D. (eds.) AMAST 2010. LNCS, vol. 6486, pp. 142–162. Springer, Heidelberg (2011)
10. Roşu, G., Ştefănescu, A.: Matching logic: a new program verification approach (NIER track). In: ICSE 2011: Proceedings of the 30th International Conference on Software Engineering, pp. 868–871. ACM (2011)

11. Roşu, G.: Matching logic — extended abstract. In: Proceedings of the 26th International Conference on Rewriting Techniques and Applications (RTA 2015). Leibniz International Proceedings in Informatics (LIPIcs), vol. 36, pp. 5–21. Schloss Dagstuhl–Leibniz-Zentrum fuer Informatik, Dagstuhl, July 2015
12. Verification of the KMP algorithm. https://fmse.info.uaic.ro/imgs/kmp.pdf
13. Lucanu, D., Rusu, V., Arusoaie, A., Nowak, D.: Verifying reachability-logic properties on rewriting-logic specifications. In: Martí-Oliet, N., Ölveczky, P.C., Talcott, C. (eds.) Meseguer Festschrift. LNCS, vol. 9200, pp. 451–474. Springer, Heidelberg (2015)
14. Visser, W., Havelund, K., Brat, G.P., Park, S., Lerda, F.: Model checking programs. Autom. Softw. Eng. **10**(2), 203–232 (2003)
15. Filliâtre, J.-C., Paskevich, A.: Why3 — where programs meet provers. In: Felleisen, M., Gardner, P. (eds.) ESOP 2013. LNCS, vol. 7792, pp. 125–128. Springer, Heidelberg (2013)
16. de Roever, W.P., de Boer, F.S., Hannemann, U., Hooman, J., Lakhnech, Y., Poel, M., Zwiers, J.: Concurrency Verification: Introduction to Compositional and Noncompositional Methods. Cambridge Tracts in Theoretical Computer Science, vol. 54. Cambridge University Press, Cambridge (2001)

Maximally Parallel Contextual String Rewriting

Traian Florin Şerbănuţă[(⊠)] and Liviu P. Dinu

Faculty of Mathematics and Computer Science,
University of Bucharest, Bucharest, Romania
{traian.serbanuta,ldinu}@fmi.unibuc.ro

Abstract. This paper introduces contextual string rewriting as a special kind of parallel string rewriting in which each rule defines a context which is not changed by the application of the rule and can be read (but not modified) by other rules applying concurrently. We study maximal parallel rewriting in this setting and provide a method to encode the computation of a maximally parallel instance for a contextual string rewrite system as a decidable normal form problem for a particular term rewrite system.

1 Introduction and Motivation

One of the main problems of structural linguistics is segmentation, i.e. how to divide a linguistic construct into its constituents, on different levels (e.g. phonemes, morphemes, etc.). This segmentation has various applications, from correctly identifying words in the presence of ambiguity (e.g., Arabic script), to the more recent theories of Levelt and Indefrey [8] according to which an important role in producing words is played by the way the brain segments them into syllables. The necessity of segmenting linguistic constructs brings a new challenge: can this segmentation be performed sequentially or parallel? When attempting a computational approach to segmentation, parallelism seems more natural; this is strengthen by Mitchell who proposes the brain as being a super-computer able to process data in parallel: "Many of the brains activities have been thought to work in parallel. For example, the fast processing abilities of the brain in tasks such as face recognition may follow from a highly parallel process" [13]. However, linguists seem more reserved regarding sequential vs. parallel segmentation. Recently, Hopf et al. [6] tackling the question "Is human sentence parsing serial or parallel?" give the following answer "These data are taken as evidence for a strictly serial parser".

Dinu and Dinu [3] propose *insertion grammars with maximal parallel derivation* as a formalization for parallel syllabification, noticing a connection between syllabification and word generation using Marcus' contextual grammars [10,11]. This parallel syllabification uses an insertion mechanism dual to that of contextual grammars, introduced by Galiuschov [5], which is enhanced by introducing a parallel derivation, and additionally constraining the number of insertion in a single parallel step to be maximal. This parallel approach to syllabification can constitute an argument for parallel segmentation of words at brain level in the context of the recent cognitive theory of speech production [8].

© Springer International Publishing Switzerland 2016
D. Lucanu (Ed.): WRLA 2016, LNCS 9942, pp. 152–166, 2016.
DOI: 10.1007/978-3-319-44802-2_9

The expressive power of this formalization and comparisons with existing formal languages classes is further studied by Dinu [4]. However, results were purely theoretical, lacking a computational implementation mechanism.

This paper comes to address this limitation by proposing *contextual string rewriting* as a generalization of maximally parallel insertion grammars, as well as a concrete mechanism for implementing and experimenting with them through translations to traditional term rewriting systems.

Our Approach. Inspired from several approaches in the theory of formal languages and computation [1,4,7,12,15,16] defining contextual application of rules we introduce contextual string rewriting as a generalization of insertion-deletion systems [7] and study concurrent application of rules with sharing of context in the spirit of maximally parallel insertion grammars [4].

We define the notion of a *parallel instance* of the application of multiple concurrent contextual string rewrite rules on a word and a refinement relation among such parallel instances increasing the degree of parallelism. Maximal parallel rewriting is defined as transforming a word according to a "maximally refined" parallel instance.

Finally, we tackle the problem of computing a maximal parallel instance with the aim of allowing simulation, execution, and analysis of the behavior of maximal parallel rewriting for contextual string rewrite systems. Two encodings of the problem as a normal forms computation problem for regular term rewriting (modulo associativity and identity axioms), one more explicit, and an optimized one, are proposed and shown adequate.

2   Preliminaries and Related Work

In this section we introduce some basic formal-language notions and review several contextual derivation methods (mostly for words) with various degrees of parallelism and sharing.

An *alphabet* is a finite non-empty set. The elements of an alphabet Σ are called *letters* or *symbols*. A *word* over alphabet Σ is a finite sequence of zero or more letters of Σ; the word with zero letters is called the *empty* word and is denoted by λ.

The set of all words over Σ is denoted by Σ^*, while $\Sigma^+ = \Sigma^* \setminus \{\lambda\}$ represents the set of non-empty words over Σ. Given two words u and w, their *concatenation* is denoted uw and is obtained by juxtaposition. Thus, $(\Sigma^*, \cdot, \lambda)$ is the free monoid generated by Σ. A *language* over the alphabet Σ is a subset of Σ^*.

Insertion-Deletion Systems. A reasonably well studied example of contextual rewriting/derivation of strings is that of insertion-deletion systems introduced by Kari and Thierrin [7].

An *insertion-deletion system* is a tuple $\Gamma = (\Sigma, T, A, I, D)$, where Σ is an alphabet, $T \subseteq \Sigma$ is the *terminal* alphabet (symbols from $\Sigma \setminus T$ are called *nonterminals*), $A \subseteq \Sigma^*$ is the set of *axioms*, while I (the insertion rules) and D (the deletion rules) are finite sets of triples of the form (u, x, v), where $u, x, v \in \Sigma^*$ with $x \neq \lambda$, having the following semantics: an insertion rule (u, x, v) specifies the insertion of x in the context (u, v), while a deletion rule (u, x, v) specifies a deletion of x in the context (u, v).

Formally, for $w, z \in \Sigma^*$, we write $w \Rightarrow_I z$ if $w = w_1 u v w_2$ and $z = w_1 u x v w_2$, for some insertion rule (u, x, v) in I and $w_1, w_2 \in \Sigma^*$; if (u, x, v) in D, this induces $z \Rightarrow_D w$. Therefore, an insertion rule is similar to the string rewriting rule $uv \to uxv$, while a deletion rule is similar to the reverse rule $uxv \to uv$.

Let $\Rightarrow_\Gamma$ denote $\Rightarrow_I \cup \Rightarrow_D$ and $\Rightarrow_\Gamma^*$ be its reflexive and transitive closure. The language generated by Γ is defined by the set of terminal words which can be derived through $\Rightarrow_\Gamma^*$ from the axioms A:

$$L(\Gamma) = \{z \in T^* | w \Rightarrow_\Gamma^* z, \text{ for } w \in A\}$$

Insertion Grammars with Maximum Parallel Derivation. Insertion grammars are a special case of insertion-deletion systems, without non-terminals $(T = \Sigma)$ and deletion rules $(D = \varnothing)$.

Introduced by Dinu [4] for defining a cognitive model for syllabification, parallel derivation with shared context of an insertion grammar Γ, here denoted as $\Rightarrow_\Gamma$, is defined by: $w \Rightarrow_\Gamma z$ iff $w = w_0 w_1 \ldots w_r$, for some $r \geqslant 1$, $z = w_0 x_1 w_1 x_2 w_2 \ldots x_r w_r$ and, for all $1 \leqslant i \leqslant r$, there exist $(u_i, x_i, v_i) \in I$ and $\alpha_i, \beta_i \in \Sigma^*$ such that $w_{i-1} = \alpha_i u_i$, $w_i = v_i \beta_i$.

Maximum parallel derivation for insertion grammars is defined as parallel derivation with a maximum number of rules (i.e., maximum r in the decomposition above).

Example 1. Let $\Sigma = \{a_1, a_2, \ldots, a_k\}$ $(k \geqslant 2)$, $A = \{a_1 a_2 \cdots a_k\}$, and

$$I = \{(a_i, a_i, a_{i+1}) \mid i \in \{1, \ldots, k-2\}\} \cup \{(a_{k-1}, a_{k-1} a_k, a_k)\}.$$

If using non-maximally parallel derivation, this grammar generates the context-free language $a_1^+ a_2^+ \cdots a_{k-2}^+ a_{k-1}^n a_k^n$. However, under maximum parallel derivation, the generated language is $a_1^n a_2^n \cdots a_k^n$.

The next example exhibits the generation of Fibonacci sequences.

Example 2. Let $\Sigma = \{a, b\}$, $A = \{a, b\}$, and $I = \{(a, b, \lambda), (\lambda, ba, b)\}$.

If using non-maximally parallel derivation, this grammar generates the language $\{a\} \cup \{(ab^+)^+\} \cup \{b(ab^+)^*\}$. However, under maximum parallel derivation, the generated language is the so called set of "Fibonacci words":

$$\{a, b, ab, bab, abbab, bababbab, abbabbababbab, bababbabbabbabbababbab \ldots\}$$

The $\mathbb{K}$ semantic framework [16] proposes a semantics for concurrent term rewriting with sharing of context based on graph transformation, again with no focus on maximality.

A $\mathbb{K}$ rule is of the form $k[l_1 \to r_1, \ldots, l_n \to r_n]$ where k is an n-ary context (which can be shared by concurrent rule applications), $l_1, \ldots, l_n$ are the parts to be rewritten, and $r_1, \ldots, r_n$ are their corresponding replacements. The "flattening" of a $\mathbb{K}$ rule as a rewrite rule is: $k[l_1, \ldots, l_n] \to k[r_1, \ldots, r_n]$.

$\mathbb{K}$ rules can be written in a visual form as $k[\,\underset{r_1}{\underline{l_1}}\,, \ldots,\, \underset{r_n}{\underline{l_n}}\,]$ where in the term $k[l_1, \ldots, l_n]$ the parts to be rewritten $(l_1, \ldots, l_n)$ are underlined and their corresponding replacements $(r_1, \ldots, r_n)$ are written under the lines.

Other Related Work

The object semantics of rewriting logic [12] allows concurrent rewriting with sharing of context in the setting of multi-set rewriting of objects, but without studying maximality.

Context-sensitive Lindenmayer systems, also termed IL-systems [9,15] also exhibit a form of maximally parallel contextual rewriting in which the context is shared by rules; however, unlike the above approaches, the context itself can be rewritten by the concurrent rule applications.

Membrane systems with promoters [1] are a variation of membrane computing [14] whose semantics resembles some form of multiset rewriting over structured nested cells in which rules (local to each cell) are applied in a maximally parallel way and where promoters (special atoms) can be shared by multiple rule instances. Our goals are somehow similar, but our setting is different: we study maximal parallelism with sharing on plain strings instead of structured multisets.

3 Concurrent Contextual String Rewriting

In this section we introduce contextual string rewriting systems, a generalization of string rewriting systems inspired by the approaches presented in Sect. 2.

A string rewriting system (SRS) is a tuple $S = (\Sigma, R)$ where Σ is an alphabet and R is a finite set of rewrite rules $x \to y$. The rewriting relation induced by R is the reflexive and transitive closure $\Rightarrow_R^*$ of the relation $w \Rightarrow_R z$ given by $w = w_1 x w_2$ and $z = w_1 y w_2$ for some rule $x \to y \in R$ and some $w_1, w_2 \in \Sigma^*$.

3.1 Contextual String Rewriting

In this section we generalize the concept of parallel derivation from the contextual insertion grammars to SRSs, with the aim to obtain a rewrite relation which allows both parallel rewriting and sharing of context.

Noting that multiple concurrent instances of string rewriting can only share the prefixes and suffixes of each rule, we define the a *contextual string rewrite rule* as a string rewrite rule in a (shared) context.

Definition 1. *A contextual string rewrite rule is defined as a tuple (u, x, y, v) of words over Σ, such that $uxv, xy \in \Sigma^+$, written $u \langle x \to y \rangle v$ and read as x rewrites to y in the context (u, v). A set $\mathcal{R}$ of contextual string rewrite rules is called a contextual string rewrite system.*

Thus, a contextual string rewrite rule can be viewed as both a generalization of an insertion-deletion systems [7] (insertion rules correspond to $x = \lambda$, while deletion rules correspond to $y = \lambda$) and a specialization of a $\mathbb{K}$ term rewrite rule [16] to strings.

A contextual string rewrite rule $u \langle x \to y \rangle v$ can be flattened to the regular string rewrite rule $uxv \to uyv$, allowing us to define $\Rightarrow_{\mathcal{R}}$ as $\Rightarrow_R$, the rewrite relation corresponding to the SRS R consisting of the flattened rules of $\mathcal{R}$.

Let us now generalize the notion of parallel derivation from insertion grammars [4] to contextual SRSs.

Definition 2. *Let $\mathcal{R}$ be an contextual SRS. We define the parallel rewriting relation, denoted $\Rightarrow_{\mathcal{R}}$, by: $w \Rightarrow_{\mathcal{R}} z$ iff $w = w_0 x_1 w_1 x_2 w_2 \ldots x_r w_r$, for some $r \geqslant 1$, $z = w_0 y_1 w_1 y_2 w_2 \ldots y_r w_r$ and, for all $1 \leqslant i \leqslant r$, there exist $u_i \langle x_i \to y_i \rangle v_i \in \mathcal{R}$ and $\alpha_i, \beta_i \in \Sigma^*$ such that $w_{i-1} = \alpha_i u_i$, $w_i = v_i \beta_i$.*

It is easy to see that regular string rewriting is a particular instance of contextual string rewriting:

Proposition 1. *Let $\mathcal{R}$ be a contextual SRS. Then $\Rightarrow_{\mathcal{R}} \subseteq \Rightarrow_{\mathcal{R}}$.*

3.2 Comparison with Existing Approaches

Insertion/Deletion Systems rules can be seen as particular forms of contextual string rewriting rules. Insertion rules are contextual string rewriting rules of the form $u \langle \lambda \to y \rangle v$. Deletion rules are contextual string rewriting rules of the form $u \langle x \to \lambda \rangle v$. Contextual string rewriting can be seen as a slight relaxation of insertion/deletion systems. Conversely, the application of a contextual string rewriting rule $u \langle x \to y \rangle v$ can be seen as an application of the deletion rule $u \langle x \to \lambda \rangle v$ followed by an application of the insertion rule $u \langle \lambda \to y \rangle v$. Therefore, in a sequential rewriting setting, any of them can simulate the other. However, if considering (maximally) concurrent application of rules, insertion/deletion systems can no longer simulate contextual string rewriting. As pointed out by Dinu [4], the languages generated by insertion/deletion systems are incomparable with those generated through maximall parallel derivation.

$\mathbb{K}$ *Rewriting.* Contextual string rewriting can be seen as a particular form of $\mathbb{K}$ rewriting over a signature defining strings and using only "ground" rules, i.e., rules with no variables. The fact that the context k involved in a $\mathbb{K}$ rule can have multiple holes is not relevant, as the "shared" parts between two holes cannot in fact be shared by any other rule applications. Therefore, the $\mathbb{K}$ rule $\dfrac{x_1}{y_1} \dfrac{w_1}{y_2} \dfrac{x_2}{\cdots} \dfrac{x_n}{y_n} \dfrac{w_n}{}$, where x_i, y_i, w_i are all (ground) words, is similar (semantic-wise) with the contextual string rewrite rule

$$w_0 \langle x_1 w_1 \cdots x_{n-1} w_{n-1} x_n \to y_1 w_1 \cdots y_{n-1} w_{n-1} y_n \rangle w_n.$$

3.3   Maximally Concurrent Contextual String Rewriting

In order to capture the maximal parallel rewriting we extract from the definition above the notion of a parallel instance of a contextual SRS and we subsequently define a refinement relation among such parallel instances.

Definition 3. *A sequence* π : $w_0\langle y_1\rangle^{\rho_1} w_1\langle y_2\rangle^{\rho_2} w_2 \dots w_{r-1}\langle y_r\rangle^{\rho_r} w_r$ *is an r-parallel instance of system $\mathcal{R}$ on word w if for all $1 \leqslant i \leqslant r$, $\rho_i \in \mathcal{R}$ is of the form $u_i \langle x_i \to y_i \rangle v_i$ and there exist $\alpha_i, \beta_i \in \Sigma^*$ such that $w_{i-1} = \alpha_i u_i, w_i = v_i \beta_i$, and $w = w_0 x_1 w_1 x_2 w_2 \dots x_r w_r$. In this case r is called the* length *of π. A parallel instance of non-zero length is termed* proper.
Let $w_0 x_1 w_1 x_2 w_2 \dots x_r w_r \Rightarrow_{\mathcal{R},\pi} w_0 y_1 w_1 y_2 w_2 \dots y_r w_r$ denote the parallel rewriting step induced by π.

Note that the sequence defining a r-parallel instance on w uniquely determines both r and w, allowing us to omit the mentioning either of them in the sequel. Also note that if the length of π is 0 then π is just a word w_0 over Σ and $\Rightarrow_{\mathcal{R},\pi}$ rewrites w_0 to itself.

It follows straight from the definition that:

Proposition 2.

$$\Rightarrow_{\mathcal{R}} = \bigcup_{\pi \text{ proper parallel instance}} \Rightarrow_{\mathcal{R},\pi} \quad and \quad \Rightarrow_{\mathcal{R}} = \bigcup_{\pi \text{ 1-parallel instance}} \Rightarrow_{\mathcal{R},\pi}.$$

Next result shows that parallel string rewriting is sound and complete for regular string rewriting.

Theorem 1.

$$\Rightarrow_{\mathcal{R}} \subseteq \Rightarrow_{\mathcal{R}}^*. \text{ Therefore, } \Rightarrow_{\mathcal{R}}^* = \Rightarrow_{\mathcal{R}}^*$$

We define a maximal parallel instance as a maximal element of a refinement relation between parallel instances.

Definition 4. *An r-parallel instance π: $w_0\langle y_1\rangle^{\rho_1} w_1\langle y_2\rangle^{\rho_2} w_2 \dots w_{r-1}\langle y_r\rangle^{\rho_r} w_r$ on a word w is* refinable *if there exists an index $0 \leqslant i \leqslant r$ and an 1-parallel instance π_i: $w_{i,0}\langle y_{i,1}\rangle^{\rho_{i,1}} w_{i,1}$ on w_i such that replacing w_i by π_i in π we obtain an $r + 1$-parallel instance of w, say π'. We denote this by $\pi \gg \pi'$ and let $\succ$ denote the refinement relation obtained as the transitive closure of $\gg$.*
A parallel instance π of $\mathcal{R}$ is maximal *if there exists no other parallel instance of $\mathcal{R}$ refining it.*

Let us also show that all parallel instances can be obtained through successive refinements from 0-parallel instances, i.e., words over Σ, which are the *minimal* parallel instances, refining no other parallel instance.

Proposition 3. *Let π' be a $r + 1$-parallel instance, $r \geqslant 0$. Then there exists a r-parallel instance π such that π' refines π.*

The following result relates the length of a parallel instance over a word w to the length of w.

Proposition 4. *Any r-parallel instance on a word w satisfies that $r \leqslant 2|w|$.*

Corollary 1. $>$ *is Noetherian. Therefore, the set of maximal parallel instances over any word w is nonempty and finite.*

Proof. The length of any $>$ chain is at most $2|w| + 1$, hence maximal elements must exist. Moreover, given the finiteness of both the length of a parallel instance and of the set of rules $\mathcal{R}$, $>$ is finitely branching, which corroborated with the above guarantees finiteness.

The following (insertion grammar) example shows that multiple maximal parallel instances are possible, as well as having maximal instances with the "maximal" length $2|w|$:

Example 3. Consider $\Sigma = \{a, b, c\}$, $\mathcal{R} = \{\rho_1 : b \langle \lambda \rightarrow c \rangle \lambda, \rho_2 : \lambda \langle \lambda \rightarrow a \rangle b, \rho_3 : b \langle \lambda \rightarrow b \rangle b\}$, and the word $w = bbb$. Then $\langle a \rangle^{\rho_2} bb \langle c \rangle^{\rho_1} \langle a \rangle^{\rho_2} b \langle c \rangle^{\rho_1}$ is a 4-parallel instance over w, which can be refined directly to the maximal 5-parallel instance $\langle a \rangle^{\rho_2} b \langle b \rangle^{\rho_3} b \langle c \rangle^{\rho_1} \langle a \rangle^{\rho_2} b \langle c \rangle^{\rho_1}$, or in two steps to the maximal 6-parallel instance $\langle a \rangle^{\rho_2} b \langle c \rangle^{\rho_1} \langle a \rangle^{\rho_2} b \langle c \rangle^{\rho_1} \langle a \rangle^{\rho_2} b \langle c \rangle^{\rho_1}$. There is even a maximal 4-parallel instance over w: $\langle a \rangle^{\rho_2} b \langle b \rangle^{\rho_3} b \langle b \rangle^{\rho_3} b \langle c \rangle^{\rho_1}$.

Definition 5. *Let $\mathcal{R}$ be a contextual string rewriting system. We define the maximal parallel rewriting relation induced by $\mathcal{R}$, denoted $\Rightarrow_{m\mathcal{R}}$, by:*

$$\Rightarrow_{m\mathcal{R}} = \bigcup_{\pi \text{ maximal parallel instance of } \mathcal{R}} \Rightarrow_{\mathcal{R}, \pi}$$

Since maximal parallel rewriting is a special case of parallel rewriting, it is easy to see that regular rewriting simulates maximal parallel rewriting.

Proposition 5. *If $\mathcal{R}$ is non empty, then*

$$\Rightarrow_{m\mathcal{R}} \subsetneq \Rightarrow_{\mathcal{R}}^* = \Rightarrow_{\mathcal{R}}^*$$

In the remainder of this paper we will attempt simulating maximal parallel rewriting for contextual SRS by regular string rewriting (with strategies). A way to achieve this is by computing a maximal parallel instance followed by extracting the result of rewriting from it.

4   Computing a Maximal Parallel Instance

In this section we would like to derive rewrite rules for defining the refinement relation between parallel instances. But first, let us recall a formalization of strings as a multi-sorted signature.

Strings over an alphabet Σ (with unit λ and concatenation) can be defined as the canonical (initial) model associated to the ordered-sorted signature (S, F, A) where $S = \{Alphabet < Words\}$ (specifying that the interpretation of the Alphabet sort is included in the interpretation of the Words sort), $F = \{a : \lambda \rightarrow Alphabet \mid a \in \Sigma\} \cup \{\_\_ : Words\ Words \rightarrow Words\} \cup \{\lambda : \lambda \rightarrow Words\}$, and A specifies the monoid axioms: $\_\_$ is associative with identity λ.

4.1   Encoding Parallel Instances

Consider a contextual string rewrite rule $u \langle x \to y \rangle v$. To be able to use this rule to refine an existing parallel instance, we must ensure that (1) we are matching inside a w_i and (2) the letters of x must not have been previously matched by any rule (i.e., they don't belong to u_i and v_{i+1}), since they will be rewritten. Thus any encoding of parallel instances would need to (1) distinguish letters corresponding to w_is from those corresponding to y_is and (2) mark those letters which were previously matched by other rules.

Now, if u, x, and v are all non-empty, the above two conditions would be sufficient during the matching process, and the rule defining refinement would simply have to replace x with y, mark y as non-matchable, and mark the letters from u and v as matched.

However, when u, x, or v are empty, things are less straightforward.

Consider first that x is empty (insertion grammars case) and take rules $aa \langle \lambda \to c \rangle bb$ and $a \langle \lambda \to d \rangle a$ on word $aabbcc$. Suppose now we use the first rule to refine it into $aa\langle c\rangle bbcc$. The reasoning above would allow aa to be further refined to $a\langle d\rangle a$ which would be wrong as both as were matched by the same u and thus need to be kept together.

To address this issue, note that in a parallel instance a letter can be matched at most twice: once as part of a u and once as part of a v. Let us incorporate this into our designs, and mark for each letter inside a w_i whether it is matched as part of a v in the left side of w_i or as part of a u in the right side of w_i, or both. Then, in the matching process, we additionally require that a letter can only be matched by u if it hasn't been previously matched by a u, and similarly for v, making sure to propagate this information into the refinement.

Consider now the case when, in addition to x being empty, one of u or v are also empty. Let us assume u is empty, and use the rules $aa \langle \lambda \to c \rangle bb$ and $\lambda \langle \lambda \to d \rangle a$ to refine word $aabbcc$. Again, using the first rule we can refine it to $aa\langle c\rangle bbcc$. Using the second rule we could correctly refine this to $\langle d\rangle aa\langle c\rangle bbcc$; however, the reasoning above does not prevent the refinement $a\langle d\rangle a\langle c\rangle bbcc$ either, which again breaks the fact that aa needs to stay atomic.

Analyzing this, we can notice that the problem occurs from the fact that either x or u would have ensured that the existing match would not be broken; to maintain this property, it is enough to analyze one additional letter to the left of the match, to ensure our match is not inside of an atomic sequence. However, to do so, we would also need to have markers to account for matching at the beginning or at the end of the word.

Note that, if for any rule $u \langle x \to y \rangle v$ both u and v are ensured to be non-empty, then the above property could be easier ensured by marking the first letter of u and last letter of v.[1]

With this understanding it becomes clear that if an instance component of the form w_i contains a letter which was matched both by an u and a v, then w_i cannot be further refined.

---

[1] As signaled by an annonymous reviewer of an earlier draft.

In the sequel, we will try to formalize the above intuitions into an appropriate encoding.

To be able to track the rules involved in a parallel instance, let n be the number of rules in $\mathcal{R}$, and let $\varrho : \{1, \ldots, n\} \to \mathcal{R}$ be an indexing bijection for the rules of $\mathcal{R}$. We extend the above signature with two new sorts $MAlphabet <$ $MWords$ and operations $\{\_\_ : MWords\, MWords \to MWords\}$ and $\{\lambda : \lambda \to MWords\}$ satisfying the same associativity and identity axioms.

Now, define an operation $\overline{(\_,\_,\_)} : Nat\, Alphabet\, Nat \to MAlphabet$ to track how the letters are matched by contexts (u, v). Thus a matching letter $\overline{(i, a, j)}$ represents a letter which is part of the original word being rewritten, embellished with numbers to its left and right denoting the index of the rule matching it from that (left/right) side. The index 0 means no rule is matching it yet.

Also define $instance : Word\, Nat \to MAlphabet$ to represent the encoding of a y_i part. The reason an entire word is encoded as a single matching letter is that y_is play no role in instance refinement other than indicating the rule introducing the wrapped word and delimiting w_is which can potentially be further refined. To improve the visual resemblance between parallel instances and their encodings, we will display $instance(y_i, k)$ as $\langle\!\langle k\, y_i\, k\rangle\!\rangle$.

Before concluding this section, let us present the encodings of 0-instances, as they will be the starting point for our refinement process.

A 0 instance is simply a word w. Every letter a of this w was not yet matched by any rule, thus its encoding is $\overline{(0, a, 0)}$. To formalize this, let $\overline{\cdot} : Word \to MWord$ be the word (monoid) morphism defined on $Alphabet$ by $\overline{a} = \overline{(0, a, 0)}$.

However, as it will become clearer in the sequel, we need to be able to determine the borders of the word. And since for inner w_is in a parallel instance this role is played by $\langle\!\langle k \cdot k\rangle\!\rangle$ matching letters, we will use $\langle\!\langle 0\, \lambda\, 0\rangle\!\rangle$ as delimiters.

Therefore, the encoding of a 0-instance w is $\langle\!\langle 0\, \lambda\, 0\rangle\!\rangle\, \overline{w}\, \langle\!\langle 0\, \lambda\, 0\rangle\!\rangle$.

Let $\_(\_) : Word \times Nat \to \{0, 1\}$ be the mapping defined by

$$w(k) = \begin{cases} 1 \text{ if } k <= |w| \\ 0 \text{ otherwise} \end{cases}$$

checking whether positive k can be an index in word w, and let $w(k)i$ denote the (integer) multiplication between $w(k)$ and i. For each i, let u_i, v_i, x_i, y_i be such that $\varrho(i) : u_i \langle x_i \to y_i \rangle v_i$. Conveniently let $u_0 = v_0 = \lambda$.

To encode a general parallel instance we define a mapping ${}^{i}\overline{\cdot}^{j} : Word \to MWord$ for each $0 \leqslant i, j \leqslant n$, where n is the number of rules, encoding a w-word in a parallel instance whose prefix is matched by v_i of rule $\varrho(i)$ and whose suffix is matched by u_j of rule $\varrho(j)$. For every $w = a_1 a_2 \ldots a_m$, let

$${}^{i}\overline{w}^{j} = \overline{(v_i(1)i, a_1, u_j(m)j)}\, \overline{(v_i(2)i, a_2, u_j(m-1)j)} \cdots \overline{(v_i(m)i, a_m, u_j(1)j)}$$

An obvious (but useful) property of the above encoding is that

Proposition 6.

$${}^{i}\overline{v_i w u_j}^{j} = {}^{i}\overline{v_i}^{0}\ \overline{w}\ {}^{0}\overline{u_j}^{j} \text{ and } {}^{0}\overline{w}^{0} = \overline{w}$$

Finally, given a parallel instance $\pi : w_0\langle y_1\rangle^{\rho_1} w_1 \langle y_2\rangle^{\rho_2} w_2 \ldots w_{r-1}\langle y_r\rangle^{\rho_r} w_r$, define its encoding $\overline{\pi}$ as:

$$\overline{\pi} = \langle\!\langle 0\,\lambda\,0\rangle\!\rangle\, {}^{0}\overline{w_0}{}^{k_1}\, \langle\!\langle k_1\, y_1\, k_1\rangle\!\rangle\, {}^{k_1}\overline{w_1}{}^{k_2}\, \langle\!\langle k_2\, y_2\, k_2\rangle\!\rangle\, {}^{k_2}\overline{w_2}{}^{k_3}\, \ldots\, {}^{k_{r-1}}\overline{w_{r-1}}{}^{k_r}\, \langle\!\langle k_r\, y_r\, k_r\rangle\!\rangle\, {}^{k_r}\overline{w_r}{}^{0}\, \langle\!\langle 0\,\lambda\,0\rangle\!\rangle$$

For example, the encoding of $\langle a\rangle^{\rho_2} b\langle c\rangle^{\rho_1} \langle a\rangle^{\rho_2} b\langle c\rangle^{\rho_1} \langle a\rangle^{\rho_2} b\langle c\rangle^{\rho_1}$, the maximal parallel instance presented in Example 3, would be

$$\langle\!\langle 0\,\lambda\,0\rangle\!\rangle\langle\!\langle 2\,a\,2\rangle\!\rangle\overline{(2,b,1)}\langle\!\langle 1\,c\,1\rangle\!\rangle\langle\!\langle 2\,a\,2\rangle\!\rangle\overline{(2,b,1)}\langle\!\langle 1\,c\,1\rangle\!\rangle\langle\!\langle 2\,a\,2\rangle\!\rangle\overline{(2,b,1)}\langle\!\langle 1\,c\,1\rangle\!\rangle\langle\!\langle 0\,\lambda\,0\rangle\!\rangle,$$

while that of the non-maximal 4-parallel instance $\langle a\rangle^{\rho_2} bb\langle c\rangle^{\rho_1} \langle a\rangle^{\rho_2} b\langle c\rangle^{\rho_1}$ would be $\langle\!\langle 0\,\lambda\,0\rangle\!\rangle\langle\!\langle 2\,a\,2\rangle\!\rangle\overline{(2,b,0)(0,b,1)}\langle\!\langle 1\,c\,1\rangle\!\rangle\langle\!\langle 2\,a\,2\rangle\!\rangle\overline{(2,b,1)}\langle\!\langle 1\,c\,1\rangle\!\rangle\langle\!\langle 0\,\lambda\,0\rangle\!\rangle$.

4.2   Encoding Refinement

In this section we will encode contextual string rewrite rules $\varrho(k) : u\langle x \to y\rangle v$ into rules refining encoding of instances.

As deduced in our informal analysis above, all letters in u, x, v must belong to a w, thus their encodings would need to match $\overline{(i,a,j)}$ letters. Furthermore, x needs to be encoded as $\overline{x}$.

Now, for the encoding of u (and dually for v), we need to make sure all its letters have not been previously matched from the left side; we don't care about their right side. Moreover, in the refined version, the right sides need to stay unchanged while the left sides will be marked with the index of the rule, k.

Define therefore two families of mappings $\overset{l\sim}{}$ and $\overset{\sim r}{}$ from $Word$ to $MWord$ with variables, defined for each word $w = a_1 a_2 \cdots a_m$ by:

$$\overset{l\sim}{w} = \overline{(l,a_1,r_1)}\,\overline{(l,a_2,r_2)}\,\cdots\,\overline{(l,a_m,r_m)} \text{ and}$$
$$\overset{\sim r}{w} = \overline{(l_1,a_1,r)}\,\overline{(l_2,a_2,r)}\,\cdots\,\overline{(l_m,a_m,r)},$$

where l, r are $Nats$, $l_1, \ldots, l_m, r_1, \ldots, r_m$ are distinct Nat variables. A pattern $\overline{l, a_i, r_i}$ matches a letter a_1 which has been previously matched "from the left side" by rule ρ_l, (or by no rule, if $l = 0$), while variable r_i is used to record what rule matched letter a_i "from the right side" (or whether it was not yet matched).

If both ux and xv are non-empty, we will encode rule k as the refinement rule

$$\overset{l\sim}{u}{}^{0}\, \overline{x}\, \overset{\sim 0}{v}\, \to\, \overset{l\sim}{u}{}^{k}\, \langle\!\langle k\, y\, k\rangle\!\rangle\, \overset{k\sim}{v}$$

Assuming $u = a_1 \cdots a_m$, $v = b_1 \cdots b_n$, and $x = c_1 \cdots c_p$, the complete form of the rule above is:

$$\overline{(l_1,a_1,0)} \cdots \overline{(l_m,a_m,0)}\,\overline{(0,c_1,0)} \cdots \overline{(0,c_p,0)}\,\overline{(0,b_1,r_1)} \cdots \overline{(0,b_n,r_n)}$$
$$\to \overline{(l_1,a_1,k)} \cdots \overline{(l_m,a_m,k)}\,\langle\!\langle k\, y\, k\rangle\!\rangle\,\overline{(k,b_1,r_1)} \cdots \overline{(k,b_n,r_n)}$$

Therefore, the encoded rule matches a segment of an encoded instance for which the u-part is not matched from the right side, the x-part is not matched from any side, and the v-part is not matched from the left side, and transforms it by marking that u is now matched from the right side by rule k (the left matching information is preserved by the l_i variables), v is now matched from the left side by rule k (the right matching information is preserved by the r_i variables), and the x part is replaced by the $instance(y, k)$.

For example, the encoding of rule $\rho_3 : b \langle \lambda \rightarrow b \rangle b$ from Example 3 would be:

$$\overline{(l_1, b, 0)} \, \overline{(0, b, r_1)} \rightarrow \overline{(l_1, b, 3)} \, \langle\!3\, b\, 3\!\rangle \, \overline{(3, b, r_1)}$$

If ux is empty, i.e., the rewrite rule is of the form $\lambda \langle \lambda \rightarrow y \rangle v$, we need to match the immediate letter to the left, which can be either a matchable letter or an instance letter, thus requiring two rules:

$$\langle\!j\, z\, j\!\rangle \, \overset{0}{\widetilde{v}} \rightarrow \langle\!j\, z\, j\!\rangle \, \langle\!k\, y\, k\!\rangle \, \overset{k}{\widetilde{v}}, \text{ and}$$
$$\overset{\sim 0}{?} \, \overset{0\sim}{v} \rightarrow \overset{\sim 0}{?} \, \langle\!k\, y\, k\!\rangle \, \overset{k\sim}{v},$$

where j is a *Nat* variable, z is a *Word* variable, and ? is an *Alphabet* variable. Obviously, the additionally matched letter is used only for giving context and is thus left unchanged.

For example, the two rules encoding rule $\rho_2 : \lambda \langle \lambda \rightarrow a \rangle b$ are:

$$\langle\!j\, z\, j\!\rangle \, \overline{(0, b, r_1)} \rightarrow \langle\!j\, z\, j\!\rangle \, \langle\!2\, a\, 2\!\rangle \, \overline{(2, b, r_1)}, \text{ and}$$
$$\overline{(l_1, ?, 0)} \, \overline{(0, b, r_1)} \rightarrow \overline{(l_1, ?, 0)} \, \langle\!2\, a\, 2\!\rangle \, \overline{(2, b, r_1)}$$

Dually, when the initial rule is of the form $u \langle \lambda \rightarrow y \rangle \lambda$, we need to match the immediate letter to the right:

$$\widetilde{u}^0 \, \langle\!j\, z\, j\!\rangle \rightarrow \widetilde{u}^k \, \langle\!k\, y\, k\!\rangle \, \langle\!j\, z\, j\!\rangle, \text{ and}$$
$$\overset{\sim 0}{u} \, \overset{0\sim}{?} \rightarrow \overset{\sim k}{u} \, \langle\!k\, y\, k\!\rangle \, \overset{0\sim}{?},$$

where j is a *Nat* variable, z is a *Word* variable, and ? is an *Alphabet* variable.

For example, the two rules encoding rule $\rho_1 : b \langle \lambda \rightarrow c \rangle \lambda$ are:

$$\overline{(l_1, b, 0)} \, \langle\!j\, z\, j\!\rangle \rightarrow \overline{(l_1, b, 1)} \, \langle\!1\, c\, 1\!\rangle \, \langle\!j\, z\, j\!\rangle, \text{ and}$$
$$\overline{(l_1, b, 0)} \, \overline{(0, ?, r_1)} \rightarrow \overline{(l_1, b, 1)} \, \langle\!1\, c\, 1\!\rangle \, \overline{(0, ?, r_1)}$$

Let $\mathcal{R}_r$ be the set of rules encoding refinement for all rules of $\mathcal{R}$, and let $\Rightarrow_r$ be the rewrite relation induced by $\mathcal{R}_r$.

Finally, let us show that the above rules correctly encode refinement.

Theorem 2. *Let π be a parallel instance. Then*

(Completeness). *If $\pi \gg \pi'$ then $\overline{\pi} \Rightarrow_r \overline{\pi'}$; and*
(Soundness). *If $\overline{\pi} \Rightarrow_r \varpi'$ then there exists π' such that $\overline{\pi'} = \varpi'$ and $\pi \gg \pi'$*
(Termination). *$\Rightarrow_r$ terminates for the encoding of any parallel instance.*

Therefore, maximal parallel rewriting can be simulated by the encoding presented in this section.

Corollary 2. $w \Rightarrow_m w'$ *iff there exists a proper parallel instance*

$$\pi' = w_0 \langle y_1 \rangle^{\varrho(k_1)} w_1 \langle y_2 \rangle^{\varrho(k_2)} w_2 \ldots w_{r-1} \langle y_r \rangle^{\varrho(k_r)} w_r$$

such that $w' = w_0 y_1 w_1 y_2 w_2 \cdots w_{r-1} y_r w_r$ *and*

$$\langle_0 \lambda_0 \rangle \, \overline{w} \, \langle_0 \lambda_0 \rangle \Rightarrow_r^! \, \overline{\pi'},$$

where $\Rightarrow_r^!$ *denotes rewriting to a normal form (using the refinement encoding system $\mathcal{R}_r$.*

4.3   An Optimized Encoding

The encoding above was designed to help prove the correspondence between parallel instances and their encodings by tracking which rules match and refine an instance.

Note however that the only property tested by the rules encoding refinement for the indices added to letters is whether they are zero or not. Assume sorts *BAlphabet* and *BWord* and operations defined on them such that *BWord* represents strings over *BAlphabet*.

We define $\overline{(\_, \_, \_)} : Bool\,Alphabet\,Bool \to BAlphabet$ to encode letters which are part of the original word being matched, where the booleans to the left and right of a letter denoting whether the letter is matched by a rule from that side.

Additionally, no rule uses the index denoting the rule associated for any $\langle_k y_k \rangle$. Therefore we can define $\langle \cdot \rangle : Word \to BAlphabet$ to encode words to be added by rule instances.

Let $\widehat{\cdot} : Word \to BWord$ be the monoid morphism defined by $\overline{\widehat{(i, a, j)}} = \overline{(\delta(i), a, \delta(j))}$, and $\widehat{\langle_i w_i \rangle} = \langle w \rangle$, where $\delta(i) = \begin{cases} false \text{ if } i = 0 \\ true \text{ otherwise} \end{cases}$

Then the boolean encoding of a parallel instance π is defined as $\widehat{\overline{\pi}}$.

To transform index-based rules into boolean rules, we need to extend our transformation $\widehat{\cdot}$ to letters with variables as follows:

- $\overline{\widehat{(l_i : Nat, a, i)}} = \overline{(l_i : Bool, a, \delta(i))}$
- $\overline{\widehat{(i, a, r_i : Nat)}} = \overline{(\delta(i), a, r_i : Bool)}$
- $\overline{\widehat{(l_i : Nat, ? : Alphabet, 0)}} = \overline{(l_i : Bool, ? : Alphabet, false)}$
- $\overline{\widehat{(0, ? : Alphabet, r_i : Nat)}} = \overline{(false, ? : Alphabet, r_i : Bool)};$
- $\widehat{\langle_{j:Nat} w : Word_{j:Nat} \rangle} = \langle w : Word \rangle$

With these additions, we can transform each index based rule $l \to r$ to a boolean encoding rule $\widehat{l} \to \widehat{r}$.

Let $\mathcal{R}_b$ be the set of rules encoding refinement for all rules of $\mathcal{R}$, and let $\Rightarrow_b$ be the rewrite relation induced by $\mathcal{R}_b$.

Since, as already mentioned above, the index-based rules only transform 0 indexes into non-0 indexes, leaving all other indexes unchanged, it is relatively easy to prove that $\Rightarrow_b$ is sound and complete for $\Rightarrow_r$.

Theorem 3. Completeness. *If* $\varpi \Rightarrow_r \varpi'$ *then* $\widehat{\varpi} \Rightarrow_b \widehat{\varpi'}$
Soundness. *If* $\widehat{\varpi} \Rightarrow_b \varpi'_b$ *then there exists* ϖ' *such that* $\widehat{\varpi'} = \varpi'_b$ *and* $\varpi \Rightarrow_r \varpi'$.

Therefore, $\Rightarrow_b$ can be used instead of $\Rightarrow_r$ to simulate the derivation of a maximally parallel instance for contextual string rewriting.

5 On Implementing Maximal Concurrent Rewriting

In this section we give a couple of pointers for how an implementation of maximal concurrent rewriting making use of the above encodings could be achieved. For simplicity we assume below a rewrite language with the capabilities of Maude [2] (including matching modulo associativity and the distinction between equations and rules), although we believe this could be implemented in any language with basic support for rewrite strategies [17].

It is relatively easy to define a function for transforming an word w into its encoding as an 0 instance $\langle\lambda\rangle\overline{w}\langle\lambda\rangle$. Let us call the set of equations allowing us to achieve this encoding E_e:

$$encode, encode' : Word \rightarrow BWord$$
$$\forall w : BWord . \qquad\qquad encode(w) = \langle\lambda\rangle \ encode'(w) \ \langle\lambda\rangle$$
$$\forall w : BWord, a : Alphabet . \ encode'(a \ w) = \overline{false, a, false} \ encode'(w)$$
$$encode'(\lambda) = \lambda$$

Let $\Rightarrow_e$ be the rewrite relation generated by $\mathcal{R}_e$.

Similarly, it is quite straightforward to define a function for flattening an instance to the word corresponding to rewriting the original word using this instance. Let us call the set of equations allowing us to achieve this flattening E_f:

$$flatten : BWord \rightarrow Word$$
$$\forall y : Word, w : BWord . \qquad\qquad flatten(\langle y \rangle \ w) = y \ flatten(w)$$
$$\forall l, r : Bool, a : Alphabet, w : BWord . \ flatten(\overline{l, a, r} \ w) = a \ flatten(w)$$
$$flatten(\lambda) = \lambda$$

Let $\Rightarrow_f$ be the rewrite relation generated by $\mathcal{R}_f$.

Therefore we have a set of equations E_e for encoding a word into its 0-instance representation, a set of rules $\mathcal{R}_b$ for computing a maximal instance, and a set of equations E_f for flattening this instance back to a regular word. We can define the maximally parallel rewrite step as:

$$\forall w_1, w_2 : Word, w' : BWord . \ w_1 \rightarrow w_2 \ \textbf{if} \ encode(w) \Rightarrow_b^! w' \wedge w_1 := flatten(w')$$

Above $\Rightarrow_b^!$ means rewriting to a normal form. This can either be achieved by means of strategies or reflection, or by defining a predicate $match_b(w')$ which is true iff any of the rules in $\mathcal{R}_b$ can match w', and changing $encode(w) \Rightarrow^!_b w'$ to $encode(w) \to w' \wedge not(match_b(w'))$. A way to define $match_b$ would be adding an equation

$$\forall X \cup \{init, end : BWord\}.match_b(init\ l\ end) = true$$

for any rule $\forall X.l \to r$, where l and r are terms with variables from set X, and *init* and *end* are variable symbols not occurring in X, together with a "default" equation defining $match_b$ to be *false* for all other terms.

$$\forall w' : BWord.match_b(w') = false\ [\textbf{owise}]$$

6   Conclusion and Future Work

We have introduced the concept of concurrent contextual string rewriting and studied maximal parallel rewriting in this context. We presented a method for simulating maximal parallel rewriting for contextual string rewriting systems through an encoding of the problem into regular (associative) term rewriting.

A proper interface for defining, executing and analyzing contextual string-rewrite systems using Maude's "LOOP"-mode and reflection [2] is under development.

The focus of this paper was on introducing contextual string rewriting and its implementation. The study of its relation with other systems as well as it expressive power is left as future work.

An interesting addition to the above work would be the ability to structure strings similarly to the usage of brackets in L-systems [15] and the use of membranes in membrane computing [14], and to allow matching context by skipping over nested structures.

Acknowledgement. The authors would like to thank the anonymous reviewers for their valuable feedback and suggestions. Liviu P. Dinu was supported by UEFISCDI, PNII-ID-PCE-2011-3-0959.

References

1. Bottoni, P., Martín-Vide, C., Păun, G., Rozenberg, G.: Membrane systems with promoters/inhibitors. Acta Inform. **38**(10), 695–720 (2002)
2. Clavel, M., Durán, F., Eker, S., Lincoln, P., Martí-Oliet, N., Meseguer, J., Quesada, J.F.: Maude: specification and programming in rewriting logic. Theor. Comput. Sci. **285**(2), 187–243 (2002). doi:10.1016/S0304-3975(01)00359-0
3. Dinu, A., Dinu, L.P.: A parallel approach to syllabification. In: Gelbukh, A.F. (ed.) CICLing 2005. LNCS, vol. 3406, pp. 83–87. Springer, Heidelberg (2005). doi:10.1007/978-3-540-30586-6_7. ISBN 3-540-24523-5
4. Dinu, L.P.: On insertion grammars with maximum parallel derivation. Fundam. Inf. **93**(4), 357–369 (2009)
5. Galiukschov, B.S.: Semicontextual grammars. In: Matematika Logica i Matematika Linguistika, pp. 38–50. Tallin University (1981)

6. Hopf, J.-M., Bader, M., Meng, M., Bayer, J.: Is human sentence parsing serial or parallel? Evidence from event-related brain potentials. Cogn. Brain Res. **15**(2), 165–177 (2003)

7. Kari, L., Thierrin, G.: Contextual insertions, deletions, computability. Inf. Comput. **131**(1), 47–61 (1996). ISSN 0890-5401

8. Levelt, W.J.M., Indefrey, P.: The speaking mind/brain: where do spoken words come from, pp. 77–93 (2000)

9. Lindenmayer, A., Rozenberg, G. (eds.): Automata, Languages, Development. North-Holland Publishing Co., Amsterdam (1976)

10. Marcus, S.: Contextual grammars. In: Proceedings of the 1969 Conference on Computational Linguistics, pp. 1–18. Association for Computational Linguistics (1969)

11. Marcus, S.: Contextual grammars and natural languages. In: Rozenberg, G., Salomaa, A. (eds.) Handbook of Formal Languages, pp. 215–235. Springer, Heidelberg (1997)

12. Meseguer, J.: Rewriting logic as a semantic framework for concurrency: a progress report. In: Sassone, V., Montanari, U. (eds.) CONCUR 1996. LNCS, vol. 1119, pp. 331–372. Springer, Heidelberg (1996). ISBN 3-540-61604-7

13. Mitchell, T.M.: Machine Learning, vol. 45, p. 995. McGraw Hill, Burr Ridge (1997)

14. Păun, G.: Computing with membranes. J. Comput. Syst. Sci. **61**(1), 108–143 (2000)

15. Prusinkiewicz, P., Lindenmayer, A.: The Algorithmic Beauty of Plants. Springer Science & Business Media, New York (2012)

16. Roşu, G., Şerbănuţă, T.F.: An overview of the $\mathbb{K}$ semantic framework. J. Log. Algebr. Program. **79**(6), 397–434 (2010)

17. Visser, E., Benaissa, Z.A., Tolmach, A.: Building program optimizers with rewriting strategies. In: Proceedings of the Third ACM SIGPLAN International Conference on Functional Programming, ICFP 1998, pp. 13–26. ACM, New York (1998). doi:10.1145/289423.289425. ISBN 1-58113-024-4. http://doi.acm.org/10.1145/289423.289425

Metalevel Algorithms for Variant Satisfiability

Stephen Skeirik$^{(\boxtimes)}$ and José Meseguer

Department of Computer Science,
University of Illinois at Urbana-Champaign, Champaign, USA
skeirik2@illinois.edu

Abstract. Variant satisfiability is a theory-generic algorithm to decide quantifier-free satisfiability in an initial algebra $T_{\Sigma/E}$ when the theory (Σ, E) has the finite variant property and its constructors satisfy a compactness condition. This paper: (i) gives a precise definition of several *meta-level sub-algorithms* needed for variant satisfiability; (ii) proves them correct; and (iii) presents a *reflective implementation* in Maude 2.7 of variant satisfiability using these sub-algorithms.

Keywords: Finite variant property (FVP) · Folding variant narrowing · Satisfiability in initial algebras · Metalevel algorithms · Reflection · Maude

1 Introduction

SMT solving is at the heart of some of the most effective theorem proving and infinite-state model checking formal verification methods that can scale up to impressive verification tasks. A current limitation, however, is its *lack of extensibility*: current SMT solvers support a (typically small) library of decidable theories. Although these theories can be combined by the Nelson-Oppen (NO) [30,31] or Shostak [33] methods under some conditions, only the theories in the SMT solver library and their combinations are available to the user: any other theories extending the tool must be implemented by the tool builders.

In practice, of course, the problem a user has to solve may not be expressible by the theories available in an SMT solver's library. Therefore, the goal of making SMT solvers *user-extensible*, so that a *user* can easily *define* new decidable theories and use them in the verification process is highly desirable.

For a well-known *subproblem* of SMT solving, such user extensibility has recently been achieved: *E-unifiability* is the subproblem of *satisfiability* defined by: (i) considering theories of the form $th(T_{\Sigma/E}(X))$, associated to equational theories (Σ, E), where $th(T_{\Sigma/E}(X))$ denotes the theory of the free (Σ, E)-algebra $T_{\Sigma/E}(X)$ on countably many variables X, and (ii) restricting ourselves to *positive* (i.e., negation-free) quantifier-free (QF) formulas. Lack of extensibility was the same: a unification tool supports a usually small library of theories (Σ, E), which can be combined by methods similar to the NO one (the paper [2] explicitly relates the NO algorithm and combination algorithms for unification). Again,

© Springer International Publishing Switzerland 2016
D. Lucanu (Ed.): WRLA 2016, LNCS 9942, pp. 167–184, 2016.
DOI: 10.1007/978-3-319-44802-2_10

the *user* could not extend such *decidable* unifiability/unification algorithms by defining new theories and using a *theory-generic* algorithm. This is now possible for theories (Σ, E) satisfying the *finite variant property* (FVP) [13] thanks to *variant unification* based on *folding variant narrowing* [18]. In fact, variant unification for user-definable FVP theories is already supported by Maude 2.7.

This suggests an obvious question: could variant unification be generalized to *variant satisfiability*, so that, under suitable conditions on and FVP theory (Σ, E), satisfiability of QF formulas in the initial algebra $T_{\Sigma/E}$ becomes *decidable* by a *theory-generic* satisfiability algorithm? This would then make satisfiability *user-extensible* as desired. This question has been positively answered in [27,28] by giving general conditions under which satisfiability of QF formulas in the initial algebra $T_{\Sigma/E}$ of an FVP theory (Σ, E) is decidable. Section 3 summarizes the main results from [27,28]; but the punchline is easy to summarize: Suppose that: (i) the convergent rewrite theory $\mathcal{R} = (\Sigma, B, R)$ is a so-called FVP decomposition of (Σ, E) (which is what it means for (Σ, E) to be FVP), (ii) B has a finitary B-unification algorithm, and (ii) $\mathcal{R}$ has an *OS-compact* constructor decomposition $\mathcal{R}_\Omega$ (definition in Sect. 3). Then satisfiability of QF formulas in $T_{\Sigma/E}$ is decidable by a *theory-generic* algorithm called variant satisfiability.

What This Paper is About. The results in [27,28] do not really provide an *algorithm* in the full sense of the word, but rather a theoretical *skeleton* on which such an algorithm can be fleshed out. Specifically, they *assume* that the constructor decomposition $\mathcal{R}_\Omega$ is *OS-compact*, but do not provide a way to *automate* both the checking of OS-compactness and the implementation of the various *auxiliary functions* needed for variant satisfiability based on OS-compactness. They also use the notions of *constructor variant* and *constructor unifier* (see Sect. 3), but give only their theoretical definitions instead of algorithms to compute them.

Main Contributions. A *theory-generic* algorithm such as variant satisfiability manipulates *metalevel* data structures such as theories, signatures, equations, disequations, rewrite rules, and the like. In this paper we provide for the first time: (i) a full-fledged algorithm for variant satisfiability with its sub-algorithms; (ii) a proof of its correctness; and (iii) a reflective Maude implementation of it. The algorithm uses the following *auxiliary functions*:

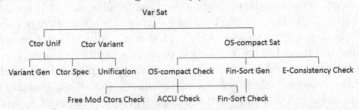

These functions automate the two main unsolved problems already mentioned: (a) checking and satisfiability in OS-compact theories; and (b) computing constructor variants and constructor unifiers. These sub-algorithms are defined and proved correct *at the metalevel of rewriting logic*. Since rewriting logic is *reflective* [10], the correctness-preserving passage from the metalevel description of the sub-algorithms to their implementations is very direct: we just *meta-represent*

them at the logic's object level as suitable meta-level theories extending Maude's META-LEVEL module [8]. Due to space limitations all proofs and some definition details are omitted. They can all be found in [34].

2   Preliminaries on Order-Sorted Algebra and Rewriting

The material is adapted from [18, 25, 28]. Due to space limitations the following elementary notions, which can be found in [25], are assume known: (i) order-sorted (OS) signature Σ; (ii) set $\widehat{S}$ of connected components (each denoted $[s] \in \widehat{S}$) of a poset of sorts $(S, \leqslant)$; (iii) sensible OS signature; (iv) order-sorted Σ-algebras and homomorphisms, and its associated category $\mathbf{OSAlg}_\Sigma$; and (v) the construction of the term algebra T_Σ and its initiality in $\mathbf{OSAlg}_\Sigma$ when Σ is sensible. Furthermore, for connected components $[s_1], \ldots, [s_n], [s] \in \widehat{S}$,

$$f^{[s_1]\ldots[s_n]}_{[s]} = \{f : s_1' \ldots s_n' \to s' \in \Sigma \mid s_i' \in [s_i],\ 1 \leqslant i \leqslant n,\ s' \in [s]\}$$

denotes the family of "subsort polymorphic" operators f.

T_Σ will (ambiguously) denote: (i) the term algebra; (ii) its underlying S-sorted set; and (iii) the set $T_\Sigma = \bigcup_{s \in S} T_{\Sigma,s}$. For $[s] \in \widehat{S}$, $T_{\Sigma,[s]} = \bigcup_{s' \in [s]} T_{\Sigma,s'}$. An OS signature Σ is said to *have non-empty sorts* iff for each $s \in S$, $T_{\Sigma,s} \neq \varnothing$. *We will assume throughout that* Σ *has non-empty sorts.* An OS signature Σ is called *preregular* [19] iff for each $t \in T_\Sigma$ the set $\{s \in S \mid t \in T_{\Sigma,s}\}$ has a least element, denoted $ls(t)$. *We will assume throughout that* Σ *is preregular.*

An S-sorted set $X = \{X_s\}_{s \in S}$ of *variables*, satisfies $s \neq s' \Rightarrow X_s \cap X_{s'} = \varnothing$, and the variables in X are always assumed disjoint from all constants in Σ. The Σ-*term algebra* on variables X, $T_\Sigma(X)$, is the *initial algebra* for the signature $\Sigma(X)$ obtained by adding to Σ the variables X as *extra constants*. Since a $\Sigma(X)$-algebra is just a pair (A, α), with A a Σ-algebra, and α an *interpretation of the constants* in X, i.e., an S-sorted function $\alpha \in [X \to A]$, the $\Sigma(X)$-initiality of $T_\Sigma(X)$ can be expressed as the following theorem:

Theorem 1 *(Freeness Theorem). If* Σ *is sensible, for each* $A \in \mathbf{OSAlg}_\Sigma$ *and* $\alpha \in [X \to A]$, *there exists a unique* Σ-*homomorphism,* $\_\alpha : T_\Sigma(X) \to A$ *extending* α, *i.e., such that for each* $s \in S$ *and* $x \in X_s$ *we have* $x\alpha_s = \alpha_s(x)$.

In particular, when $A = T_\Sigma(X)$, an interpretation of the constants in X, i.e., an S-sorted function $\sigma \in [X \to T_\Sigma(X)]$ is called a *substitution*, and its unique homomorphic extension $\_\sigma : T_\Sigma(X) \to T_\Sigma(X)$ is also called a substitution. Define $dom(\sigma) = \{x \in X \mid x \neq x\sigma\}$, and $ran(\sigma) = \bigcup_{x \in dom(\sigma)} vars(x\sigma)$. A *variable specialization* is a substitution ρ that just renames a few variables and may lower their sort. More precisely, $dom(\rho)$ is a finite set of variables $\{x_1, \ldots, x_n\}$, with respective sorts $s_1, \ldots, s_n$, and ρ injectively maps the $x_1, \ldots, x_n$ to variables $x_1', \ldots, x_n'$ with respective sorts $s_1', \ldots, s_n'$ such that $s_i' \leqslant s_i$, $1 \leqslant i \leqslant n$.

The first-order language of *equational* Σ-*formulas* is defined in the usual way: its atoms are Σ-*equations* $t = t'$, where $t, t' \in T_\Sigma(X)_{[s]}$ for some $[s] \in$

$\widehat{S}$ and each X_s is assumed countably infinite. The set $Form(\Sigma)$ of *equational Σ-formulas* is then inductively built from atoms by: conjunction ($\wedge$), disjunction ($\vee$), negation ($\neg$), and universal ($\forall x{:}s$) and existential ($\exists x{:}s$) quantification with sorted variables $x{:}s \in X_s$ for some $s \in S$. The literal $\neg(t = t')$ is denoted $t \neq t'$. Given a Σ-algebra A, a formula $\varphi \in Form(\Sigma)$, and an assignment $\alpha \in [Y{\to}A]$, with $Y = fvars(\varphi)$ the free variables of φ, the *satisfaction relation* $A, \alpha \models \varphi$ is defined inductively as usual: for atoms, $A, \alpha \models t = t'$ iff $t\alpha = t'\alpha$; for Boolean connectives it is the corresponding Boolean combination of the satisfaction relations for subformulas; and for quantifiers: $A, \alpha \models (\forall x{:}s)\ \varphi$ (resp. $A, \alpha \models (\exists x{:}s)\ \varphi$) holds iff for all $a \in A_s$ (resp. some $a \in A_s$) we have $A, \alpha \uplus \{(x{:}s, a)\} \models \varphi$, where the assignment $\alpha \uplus \{(x{:}s, a)\}$ extends α by mapping $x{:}s$ to a. Finally, $A \models \varphi$ holds iff $A, \alpha \models \varphi$ holds for each $\alpha \in [Y{\to}A]$, where $Y = fvars(\varphi)$. We say that φ is *valid* (or *true*) in A iff $A \models \varphi$. We say that φ is *satisfiable* in A iff $\exists \alpha \in [Y{\to}A]$ such that $A, \alpha \models \varphi$, where $Y = fvars(\varphi)$. For a subsignature $\Omega \subseteq \Sigma$ and $A \in \mathbf{OSAlg}_\Sigma$, the *reduct* $A|_\Omega \in \mathbf{OSAlg}_\Omega$ agrees with A in the interpretation of all sorts and operations in Ω and discards everything in $\Sigma - \Omega$. If $\varphi \in Form(\Omega)$ we have the equivalence $A \models \varphi \Leftrightarrow A|_\Omega \models \varphi$.

An OS *equational theory* is a pair $T = (\Sigma, E)$, with E a set of Σ-equations. $\mathbf{OSAlg}_{(\Sigma,E)}$ denotes the full subcategory of $\mathbf{OSAlg}_\Sigma$ with objects those $A \in \mathbf{OSAlg}_\Sigma$ such that $A \models E$, called the (Σ, E)-*algebras*. $\mathbf{OSAlg}_{(\Sigma,E)}$ has an *initial algebra* $T_{\Sigma/E}$ [25]. Given $T = (\Sigma, E)$ and $\varphi \in Form(\Sigma)$, we call φ T-*valid*, written $E \models \varphi$, iff $A \models \varphi$ for each $A \in \mathbf{OSAlg}_{(\Sigma,E)}$. We call φ T-*satisfiable* iff there exists $A \in \mathbf{OSAlg}_{(\Sigma,E)}$ with φ satisfiable in A. Note that φ is T-*valid* iff $\neg\varphi$ is T-*unsatisfiable*. The inference system in [25] is *sound and complete* for OS equational deduction, i.e., for any OS equational theory (Σ, E), and Σ-equation $u = v$ we have an equivalence $E \vdash u = v \Leftrightarrow E \models u = v$. Deducibility $E \vdash u = v$ is abbreviated as $u =_E v$, called E-*equality*. An E-*unifier* of a system of Σ-equations, i.e., a conjunction $\phi = u_1 = v_1 \wedge \ldots \wedge u_n = v_n$ of Σ-equations is a substitution σ such that $u_i\sigma =_E v_i\sigma$, $1 \leqslant i \leqslant n$. An E-*unification algorithm* for (Σ, E) is an algorithm generating a *complete set* of E-unifiers $Unif_E(\phi)$ for any system of Σ equations ϕ, where "complete" means that for any E-unifier σ of ϕ there is a $\tau \in Unif_E(\phi)$ and a substitution ρ such that $\sigma =_E \tau\rho$, where $=_E$ here means that for any variable x we have $x\sigma =_E x\tau\rho$. The algorithm is *finitary* if it always terminates with a *finite set* $Unif_E(\phi)$ for any ϕ.

Given a set of equations B used for deduction modulo B, a preregular OS signature Σ is called B-*preregular*[1] iff for each $u = v \in B$ and variable specialization ρ, $ls(u\rho) = ls(v\rho)$.

---

[1] When the axioms B consist of a combination of associativity, commutativity, and (left and/or right) identity axioms, we can decompose B into the disjoint union $B = B_0 \uplus U$, where B_0 are associativity and/or commutativity axioms, and U are left and/or right identity axioms. The equations in U, of the general form $f(e, x) = x$ and/or $f(x, e) = x$, can be oriented as rewrite rules $R(U)$ of the form $f(e, x) \to x$ and/or $f(x, e) \to x$ to be applied *modulo* B_0. The B-preregularity notion can then be *broadened* by requiring only that: (i) Σ is preregular; (ii) Σ is B_0-preregular in the standard sense that $ls(u\rho) = ls(v\rho)$ for all $u = v \in B_0$ and sort specializations ρ; and (iii) the rules $R(U)$ are *sort-decreasing* in the sense of Definition 1. Maude automatically checks B-preregularity of an OS signature Σ in this broader sense [8].

In the above logical notions the lack of predicate symbols is only *apparent*: full order-sorted first-order logic can be *reduced* to order-sorted algebra and equational formulas. The essential idea is to view a predicate $p(x_1:s_1, \ldots, x_n:s_n)$ as a function symbol $p : s_1 \ldots s_n \to Pred$, with $Pred$, a new sort having a constant tt. An atomic formula $p(t_1, \ldots, t_n)$ is then expressed as the equation $p(t_1, \ldots, t_n) = tt$. We refer the reader to [27,28] for a detailed account of this reduction of predicate symbols to function symbols.

Recall the notation for term positions, subterms, and term replacement from [14]: (i) positions in a term viewed as a tree are marked by strings $p \in \mathbb{N}^*$ specifying a path from the root, (ii) $t|_p$ denotes the subterm of term t at position p, and (iii) $t[u]_p$ denotes the result of *replacing* subterm $t|_p$ at position p by u.

Definition 1. *A rewrite theory is a triple* $\mathcal{R} = (\Sigma, B, R)$ *with* (Σ, B) *an order-sorted equational theory and* R *a set of* Σ-*rewrite rules, i.e., sequents* $l \to r$, *with* $l, r \in T_\Sigma(X)_{[s]}$ *for some* $[s] \in \widehat{S}$. *In what follows it is always assumed that:*

1. *For each* $l \to r \in R$, $l \notin X$ *and* $vars(r) \subseteq vars(l)$.
2. *Each rule* $l \to r \in R$ *is sort-decreasing, i.e., for each variable specialization* ρ, $ls(l\rho) \geqslant ls(r\rho)$.
3. Σ *is* B-*preregular (if* $B = B_0 \uplus U$, *in the broader sense of Footnote 1).*
4. *Each equation* $u = v \in B$ *is regular, i.e.,* $vars(u) = vars(v)$, *and* linear, *i.e., there are no repeated variables in* u, *and no repeated variables in* v.

The one-step R, B-*rewrite relation* $t \to_{R,B} t'$, *holds between* $t, t' \in T_\Sigma(X)_{[s]}$, $[s] \in \widehat{S}$, *iff there is a rewrite rule* $l \to r \in R$, *a substitution* $\sigma \in [X \to T_\Sigma(X)]$, *and a term position* p *in* t *such that* $t|_p =_B l\sigma$, *and* $t' = t[r\sigma]_p$. *Note that, by assumptions (2)–(3) above,* $t[r\sigma]_p$ *is always a well-formed* Σ-*term.*

$\mathcal{R}$ *is called: (i)* terminating *iff the relation* $\to_{R,B}$ *is well-founded; (ii)* strictly B-coherent [26] *iff whenever* $u \to_{R,B} v$ *and* $u =_B u'$ *there is a* v' *such that* $u' \to_{R,B} v'$ *and* $v =_B v'$; *(iii)* confluent *iff* $u \to_{R,B}^* v_1$ *and* $u \to_{R,B}^* v_2$ *imply that there are* w_1, w_2 *such that* $v_1 \to_{R,B}^* w_1$, $v_2 \to_{R,B}^* w_2$, *and* $w_1 =_B w_2$ *(where* $\to_{R,B}^*$ *denotes the reflexive-transitive closure of* $\to_{R,B}$); *and (iv)* convergent *if (i)–(iii) hold. If* $\mathcal{R}$ *is convergent, for each* Σ-*term* t *there is a term* u *such that* $t \to_{R,B}^* u$ *and* $(\nexists v) \ u \to_{R,B} v$. *We then write* $u = t!_{R,B}$, *and call* $t!_{R,B}$ *the* R, B-*normal form of* t, *which, by confluence, is unique up to* B-*equality.*

Given a set E of Σ-equations, let $R(E) = \{u \to v \mid u = v \in E\}$. A *decomposition* of an order-sorted equational theory (Σ, E) is a convergent rewrite theory $\mathcal{R} = (\Sigma, B, R)$ such that $E = E_0 \uplus B$ and $R = R(E_0)$. The key property of a decomposition is the following:

Theorem 2 *(Church-Rosser Theorem)* [22,26]. *Let* $\mathcal{R} = (\Sigma, B, R)$ *be a decomposition of* (Σ, E). *Then we have an equivalence:*

$$E \vdash u = v \iff u!_{R,B} =_B v!_{R,B}.$$

If $\mathcal{R} = (\Sigma, B, R)$ is a decomposition of (Σ, E), and X an S-sorted set of variables, the *canonical term algebra* $C_\mathcal{R}(X)$ has $C_\mathcal{R}(X)_s = \{[t!_{R,B}]_B \mid t \in T_\Sigma(X)_s\}$, and interprets each $f : s_1 \ldots s_n \to s$ as the function $C_\mathcal{R}(X)_f : ([u_1]_B, \ldots, [u_n]_B) \mapsto [f(u_1, \ldots, u_n)!_{R,B}]_B$. By the Church-Rosser Theorem we then have an isomorphism $h : T_{\Sigma/E}(X) \cong C_\mathcal{R}(X)$, where $h : [t]_E \mapsto [t!_{R,B}]_B$. In particular, when X is the empty family of variables, the canonical term algebra $C_\mathcal{R}$ is an initial algebra, and is the most intuitive possible model for $T_{\Sigma/E}$ as an algebra of *values* computed by R, B-simplification.

Quite often, the signature Σ on which $T_{\Sigma/E}$ is defined has a natural decomposition as a disjoint union $\Sigma = \Omega \uplus \Delta$, where the elements of $C_\mathcal{R}$, that is, the *values* computed by R, B-simplification, are Ω-terms, whereas the function symbols $f \in \Delta$ are viewed as *defined functions* which are *evaluated away* by R, B-simplification. Ω (with same poset of sorts as Σ) is then called a *constructor subsignature* of Σ. Call a decomposition $\mathcal{R} = (\Sigma, B, R)$ of (Σ, E) *sufficiently complete* with respect to the *constructor subsignature* Ω iff for each $t \in T_\Sigma$ we have: (i) $t!_{R,B} \in T_\Omega$, and (ii) if $u \in T_\Omega$ and $u =_B v$, then $v \in T_\Omega$. This ensures that for each $[u]_B \in C_\mathcal{R}$ we have $[u]_B \subseteq T_\Omega$. Of course, we want Ω *as small as possible* with these properties. In Example 1 below, $\Omega = \{\top, \bot\}$ and $\Delta = \{\_ \wedge \_, \_ \vee \_\}$. Tools based on tree automata [11], equational tree automata [21], or narrowing [20], can be used to automatically check sufficient completeness of a decomposition $\mathcal{R}$ with respect to constructors Ω under some assumptions.

Sufficient completeness is closely related to the notion of a *protecting* theory inclusion.

Definition 2. *An equational theory (Σ, E) protects another theory (Ω, E_Ω) iff $(\Omega, E_\Omega) \subseteq (\Sigma, E)$ and the unique Ω-homomorphism $h : T_{\Omega/E_\Omega} \to T_{\Sigma/E}|_\Omega$ is an isomorphism $h : T_{\Omega/E_\Omega} \cong T_{\Sigma/E}|_\Omega$.*

A decomposition $\mathcal{R} = (\Sigma, B, R)$ protects another decomposition $\mathcal{R}_0 = (\Sigma_0, B_0, R_0)$ iff $\mathcal{R}_0 \subseteq \mathcal{R}$, i.e., $\Sigma_0 \subseteq \Sigma$, $B_0 \subseteq B$, and $R_0 \subseteq R$, and for all $t, t' \in T_{\Sigma_0}(X)$ we have: (i) $t =_{B_0} t' \Leftrightarrow t =_B t'$, (ii) $t = t!_{R_0, B_0} \Leftrightarrow t = t!_{R,B}$, and (iii) $C_{\mathcal{R}_0} = C_\mathcal{R}|_{\Sigma_0}$.

$\mathcal{R}_\Omega = (\Omega, B_\Omega, R_\Omega)$ is a constructor decomposition of $\mathcal{R} = (\Sigma, B, R)$ iff $\mathcal{R}$ protects $\mathcal{R}_\Omega$ and Σ and Ω have the same poset of sorts, so that by (iii) above $\mathcal{R}$ is sufficiently complete with respect to Ω. Furthermore, Ω is called a subsignature of free constructors modulo B_Ω iff $R_\Omega = \varnothing$, so that $C_{\mathcal{R}_0} = T_{\Omega/B_\Omega}$.

3   Variants and Variant Satisfiability

The notion of *variant* answers two questions: (i) how can we best describe symbolically the elements of $C_\mathcal{R}(X)$ that are *reduced substitution instances* of a given *pattern term* t? and (ii) when is such a symbolic description *finite*?

Definition 3. *Given a decomposition $\mathcal{R} = (\Sigma, B, R)$ of an OS equational theory (Σ, E) and a Σ-term t, a variant[2] [13,18] of t is a pair (u, θ) such that: (i)*

---

[2] For a discussion of similar but not exactly equivalent versions of the variant notion see [7]. Here we follow the formulation in [18].

$u =_B (t\theta)!_{R,B}$, *(ii) if* $x \notin vars(t)$, *then* $x\theta = x$, *and (iii)* $\theta = \theta!_{R,B}$, *that is,* $x\theta = (x\theta)!_{R,B}$ *for all variables* x. (u, θ) *is called a* ground variant *iff* $u \in T_\Sigma$. *Note that if* (u, θ) *is a ground variant of some* t, *then* $[u]_B \in C_\mathcal{R}$. *Given variants* (u, θ) *and* (v, γ) *of* t, (u, θ) *is called* more general *than* (v, γ), *denoted* $(u, \theta) \sqsupseteq_{R,B}$ (v, γ), *iff there is a substitution* ρ *such that: (i)* $\theta\rho =_B \gamma$, *and (ii)* $u\rho =_B v$. *Let* $[\![t]\!]_{R,B} = \{(u_i, \theta_i) \mid i \in I\}$ *denote a* most general complete set of variants *of* t, *that is, a set of variants such that: (i) for any variant* (v, γ) *of* t *there is an* $i \in I$, *such that* $(u_i, \theta_i) \sqsupseteq_{R,B} (v, \gamma)$; *and (ii) for* $i, j \in I$, $i \neq j \Rightarrow ((u_i, \theta_i) \not\sqsupseteq_{R,B}$ $(u_j, \theta_j) \wedge (u_j, \theta_j) \not\sqsupseteq_{R,B} (u_i, \theta_i))$. *A decomposition* $\mathcal{R} = (\Sigma, B, R)$ *of* (Σ, E) *has the* finite variant property [13] *(FVP) iff for each* Σ*-term* t *there is a finite most general complete set of variants* $[\![t]\!]_{R,B} = \{(u_1, \theta_1), \ldots, (u_n, \theta_n)\}$.

If B has a finitary unification algorithm, the *folding variant narrowing* strategy described in [18] provides an effective method to generate $[\![t]\!]_{R,B}$. Furthermore, $[\![t]\!]_{R,B}$ is finite for each t, so that the strategy *terminates* iff $\mathcal{R}$ is FVP.

Example 1. Let $\mathcal{B} = (\Sigma, B, R)$ with Σ having a single sort, say *Bool*, constants $\top, \bot$, and binary operators $\_\wedge\_$ and $\_\vee\_$, B the associativity and commutativity (AC) axioms for both $\_\wedge\_$ and $\_\vee\_$, and R the rules: $x \wedge \top \rightarrow x$, $x \wedge \bot \rightarrow \bot$, $x \vee \bot \rightarrow x$, and $x \vee \top \rightarrow \top$. Then $\mathcal{B}$ is FVP. For example, $[\![x \wedge y]\!]_{R,B} = \{(x \wedge y, id), (y, \{x \mapsto \top\}), (x, \{y \mapsto \top\}), (\bot, \{x \mapsto \bot\}), (\bot, \{y \mapsto \bot\})\}$.

FVP is a *semi-decidable* property [7], which can be easily verified (when it holds) by checking, using folding variant narrowing, that for each function symbol f the term $f(x_1, \ldots, x_n)$, with the sorts of the $x_1, \ldots, x_n$ those of f, has a finite number of most general variants.

Folding variant narrowing provides also a method for generating a *complete set of E-unifiers* when (Σ, E) has a decomposition $\mathcal{R} = (\Sigma, B, R)$ with B having a finitary B-unification algorithm [18]. To express systems of equations, say, $u_1 = v_1 \wedge \ldots \wedge u_n = v_n$, as *terms*, we can extend Σ to a signature $\Sigma^\wedge$ by adding:

1. for each connected component $[s]$ that does not already have a top element, a fresh new sort $\top_{[s]}$ with $\top_{[s]} > s'$ for each $s' \in [s]$. In this way we obtain a (possibly extended) poset of sorts $(S_\top, \geqslant)$;
2. fresh new sorts *Lit* and *Conj* with a subsort inclusion *Lit.* $<$ *Conj*, with a binary conjunction operator $\_\wedge\_ : Lit\ Conj \rightarrow Conj$, and
3. for each connected component $[s] \in \widehat{S_\top}$ with top sort $\top_{[s]}$, binary operators $\_=\_ : \top_{[s]} \top_{[s]} \rightarrow Lit$ and $\_\neq\_ : \top_{[s]} \top_{[s]} \rightarrow Lit$.

Theorem 3 [28]. *Under the above assumptions on* $\mathcal{R}$, *let* $\phi = u_1 = v_1 \wedge \ldots \wedge$ $u_n = v_n$ *be a system of* Σ*-equations viewed as a* $\Sigma^\wedge$*-term of sort Conj. Then*

$$\{\theta\gamma \mid (\phi', \theta) \in [\![\phi]\!]_{R,B} \wedge \gamma \in \mathit{Unif}_B(\phi') \wedge (\phi'\gamma, \theta\gamma) \text{ is a variant of } \phi\}$$

is a complete set of E-unifiers for ϕ, *where* $\mathit{Unif}_B(\phi')$ *denotes a complete set of most general B-unifiers for each variant* $\phi' = u_1' = v_1' \wedge \ldots \wedge u_n' = v_n'$.

Since if $\mathcal{R} = (\Sigma, B, R)$ is FVP, then $\mathcal{R}^\wedge = (\Sigma^\wedge, B, R)$ is also FVP, Theorem 3 shows that if a finitary B-unification algorithm exists and $\mathcal{R}$ is an FVP decomposition of (Σ, E), then E has a finitary E-unification algorithm.

The key question asked and answered in [27,28] is: given an FVP decomposition $\mathcal{R} = (\Sigma, B, R)$ of an equational theory (Σ, E), under what conditions is satisfiability of QF equational Σ-formulas in the canonical term algebra $C_{\mathcal{R}}$ decidable? It turns out that: (i) $\mathcal{R}$ having a constructor decomposition $\mathcal{R}_\Omega = (\Omega, B_\Omega, R_\Omega)$, and (ii) the associated notions of *constructor variant* and *constructor unifier* [28] play a crucial role in answering this question.

Definition 4. *Let* $\mathcal{R} = (\Sigma, B, R)$ *be a decomposition of* (Σ, E), *and let* $\mathcal{R}_\Omega = (\Omega, B_\Omega, R_\Omega)$ *be a constructor decomposition of* $\mathcal{R}$. *Then an* R, B-variant (u, θ) *of a* Σ-term t *is called a* constructor R, B-variant *of* t *iff* $u \in T_\Omega(X)$.

Suppose, furthermore, that B *has a finitary* B-unification algorithm, so that, given a unification problem* $\phi = u_1 = v_1 \wedge \dots \wedge u_n = v_n$, *Theorem 3 allows us to generate the complete set of* E-unifiers

$$\{\theta\gamma \mid (\phi', \theta) \in [\![\phi]\!]_{R,B} \wedge \gamma \in \mathit{Unif}_B(\phi') \wedge (\phi'\gamma, \theta\gamma) \text{ is a variant of } \phi\}$$

Then a constructor E-unifier[3] *of* ϕ *is either: (1) a unifier* $\theta\gamma$ *in the above set with* $\phi'\gamma \in T_{\Omega^\wedge}(X)$; *or otherwise, (2) a unifier* $\theta\gamma\alpha$ *such that: (i)* $\theta\gamma$ *belongs the above set, (ii)* α *is a substitution of the variables in* $\mathrm{ran}(\theta\gamma)$ *such that* $\phi'\gamma\alpha \in T_{\Omega^\wedge}(X)$, *and (iii)* $(\phi'\gamma\alpha, \theta\gamma\alpha)$ *is a variant of* ϕ. $\mathit{mgu}_{\mathcal{R}}^\Omega(\phi)$ *denotes a set of most general constructor* E-unifiers *of* ϕ, *i.e., for any constructor* E-unifier μ *of* ϕ *there is another one* $\eta \in \mathit{mgu}_{\mathcal{R}}^\Omega(\phi)$ *and a substitution* ν *such that* $\mu =_B \eta\nu$.

Note that if (v, δ) is a ground variant of t, then $[v]_B \in C_{\mathcal{R}}$, so that v is an Ω-term. Therefore, any ground variant (v, δ) of t is "covered" by some constructor variant (u, θ) of t, i.e., $(u, \theta) \sqsupseteq_{R,B} (v, \delta)$. If (Σ, E) has a decomposition $\mathcal{R} = (\Sigma, B, R)$, B has a finitary B-unification algorithm and we are only interested in characterizing the *ground solutions* of an equation in the initial algebra $T_{\Sigma/E}$, only constructor E-unifiers are needed, since they completely cover all such solutions. Likewise, if we are only interested in *unifiability* of a system of equations only constructor E-unifiers are needed.

Theorem 4 [27,28]. *Let* (Σ, E) *have a decomposition* $\mathcal{R} = (\Sigma, B, R)$ *with* B *having a finitary* B-unification algorithm. *Then, for each system of* Σ-equations $\phi = u_1 = v_1 \wedge \dots \wedge u_n = v_n$, *where* $Y = \mathit{vars}(\phi)$, *we have:*

1. *(Completeness for Ground Unifiers). If* $\delta \in [Y \to T_\Sigma]$ *is a ground* E-unifier of ϕ, *then there is a constructor* E-unifier $\eta \in \mathit{mgu}_{\mathcal{R}}^\Omega(\phi)$ *and a substitution* β *such that* $\delta =_E \eta\beta$, *i.e.,* $x\delta =_E x\eta\beta$ *for each variable* $x \in Y$.
2. *(Unifiability).* $T_{\Sigma/E} \models (\exists Y)\,\phi$ *iff* ϕ *has a constructor* E-unifier.

Given an OS equational theory (Σ, E), call a Σ-equality $u = v$ E-trivial iff $u =_E v$, and a Σ-disequality $u \neq v$ E-consistent iff $u \neq_E v$. Likewise, call a conjunction $\bigwedge D$ of Σ-disequalities E-consistent iff each $u \neq v$ in D is so.

---

[3] [27,28,34] give examples of constructor variants and constructor unifiers.

Theorem 4 is a key step to find conditions for the decidable satisfiability of QF equational Σ-formulas in $C_{\mathcal{R}}$ for $\mathcal{R} = (\Sigma, B, R)$ an FVP decomposition of (Σ, E), where B has a finitary B-unification algorithm and $\mathcal{R}$ has a constructor decomposition $\mathcal{R}_{\Omega} = (\Omega, B_{\Omega}, R_{\Omega})$. The key idea is to reduce the problem to one of satisfiability of a conjunction of Ω-*disequalities* in the simpler canonical term algebra $C_{\mathcal{R}_{\Omega}}$. By $C_{\mathcal{R}}|_{\Omega} = C_{\mathcal{R}_{\Omega}}$, Theorem 4, and the Descent Theorems in [27,28] (see [27,28] for full details), we can apply the following algorithm to a conjunction of literals $\phi = \bigwedge G \wedge \bigwedge D$, with G equations and D disequations:

1. Thanks to Theorem 4 we need only compute the *constructor E*-unifiers $mgu_{\mathcal{R}}^{\Omega}(\bigwedge G)$, and reduce to the case of deciding the satisfiability of some conjunction of disequalities $(\bigwedge D\alpha)!_{R,B}$, for some $\alpha \in mgu_{\mathcal{R}}^{\Omega}(\bigwedge G)$, discarding any $(\bigwedge D\alpha)!_{R,B}$ containing a B-inconsistent disequality.
2. For each remaining $(\bigwedge D\alpha)!_{R,B}$ we can then compute a finite, complete set of most general R, B-variants $[\![(\bigwedge D\alpha)!_{R,B}]\!]_{R,B}$ by folding variant narrowing, and obtain for each of them its B_{Ω}-consistent constructor variants $\bigwedge D'$.
3. Then by the Descent Theorems in [27,28], ϕ will be satisfiable in $C_{\mathcal{R}}$ iff $\bigwedge D'$ is satisfiable in $C_{\mathcal{R}_{\Omega}}$ for some such $\bigwedge D'$ and some such α.

Therefore, the method hinges upon being able to decide when a conjunction of Ω-disequalities $\bigwedge D'$ is satisfiable in $C_{\mathcal{R}_{\Omega}}$. This is decidable if $\mathcal{R}_{\Omega}$ is the decomposition of an OS-*compact theory*, which generalizes the notion of *compact theory* in [12]:

Definition 5 [27,28]. *An equational theory* (Σ, E) *is called* OS-*compact iff: (i) for each sort s in Σ we can effectively determine whether $T_{\Sigma/E,s}$ is finite or infinite, and, if finite, can effectively compute a representative ground term $rep([u]) \in [u]$ for each $[u] \in T_{\Sigma/E,s}$ (ii) $=_E$ is decidable and E has a finitary unification algorithm; and (iii) any E-consistent finite conjunction $\bigwedge D$ of Σ-disequalities whose variables all have infinite sorts is satisfiable in $T_{\Sigma/E}$.*

The reason why satisfiability of a conjunction of disequalities in the initial algebra of an OS-compact theory is decidable [27,28] is fairly obvious: by (iii) it is decidable when all variables have infinite sorts; and we can always reduce to a disjunction of formulas in that case by instantiating each variable with a finite sort s by all the possible representatives in $T_{\Sigma/E,s}$. Therefore we have:

Corollary 1. *For* $\mathcal{R} = (\Sigma, B, R)$ *an FVP decomposition of* (Σ, E)*, where B has a finitary B-unification algorithm and $\mathcal{R}$ has an OS-compact constructor decomposition $\mathcal{R}_{\Omega}$, satisfiability of QF equational Σ-formulas in $C_{\mathcal{R}}$ is decidable.*

The papers [27,28] contain many examples of commonly used theories that have FVP specifications whose constructor decompositions are OS-compact. This can be established by one of the two methods discussed below.

A first method to show OS-compactness is both very simple and widely applicable to constructor decompositions of FVP theories. It applies to OS equational theories of the form $(\Omega, ACCU)$, where $ACCU$ stands for any combination of associativity and/or commutativity and/or left- or right-identity axioms, except combinations where the same operator is associative but not commutative. We also assume that if any typing for a binary operator f in a subsort-polymorphic family $f_{[s]}^{[s]\,[s]}$ satisfies some axioms in $ACCU$, then any other typing in $f_{[s]}^{[s]\,[s]}$ satisfies the *same* axioms. The following theorem generalizes to the order-sorted and $ACCU$ case a similar result in [12] for the unsorted and AC case:

Theorem 5 [27,28]. *Under the above assumptions* $(\Omega, ACCU)$ *is OS-compact. Furthermore, satisfiability of QF* Ω-*formulas in* $T_{\Omega/ACCU}$ *is decidable.*

The range of FVP theories whose initial algebras have decidable QF satisfiability is greatly increased by a second method of *satisfiability-preserving FVP parameterized theories*. For our present purposes it suffices to summarize the basic general facts and assumptions for the case of FVP parameterized data types with a *single parameter* X. That is, we can focus on parameterized FVP theories of the form $\mathcal{R}[X] = (\mathcal{R}, X)$, where $\mathcal{R} = (\Sigma, B, R)$ is an FVP decomposition of an OS equational theory (Σ, E), and X is a sort in Σ (called the *parameter sort*) such that: (i) is empty, i.e., $T_{\Sigma,X} = \varnothing$; and (ii) X is a minimal element in the sort order, i.e., there is no other sort s' with $s' < X$.

Consider an FVP decomposition $\mathcal{G} = (\Sigma', B', R')$ of a finitary OS equational theory (Σ', E'), which we can assume without loss of generality is disjoint from (Σ, E), and additionally let s be a sort in Σ'. Then the *instantiation* $\mathcal{R}[\mathcal{G}, X \mapsto s] = (\Sigma[\Sigma', X \mapsto s], B \cup B', R \cup R')$ is the decomposition of a theory $(\Sigma[\Sigma', X \mapsto s], E \cup E')$, extending (Σ', E'), where the signature $\Sigma[\Sigma', X \mapsto s]$ is defined as the union $\Sigma[X \mapsto s] \cup \Sigma'$, with $\Sigma[X \mapsto s]$ just like Σ, except for X renamed to s. Its set of sorts is $(S - \{X\}) \uplus S'$, and the poset ordering combines those of $\Sigma[X \mapsto s]$ and Σ'. Furthermore, $\mathcal{R}[\mathcal{G}, X \mapsto s]$ is also FVP under mild assumptions [27].

Suppose B, B' and $B \cup B'$ have finitary unification algorithms and both $\mathcal{R}[X] = (\mathcal{R}, X)$ and $\mathcal{G}$ protect, respectively, the two constructor theories, say $\mathcal{R}_\Omega[X] = (\Omega, B_\Omega, R_\Omega)$ and $\mathcal{G}_{\Omega'} = (\Omega', B_{\Omega'}, R_{\Omega'})$. Then $\mathcal{R}[\mathcal{G}, X \mapsto s]$ will protect $\mathcal{R}_\Omega[\mathcal{G}_{\Omega'}, X \mapsto s]$. Suppose, further, that B_Ω, $B_{\Omega'}$, and $B_\Omega \cup B_{\Omega'}$ have decidable equality. The general satisfiability-preserving method of interest is then as follows: (i) assuming that $\mathcal{G}_{\Omega'}$ is the decomposition of an OS-compact theory, then (ii) under some assumptions about the cardinality of the sort s, prove the OS-compactness of $\mathcal{R}_\Omega[\mathcal{G}_{\Omega'}, X \mapsto s]$. It then follows from our earlier reduction of satisfiability in initial FVP algebras to their constructor decompositions that satisfiability of QF formulas in the initial model of the instantiation $\mathcal{R}[\mathcal{G}, X \mapsto s]$ is decidable.

In [27] the following parameterized data types have been proved satisfiability-preserving following the just-described pattern of proof: (i) $\mathcal{L}[X]$, *parameterized lists*, which is just an example illustrating the general case of any constructor-selector-based [29] parameterized data type; (ii) $\mathcal{L}^c[X]$, *parameterized compact lists*, where any two identical contiguous list elements are identified [15,16]; (iii) $\mathcal{M}[X]$, *parameterized multisets*; (iv) $\mathcal{S}[X]$, *parameterized sets*; and (v) $\mathcal{H}[X]$, *parameterized hereditarily finite sets*.

4   Metalevel Algorithms for Variant Satisfiability

For $\mathcal{R} = (\Sigma, B, R)$ an FVP decomposition of (Σ, E), where B has a finitary B-unification algorithm and $\mathcal{R}$ has a constructor decomposition $\mathcal{R}_\Omega$, the issue of the decidable satisfiability of QF equational Σ-formulas in $C_\mathcal{R}$ has been condensed in Sect. 3 to two key sub-issues: (i) steps (1)–(3) in the high-level algorithm, which reduce satisfiability of a conjunction of Σ-literals in $C_\mathcal{R}$ to satisfiability of a conjunction of Ω-disequalities in $C_{\mathcal{R}_\Omega}$; and (ii) decidable satisfiability of conjunctions of Ω-disequalities in $C_{\mathcal{R}_\Omega}$ when $\mathcal{R}_\Omega$ is OS-compact (Corollary 1).

At a theoretical level this gives the *skeleton* of a high-level algorithm for variant satisfiability. But at a concrete, algorithmic level several important questions, essential for having an actual satisfiability *algorithm*, remain unresolved, including: (1) how can we *automatically check* that the constructor decomposition $\mathcal{R}_\Omega$ is OS-compact using the two methods for OS-compactness outlined in Sect. 3? (2) how can we *compute* constructor variants and constructor unifiers? (3) how can we *prove* that the auxiliary algorithms answering questions (1) and (2) are *correct*? and (4) how can we *implement* both the main algorithm and the auxiliary algorithms in a correctness-preserving manner?

Let us begin with question (3). The algorithm skeleton sketched in Sect. 3 manipulates metalevel entities like operators, signatures, terms, equations, and theories. Likewise, the checks for OS-compactness and the computation of constructor variants and constructor unifiers (questions (1) and(2)) are problems fully expressible in terms of such metalevel entities. Therefore, both for mathematical clarity and for simplicity of the needed correctness proofs, the definitions of the auxiliary algorithms should be carried out at the metalevel of rewriting logic.

This brings us to question (4), which has a simple answer: since rewriting logic is *reflective* [10], once we have defined and proved correct at the metalevel the auxiliary algorithms solving questions (1) and (2), we can derive correct implementations for them by *meta-representing* them at the logic's object level as equational or rewrite theories. In fact, this can be carried out in Maude by defining suitable meta-level theories extending the META-LEVEL module [8].

The previous paragraphs lead us to the main contributions of the present paper. We answer questions (1) and part of (3) by defining and proving correct at the metalevel a method to check OS-compactness, including: (a) checking which sorts s satisfy $|T_{\Omega/B_\Omega,s}| < \aleph_0$, and (b) computing for each such s a unique representative $rep([t]_{B_\Omega})$ for each $[t]_{B_\Omega} \in T_{\Omega/B_\Omega,s}$. We answer question (2) and the other part of (3) by defining and proving correct at the meta-level a method to compute constructor unifiers and constructor variants. And we answer question (4) by meta-representing both the auxiliary algorithms and the main algorithm (already proved correct at the meta-level in [27,28]) in Sect. 5.

To help guide the discussion, the reader may refer to the tree diagram in the Introduction, which describes the dependencies among different subalgorithms. Due to space limitations, we cannot describe these metalevel sub-algorithms in full detail in the body of the paper: all remaining details, together with full proofs of correctness, can be found in [34].

4.1   OS-Compact Satisfiability

E_Ω-*consistency* of a conjunction of Ω-disequalities $\bigwedge D'$ in a constructor decomposition $\mathcal{R}_\Omega = (\Omega, B_\Omega, R_\Omega)$ is easy to check: we may assume $\bigwedge D'$ in R_Ω, B_Ω-normal form and just need to check that $u \neq_{B_\Omega} v$ for each $u \neq v$ in $\bigwedge D'$.

Checking that the constructor subtheory $\mathcal{R}_\Omega$ of $\mathcal{R}$ is *OS-compact* breaks into two cases: (1) when $\mathcal{R}$ is an *unparameterized theory*; and (2) when $\mathcal{R}$ is the instantiation of a possibly *nested* collection of satisfiability-preserving *parameterized theories* such as, for example, *sets of lists of natural numbers*. In case (2) it is enough (for the parameterized theories described in Sect. 3) to check that: (i) the unparameterized theory $\mathcal{G}$ in the innermost instantiation (in our example the theory $\mathcal{N}_+$ of naturals with addition) is *OS-compact*, and the chosen sort (in our example the sort *Nat*) is *infinite*; and (ii) that the sorts chosen to instantiate each remaining parameter is the *principal sort* of the parameterized module immediately below in the nesting. In our example this is just checking that the parameter sort X for the *set* parameterized module is instantiated to the principal sort, namely *List*, of the *list* parameterized module immediately below. In this way, checking OS-compactness of $\mathcal{R}_\Omega$ in the, nested, parameterized case is reduced to checking OS-compactness of the unparameterized inner argument, plus a check of an infinite sort. All checks for the unparameterized case (1), including the two needed in case (2), are described below.

OS-Compactness Check (Unparameterized Case). As shown in Theorem 5, a sufficient condition for an unparameterized constructor decomposition $\mathcal{R}_\Omega = (\Omega, B_\Omega, R_\Omega)$ to be OS-compact is for $\mathcal{R}_\Omega$ to be of the form $\mathcal{R}_\Omega = (\Omega, ACCU, \varnothing)$. Thus, a sufficient condition is to require: (1) B_Ω to be a set of ACCU axioms, and (2) Ω to be a signature of *free constructors* modulo B_Ω. Fortunately, both of these subgoals are quite simple to check. Goal (1) can be solved by iterating over each axiom and applying a case analysis against its structure. Goal (2) can be solved by an application of propositional tree automata (PTA). In particular, if the rules R in $\mathcal{R}$ are linear and unconditional, then constructor freeness modulo B is translatable into a PTA emptiness problem; see [32] for further details.

Finite Sort Classification. Another needed algorithm takes as input a signature Ω and a sort s and checks if $|T_{\Omega/B_\Omega,s}| < \aleph_0$. We solve this problem in two phases: (1) we devise an algorithm to check $|T_{\Omega,s}| < \aleph_0$, and (2) we use this as a subroutine in an *approximate* algorithm to check $|T_{\Omega/B_\Omega,s}| < \aleph_0$ when $B_\Omega = ACCU$. If the approximate algorithm fails to classify some s as either infinite or finite, s is returned to the user as a proof obligation [34].

If Ω is finite and has non-empty sorts, we show that $|T_{\Omega,s}| = \aleph_0$ iff there exists a *cycle* in the relation $(\prec) \subseteq S^2$ reachable from s where $s \prec s'$ iff the formula $\exists f : s_1 \cdots s_n \rightarrow s'' \in \Omega \exists i \in \mathbb{N}[s'' \leqslant s \wedge s \leqslant s_i] \vee [s' < s]$ holds. We construct a rewrite theory R_F over S such that $s \rightarrow_{R_F} s'$ iff $s \prec s'$. If $cy(S) = \{s \in S \mid s \rightarrow^+_{R_F} s\}$, then $s \rightarrow^*_{R_F} s'$ with $s' \in cy(S)$ implies $|T_{\Omega,s}| = \aleph_0$. Then $\bigvee_{s' \in cy(S_{\supset \emptyset})} R_F \vdash s \rightarrow^* s'$ holds iff there is a cycle in the relation $(\prec)$ reachable from s [34].

We now lift the algorithm above to phase (2). We can show that for ACC axioms B_Ω there is an exact correspondence $|T_{\Omega/B_\Omega,s}| < \aleph_0$ iff $|T_{\Omega,s}| < \aleph_0$. The tricky case is when B_Ω contains unit axioms, since they may break this happy correspondence. For example, consider the unsorted signature $\Omega = (0, \_ + \_)$ where 0 is a unit element for $\_ + \_$. For the ACCU case, [34] describes two simple checks for $|T_{\Omega/B_\Omega,s}| < \aleph_0$ that apply in most cases. Failing that, the classification of sort s is returned to the user as a proof obligation.

Finite Sort Representative Generation. Here we require a method to do two things: (1) when $|T_{\Omega/B_\Omega,s}| < \aleph_0$, we can compute each $[t]_{B_\Omega} \in T_{\Omega/B_\Omega,s}$ (2) for each such $[t]_{B_\Omega}$, we can compute a unique representative $rep([t]_{B_\Omega})$. We first show how to generate $T_{\Omega,s}$. Recall that any order-sorted signature Ω can be viewed as a tree automaton such that the tree automaton accepts a term t in final state s iff $t \in T_{\Omega,s}$. Note also that tree automata are very simple *ground* rewrite theories. Let R_P be the ground rewrite rules for Ω's tree automaton over $T_{\Omega \cup S}$, so that $t \in T_{\Omega,s}$ iff $t \to^+_{R_P} s$. Let $R_G = R_P^{-1}$ then $T_{\Omega,s} = \{t \in T_\Omega \mid s \to^!_{R_G} t\}$ [34]. Furthermore, if $|T_{\Omega,s}| < \aleph_0$ and Ω has no empty sorts, this process will always terminate. Note that we can apply the rules R_G modulo B_Ω. Then the set $\mathrm{Rep}(T_{\Omega/B_\Omega,s}) = \{rep([t]) \mid [t] \in T_{\Omega/B_\Omega,s}\}$ is exactly the set $\mathrm{Rep}(T_{\Omega/B_\Omega,s}) = \{t \mid s \to^!_{R_G,B_\Omega} t\}$.

4.2   Constructor Variants and Constructor Unifiers

We first show how to compute a set of *most general* constructor variants of a term t (i.e. a set of constructor variants $[\![t]\!]^\Omega_{R,B}$ such that for any constructor variant (t', θ), we have $\exists (t'', \psi) \in [\![t]\!]^\Omega_{R,B}[(t'', \psi) \sqsupseteq_{R,B} (t', \phi)])$ and then show how to use this method to compute a set of *most general* constructor unifiers $mgu^\Omega_R(\phi)$. Recall that a constructor variant is just an variant (t, θ) such that $t \in T_\Omega(X)$. Thus, $[\![t]\!]^\Omega_{R,B}$ can be computed in two steps: (1) computing a set of most general variants $[\![t]\!]_{R,B}$, and (2) for each most general variant (t', θ), compute the set of its *most general* constructor instances, i.e. a set of instances $mgci_B(t') = \{t'\eta_1, \cdots, t'\eta_n\}$ where for any other instance $t'\alpha$, there exists a substitution γ and η_i with $\alpha =_B \eta_i\gamma$. Note that (1) can be solved via folding variant narrowing, so we tackle (2) by a reduction to a B-unification problem via a signature transformation $\Sigma \mapsto \Sigma^c$. In this transformed signature, the instances $mgci_B(t')$ correspond exactly to the solutions of a *single* B-unification problem.

The signature transformation $\Sigma \mapsto \Sigma^c$ splits into two steps: (i) we extend the sort poset $(S, <)$ of Σ and Ω and (ii) likewise extend the operator sets F and F_Ω, as specified by the definitions below, respectively. Recall we assume Σ (and thus Ω) are finite; otherwise these transformations would not be effective.

Definition 6. *A* constructor sort refinement *of* $(S, <)$ *is defined by the following: (a) a set $S^c = S \uplus S^\downarrow$ with $c : S \to S^\downarrow$ a bijection, (b) a relation $(<^c)$ the smallest strict order where: (i) $\forall s, s' \in S [s < s' \Leftrightarrow [s <^c s' \wedge c(s) <^c c(s')]]$ and (ii) $\forall s \in S [c(s) <^c s]$, and (c) functions $(^\bullet) : S^c \to S$ and $(_\bullet) : S^c \to S^\downarrow$ defined by $s^\bullet = s$ if $s \in S$ else $c^{-1}(s)$ and $s_\bullet = s$ if $s \in S^\downarrow$ else $c(s)$.*

We let $(<^c)$ also ambiguously denote its extension to strings $(S^c)^*$. Similarly, let $(^{\bullet})$ and $(_{\bullet})$ ambiguously denote their extensions to $(S^c)^*$ and $\mathcal{P}(S^c)$.

Definition 7. *Given* $\Sigma = ((S, <), F)$ *and* $\Omega = ((S, <), F_\Omega)$ *where* $\Omega \subseteq \Sigma$ *and* $(S^c, <^c, (^{\bullet}), (_{\bullet}))$ *is a constructor sort refinement of* $(S, <)$, *we define signatures* $\Omega^{\downarrow} = ((S^c, <^c), F_\Omega^{\downarrow})$ *and* $\Sigma^c = ((S^c, <^c), F^c)$ *such that* $F^c = F \uplus F_\Omega^{\downarrow}$ *and* $F_\Omega^{\downarrow} = \{f : w_{\bullet} \to s_{\bullet} \mid f : w \to s \in F_\Omega\}$. *Then let* $X^{\downarrow} = \{X_s\}_{s \in S^{\downarrow}}$ *and* $X^c = X \uplus X^{\downarrow}$.

In particular, we refer to signatures $\Sigma^c(X^c)$ and $\Omega^{\downarrow}(X^c)$ as the constructor sort refinement of $\Sigma(X)$ and $\Omega(X)$. It is in these signatures where we will perform unification. Also note that $(^{\bullet})$ and $(_{\bullet})$ extend naturally to signature morphisms $(^{\bullet}) : \Sigma^c \to \Sigma$ and $(_{\bullet}) : \Omega \to \Omega^{\downarrow}$. On ground terms $(^{\bullet})$ and $(_{\bullet})$ are the identity, but variables $x \in X^c$ are mapped either into X or $X^{\downarrow}$ respectively. They further extend into substitution mappings where $(x, t) \in \theta$ is mapped into $(x^{\bullet}, t^{\bullet}) \in \theta^{\bullet}$ and $(x_{\bullet}, t_{\bullet}) \in \theta_{\bullet}$ respectively.

In practice, for our unification algorithm to be efficiently used modulo a set of rewrite rules R, we want our transformed signature to be sensible and B-preregular. In general, sensibility is preserved, but preregularity (and thus B-preregularity) is not. Thus, we give a relatively mild condition which ensures B-preregularity is preserved. If $\Omega \subseteq \Sigma$, then we write $\Omega \prec \Sigma$ and say Ω is *preregular below* Σ iff Ω and Σ are preregular and $\forall t \in T_\Sigma[t \in T_\Omega \Rightarrow ls_\Omega(t) = ls_\Sigma(t)]$. Intuitively this means whenever a constructor typing is possible for a term, we need only examine its constructor typings to find its least possible typing.

Theorem 6 [34]. *Let* $R = (\Sigma, B, R)$ *be convergent and have the constructor decomposition* $R_\Omega = (\Omega, B_\Omega, R_\Omega)$ *and* $\Omega \prec \Sigma$. *Then* Σ^c *and* $\Omega^{\downarrow}$ *are sensible and* B-*preregular.*

Now we can derive the most general constructor instances via unification.

Theorem 7 [34]. *Let* $\Sigma(X)$ *and* $\Omega(X)$ *be sensible and* B-*preregular*, $\Omega \prec \Sigma$, *and* B *respect constructors. Then (a)* $\forall t \in T_\Sigma(X)_s \, \forall t' \in T_\Omega(X)_{s'}$ *with* $s \equiv_< s'$ *and* $x \notin vars(t)$, $t\alpha =_B t'$ *iff there are* $\eta \in mgu_B(t = x : c(s'))$ *and* θ *such that* $\eta^{\bullet}\theta|_{vars(t)} =_B \alpha$ *where* $\alpha \in [vars(t) \to T_\Omega(X)]$ *and* $\theta \in [X \to T_\Omega(X)]$ *and (b) the set of most general constructor instances of* t *modulo* B *is defined by* $mgci_B^{\Omega}(t) = \{t(\eta^{\bullet}) \mid \eta \in mgu_B(t = x : ls_{\Sigma(X)}(t)_{\bullet})\}$.

Now that we can obtain constructor instances, we just need to show how to compute constructor variants. But this is now straightforward, since we already know we can compute every most general variant by folding variant narrowing.

Corollary 2 [34]. *Let* (Σ, B, R) *be convergent and protect constructor decomposition* $(\Omega, B_\Omega, \varnothing)$ *and* $\Omega \prec \Sigma$. *The most general constructor variants of* $t \in T_\Sigma(X)$ *are* $[\![t]\!]_{R,B}^{\Omega} = \{(t'\eta^{\bullet}, \theta\eta^{\bullet}) \mid (t', \theta) \in [\![t]\!]_{R,B} \wedge \eta \in mgu_B(t', x : ls_{\Sigma(X)}(t')_{\bullet})\}$.

The reduction of constructor unifiers to constructor variants is simple. Recall any unification problem ϕ is a $\Sigma^{\wedge}$-term $\phi \in T_{\Sigma^{\wedge}}(X)_{Conj}$. Let $\{\alpha_i\}_{i \in I}$ denote the finite set of most general R, B-variant unifiers of ϕ obtained as explained in Theorem 3. Then the set of most general constructor unifiers of ϕ is the set $\{\alpha_i \eta^\bullet \mid \eta \in mgu_B((\phi\alpha_i)!_{R,B}, x : Conj_\bullet)\}$.

We finish with an example of constructor variants and unifiers, which illustrates some issues relating to subsort-overloading that need to be considered. Consider the theory INT of integers with addition. In our example, we have four sorts: Int, Nat, $NzNat$, and $NzNeg$ where $NzNat < Nat < Int$ and $NzNeg < Int$. There are five constructors $\_+\_ : NzNat\ NzNat \to NzNat$, $\_+\_ : Nat\ Nat \to Nat$, $0 :\to Nat$, $1 :\to NzNat$, and $- : NzNat \to NzNeg$, and one defined operator $\_+\_ : Int\ Int \to Int$, where the addition operators all satisfy associativity, commutativity, and identity axioms with unit element 0. Let $n, m : NzNat$ and $i : Int$. Then the operators satisfy four equations: $i + -(n) + -(m) = i + -(n + m)$, $i + n + -(n) = i$, $i + n + -(n + m) = i + -(m)$, $i + n + m + -(n) = i + m$.

Note that this theory is FVP and protects its constructor subtheory. Suppose that using this signature we wish to compute the constructor variants of term $i + n$ where $i : Int$ and $n : NzNat$. We start computing the most general variants of the term $i + n$ using finite variant narrowing and obtain four variants: i, $i + n$, $i + -(n)$, and $i + n + -(m)$, where $i : Int$ and $n, m : NzNat$.

We then construct the extended signatures according to Definition 7. Figure 1 below illustrates how this is done, where for each sort s, we let $s_\bullet$ denote its lowered sort. Then, for each variant t above, we just compute and apply substitutions $mgu_B(t = x : ls_{\Sigma(X)}(t)_\bullet)\}$. Thus, we obtain the four constructor variants: i, $k + n$, $0 + n$, and $0 + -(n)$ where $i : Int$, $k : Nat$, and $n : NzNat$. Now recall $(+)$ is a defined operator over Int but a constructor over Nat; therefore, for each $(+)$ variant, in order to obtain the corresponding constructor variants, we instantiate subterm $i : Int$ so the typing of the whole term lowers into Nat.

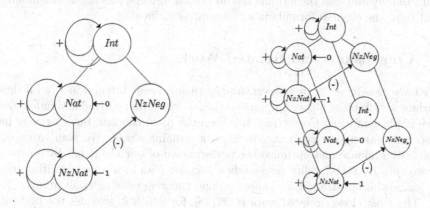

Fig. 1. INT signature Σ and its refinement Σ^c

5   Implementation and Example

Now we describe our implementation of the metalevel algorithms using Maude. Thanks to the reflective nature of rewriting logic and the fact that Maude directly implements rewriting logic, we can directly represent metalevel concepts in Maude as terms in a theory. In fact, such a library already exists in Maude's META-LEVEL module. By using META-LEVEL, we can directly write functions over meta-level constructs to implement our algorithms. Essentially, the algorithm follows the outline sketched in Sect. 4 and shown in the diagram in the Introduction, except that the finite sort checks for theories with axioms have not been implemented yet. The algorithm takes as input a reflected theory M and a formula $\phi = \bigwedge G \wedge \bigwedge D$ and returns a boolean indicating if the formula is satisfiable in M. For further details, we refer the reader to [34].

Let us see how our algorithm can be applied to a concrete example theory NATLIST of lists of natural numbers with Presburger arithmetic. It has four sorts: *Bool, Nat, NeList,* and *List* such that *NeList* < *List*, seven constructors $0 :\to Nat$, $1 :\to Nat$, $\_ + \_ : Nat\ Nat \to Nat$, $\_ : \_ : Nat\ List \to NeList$, nil $:\to List$, true $:\to Bool$, and false $:\to Bool$, and three defined operators $\_ < \_ : Nat\ Nat \to Bool$, $hd : NeList \to Nat$, and $tl : NeList \to List$ where $\_ + \_$ satisfies associativity, commutativity, and identity axioms for element 0. The theory has four equations: $m + 1 + n > n = $ true, $n > n + m = $ false, $hd(n : l) = n$ and $tl(n : l) = l$ where $n, m : Nat$ and $l : List$.

Suppose we want to show $\phi = \forall l, l' : NeList\ [hd(l) > hd(l') = true \Rightarrow l \neq l']$ is a theorem of the initial algebra of NATLIST. Usually, to solve equations in this combined theory, we would need a separate solver for each subtheory and use the Nelson-Oppen combination method to reason in the combined theory, but here, since the theory NATLIST is FVP and protects an OS-compact subtheory, we can directly reason in the combined theory. Thus, we proceed by proving the negation of $\phi\ \exists l, l' : NeList\ [hd(l) > hd(l') = true \wedge l = l']$ is unsatisfiable. But we immediately find that the formula has no variant unifiers, proving unsatisfiability, and thus, the original formula is a theorem, as claimed.

6   Conclusions and Related Work

We have presented the meta-level sub-algorithms needed to obtain a full-fledged variant satisfiability algorithm, proved them correct, and derived a Maude reflective implementation. Correctness has been the main concern, but efficiency has also been taken into account. Much work remains ahead. We plan to experimentally evaluate and optimize the performance of our algorithm by means of representative satisfiability case studies. We also plan to use the algorithm itself in various infinite-state model checking and theorem proving applications.

The most closely-related work is [27,28], for which it provides the first full-fledged algorithm and implementation. Other related topics include folding variant narrowing [18], the FVP [13], and unsorted compactness [12]. Of course, this work occurs in the larger context of decidable satisfiability algorithms and the vast literature on SMT solving, e.g., [1,3–6,6,17,23,24], and additional references in [27,28]. Finally, the literature on Maude's reflective algorithms and tools, e.g., [8,9] is also closely related.

Acknowledgements. Partially supported by NSF Grant CNS 13-19109.

References

1. Armando, A., Ranise, S., Rusinowitch, M.: A rewriting approach to satisfiability procedures. Inf. Comput. **183**(2), 140–164 (2003)
2. Baader, F., Schulz, K.U.: Combining constraint solving. In: Comon, H., Marché, C., Treinen, R. (eds.) CCL 1999. LNCS, vol. 2002, p. 104. Springer, Heidelberg (2001)
3. Barrett, C., Sebastiani, R., Seshia, S., Tinelli, C.: Satisfiability modulo theories. In: Biere, A., Heule, M.J.H., van Maaren, H., Walsh, T. (eds.) Handbook of Satisfiability, vol. 185, pp. 825–885. IOS Press, Amsterdam (2009). Chap. 26
4. Barrett, C., Shikanian, I., Tinelli, C.: An abstract decision procedure for satisfiability in the theory of inductive data types. J. Satisf. Boolean Model. Comput. **3**, 21–46 (2007)
5. Barrett, C., Tinelli, C.: Satisfiability modulo theories. In: Clarke, E., Henzinger, T., Veith, H. (eds.) Handbook of Model Checking. Springer, Berlin (2014)
6. Bradley, A.R., Manna, Z.: The Calculus of Computation - Decision Procedures with Applications to Verification. Springer, Berlin (2007)
7. Cholewa, A., Meseguer, J., Escobar, S.: Variants of variants and the finite variant property. Technical report, CS Deptartment, University of Illinois at Urbana-Champaign, February 2014. http://hdl.handle.net/2142/47117
8. Clavel, M., Durán, F., Eker, S., Lincoln, P., Martí-Oliet, N., Meseguer, J., Talcott, C. (eds.): All About Maude - A High-Performance Logical Framework. LNCS, vol. 4350. Springer, Heidelberg (2007)
9. Clavel, M., Durán, F., Eker, S., Meseguer, J., Stehr, M.-O.: Maude as a formal meta-tool. In: Wing, J.M., Woodcock, J., Davies, J. (eds.) FM 1999. LNCS, vol. 1709, p. 1684. Springer, Heidelberg (1999)
10. Clavel, M., Meseguer, J., Palomino, M.: Reflection in membership equational logic, many-sorted equational logic, horn logic with equality, and rewriting logic. Theoret. Comput. Sci. **373**, 70–91 (2007)
11. Comon, H., Dauchet, M., Gilleron, R., Löding, C., Jacquemard, F., Lugiez, D., Tison, S., Tommasi, M.: Tree automata techniques and applications (2007). http://www.grappa.univ-lille3.fr/tata. Accessed 12 October 2007
12. Comon, H.: Complete axiomatizations of some quotient term algebras. Theoret. Comput. Sci. **118**(2), 167–191 (1993)
13. Comon-Lundh, H., Delaune, S.: The finite variant property: how to get rid of some algebraic properties. In: Giesl, J. (ed.) RTA 2005. LNCS, vol. 3467, pp. 294–307. Springer, Heidelberg (2005)
14. Dershowitz, N., Jouannaud, J.P.: Rewrite systems. In: van Leeuwen, J. (ed.) Handbook of Theoretical Computer Science, vol. B, pp. 243–320. ACM, North-Holland (1990)
15. Dovier, A., Piazza, C., Rossi, G.: A uniform approach to constraint-solving for lists, multisets, compact lists, and sets. ACM Trans. Comput. Log. **9**(3), 15 (2008)
16. Dovier, A., Policriti, A., Rossi, G.: A uniform axiomatic view of lists, multisets, and sets, and the relevant unification algorithms. Fundam. Inform. **36**(2–3), 201–234 (1998)
17. Dross, C., Conchon, S., Kanig, J., Paskevich, A.: Adding decision procedures to SMT solvers using axioms with triggers. J. Autom. Reason. **56**, 387–457 (2016). https://hal.archives-ouvertes.fr/hal-01221066

18. Escobar, S., Sasse, R., Meseguer, J.: Folding variant narrowing and optimal variant termination. J. Algebr. Log. Program. **81**, 898–928 (2012)
19. Goguen, J., Meseguer, J.: Order-sorted algebra I. Theoret. Comput. Sci. **105**, 217–273 (1992)
20. Hendrix, J., Clavel, M., Meseguer, J.: A sufficient completeness reasoning tool for partial specifications. In: Giesl, J. (ed.) RTA 2005. LNCS, vol. 3467, pp. 165–174. Springer, Heidelberg (2005)
21. Hendrix, J., Meseguer, J., Ohsaki, H.: A sufficient completeness checker for linear order-sorted specifications modulo axioms. In: Furbach, U., Shankar, N. (eds.) IJCAR 2006. LNCS (LNAI), vol. 4130, pp. 151–155. Springer, Heidelberg (2006)
22. Jouannaud, J.P., Kirchner, H.: Completion of a set of rules modulo a set of equations. SIAM J. Comput. **15**, 1155–1194 (1986)
23. Kroening, D., Strichman, O.: Decision Procedures - An Algorithmic Point of View. Texts in Theoretical Computer Science. An EATCS Series. Springer, Berlin (2008)
24. Krstić, S., Goel, A., Grundy, J., Tinelli, C.: Combined satisfiability modulo parametric theories. In: Grumberg, O., Huth, M. (eds.) TACAS 2007. LNCS, vol. 4424, pp. 602–617. Springer, Heidelberg (2007)
25. Meseguer, J.: Membership algebra as a logical framework for equational specification. In: Parisi-Presicce, F. (ed.) WADT 1997. LNCS, vol. 1376. Springer, Heidelberg (1998)
26. Meseguer, J.: Strict coherence of conditional rewriting modulo axioms. Technical report, C.S. Department, University of Illinois at Urbana-Champaign, August 2014. http://hdl.handle.net/2142/50288
27. Meseguer, J.: Variant-based satisfiability in initial algebras. Technical report, University of Illinois at Urbana-Champaign, November 2015. http://hdl.handle.net/2142/88408
28. Mashauri, D., et al.: Variant-based satisfiability in initial algebras. In: Artho, C., et al. (eds.) FTSCS 2015. CCIS, vol. 596, pp. 3–34. Springer, Heidelberg (2016). doi:10.1007/978-3-319-29510-7_1
29. Meseguer, J., Goguen, J.: Order-sorted algebra solves the constructor-selector, multiple representation and coercion problems. Inf. Comput. **103**(1), 114–158 (1993)
30. Nelson, G., Oppen, D.C.: Simplification by cooperating decision procedures. ACM Trans. Program. Lang. Syst. **1**(2), 245–257 (1979)
31. Oppen, D.C.: Complexity, convexity and combinations of theories. Theor. Comput. Sci. **12**, 291–302 (1980)
32. Rocha, C., Meseguer, J.: Constructors, sufficient completeness, and deadlock freedom of rewrite theories. In: Fermüller, C.G., Voronkov, A. (eds.) LPAR-17. LNCS, vol. 6397, pp. 594–609. Springer, Heidelberg (2010)
33. Shostak, R.E.: Deciding combinations of theories. J. ACM **31**(1), 1–12 (1984)
34. Skeirik, S., Meseguer, J.: Metalevel algorithms for variant satisfiability. Technical report, C.S. Department, University of Illinois at Urbana-Champaign, June 2016. https://www.ideals.illinois.edu/handle/2142/90238

Author Index

Arusoaie, Andrei 134

Bijo, Shiji 47
Boichut, Yohan 64

Dantas, Yuri Gil 82
Dinu, Liviu P. 152
Durán, Francisco 118

Fernández, Maribel 1
Fonseca, Iguatemi E. 82

Johnsen, Einar Broch 47

Kirchner, Hélène 1

Lemos, Marcilio O.O. 82
Lucas, Salvador 26

Martín, Óscar 98
Martí-Oliet, Narciso 98

Meseguer, José 118, 167
Moreno-Delgado, Antonio 118

Nigam, Vivek 82

Pelletier, Vivien 64
Pinaud, Bruno 1
Pun, Ka I 47

Réty, Pierre 64
Rusu, Vlad 134

Şerbănuţă, Traian Florin 152
Skeirik, Stephen 167

Tapia Tarifa, Silvia Lizeth 47

Vallet, Jason 1
Verdejo, Alberto 98

Printed in the United States
By Bookmasters